# The Structure of Shakespearean Scenes

# THE STRUCTURE OF
# SHAKESPEAREAN
# SCENES

JAMES E. HIRSH

New Haven and London
Yale University Press

Published with the assistance of the Frederick W. Hilles Publication Fund

Designed by Nancy Ovedovitz and set in VIP Bodoni type.
Printed in the United States of America by
Halliday Lithograph, West Hanover, Mass.

Library of Congress Cataloging in Publication Data

Hirsh, James E., 1946–
   The structure of Shakespearean scenes.

   Includes index.
   1. Shakespeare, William, 1564–1616—Technique.   I. Title.
PR2997.S3H5        822.3'3        81-2473
ISBN 0-300-02650-1                 AACR2

10    9    8    7    6    5    4    3    2    1

*To*
*Bill Matchett*
*and*
*Stephen Booth*

# Contents

# Acknowledgments

I wish to acknowledge my debt and express my gratitude to William H. Matchett of the University of Washington and to Stephen Booth of the University of California, Berkeley. Each deserved to have the book dedicated to him alone. Professor Matchett, a friend and former colleague, read two successive drafts of each chapter of the manuscript and gave me extensive and valuable advice. Professor Booth was unaware of my existence until he was asked to evaluate the manuscript. He provided not only a generous evaluation, but a remarkably generous list of specific editorial comments. Nearly every page of this book is better than it would have been had the manuscript not fallen into Professor Booth's hands. I still await the opportunity to thank Professor Booth in person. I *have* had the opportunity to thank my wife, Kathleen, in person, but she deserves a public acknowledgment of my gratitude for her unsparing assistance, her objective counsel, and her loving encouragement. I would also like to thank Otto Reinert, Robert Bratager, Judith Kalitzki, Stephen Fink, Kathleen Burrage, Roberta Scholz, Sara Collins, Christine LesCarbeau, Mitchell LesCarbeau, Todd Sammons, Margaret Ketchum, Cheryl Colopy, Ellen Graham, and Lawrence Kenney.

J.E.H.

Honolulu, Hawaii
April 1, 1981

# One �֎ Introduction

In a passage that reminds one of Johnson's comment about the quibble being Shakespeare's "fatal Cleopatra," Levin L. Schücking complains of "Shakespeare's supreme interest in the single scene, which all his knowledge of dramatic art cannot induce him to subordinate to the interest of the whole."[1] Acknowledging Shakespeare's love of the quibble, many critics now tend to regard it as a virtue rather than a failing. Similarly, some critics regard "Shakespeare's supreme interest in the single scene" as a factor contributing to, rather than detracting from, the overall organization of his plays. In an influential essay William Empson maintains that Elizabethan dramatists, particularly Shakespeare, employed a "system of 'construction by scenes.'" This system "clearly makes the scenes, the incidents, stand out as objects in themselves, to be compared even when they are not connected," and these comparisons establish ironic relationships that hold together the disparate elements of a play.[2] Unfortunately, Empson does not explain in detail what he means by "construction by scenes." And the issue needs clarification because the study of Shakespeare's dramatic construction has been beset by a surprising degree of disagreement and confusion.

One source of that confusion is the conventional division of

1. *Character Problems in Shakespeare's Plays* (1922; rpt. Gloucester, Mass.: Peter Smith, 1959), p. 112.
2. "Double Plots: Heroic and Pastoral in the Main Plot and Sub-Plot," in *Some Versions of Pastoral* (Norfolk, Conn.: James Laughlin, n.d. [c. 1935]), p. 55.

1

Shakespeare's plays into five acts. Critics, such as Marc Hunter and T. W. Baldwin, who explicitly defend act division quite naturally tend to regard scenes as relatively minor structural elements. If the act is not a legitimate unit, however, then the scene would take on a special importance, for it would be the largest structural element that Shakespeare consistently and demonstrably uses in all his plays. Even though a majority of critics now tacitly concede that, with few exceptions, Shakespeare did not himself divide his plays into acts, almost all editions of his plays are still so divided, and most readers, including many critics, still seem to regard acts as legitimate structural divisions of the plays. A complicating factor is that some critics unaccountably have treated act division and scene division as a single issue, as if the two can only stand or fall together. J. Dover Wilson, for example, dismisses act divisions as encrustations but inexplicably lumps scene divisions in the same dismissal.[3]

If the theaters for which he wrote had intervals during a performance, Shakespeare would have been obliged to divide his plays into acts. That the evidence points in the contrary direction has baffled those inclined to believe in the legitimacy of act division:

> It is difficult to suppose that the public theatres paid no regard to act-intervals, and one cannot therefore quite understand why neither the poets nor the book-keepers were in the habit of showing them in the play-house "originals" of plays. Had they been shown there, they would almost inevitably have gotten into the prints.[4]

Nearly all of Shakespeare's plays were designed for performance at public theaters. Although the company of which Shakespeare

3. "Textual Introduction," *The New Cambridge Shakespeare*, ed. Arthur Quiller-Couch and John Dover Wilson (Cambridge: Cambridge Univ. Press, 1921–66), in *The Tempest* (1921), pp. xxxv–xxxvi.

4. E. K. Chambers, *The Elizabethan Stage* (Oxford: Clarendon Press, 1923), 3: 199–200.

was a leading shareholder occasionally presented a play at court, a public performance almost always preceded a court performance, and the company derived only a minute fraction of its income from court performances.[5] Very late in Shakespeare's career the King's Men acquired a private theater, the Blackfriars, and it is not unlikely that in his last plays Shakespeare adapted his dramatic techniques to the very different requirements of that type of theater. Suppositions that other plays were initially presented in a forum other than a public theater are in most instances highly speculative and, in any case, involve only a small number of plays.

The most significant indication of the differing practices of public and private playhouses is provided by the extant editions of plays that were produced in each during Shakespeare's career. Wilfred T. Jewkes has examined these editions and has discovered that of 236 plays probably performed between 1583 and 1616, 123 have some division into acts but only 89 of 201 plays printed before 1616 are so divided, and of 134 plays for the public theaters printed before 1616 only 30 are divided.[6] W. W. Greg once made a similar examination of all the extant plays printed between 1591 and 1610. According to the list he compiled, editions of nearly all academic plays and of plays performed by boys' companies at private theaters were divided into acts. But the opposite is true for plays probably performed at public theaters: only 19 of 102 such plays are divided, and some of those show significant irregularity in their division.[7]

5. Bernard Beckerman, *Shakespeare at the Globe, 1599–1609* (1962; rpt. London: Collier-Macmillan, 1966), pp. 20–23. Beckerman bases his calculation that only 5 percent of the company's income during Elizabeth's reign was derived from court appearances on data supplied by Chambers (*Elizabethan Stage*, 4: 166–75).

6. *Act Division in Elizabethan and Jacobean Plays, 1583–1616* (Hamden, Conn.: Shoe String Press, 1958), p. 97.

7. "Act-Divisions in Shakespeare," *Review of English Studies* 4 (April 1928): 152–58. The figures derived from Greg's list should be considered only

When an earlier terminal date is chosen, the evidence becomes even more overwhelming: according to Jewkes, of the 74 plays for the adult companies printed between 1591 and 1607, 5 plays by Ben Jonson are the only ones that are divided into acts. Jewkes concludes:

> Since the texts show every conceivable variety of textual history, it is clear, then, that neither playhouses, nor authors, nor printers, nor scribes paid any attention to act division during this period, with the glaring exception of Jonson. . . . Since division after 1616 is so uniform, it can be assumed with a fair degree of certainty that it was an established practice in the public theaters by that time. Actually since several plays after 1607 are divided, it seems likely that the practice of division was gaining ground after that time.[8]

This change in the practice of the public theaters is the source of the confusion. Shakespeare's plays remained in the repertory of the King's Men after his retirement. Thus, by the time the First Folio appeared in 1623 most of his plays had acquired act divisions either because they had come to be so divided in revival performances or because printed plays by that time were expected to be divided into acts. Over half of Shakespeare's plays appeared in quarto editions during his lifetime—none of these is divided into acts. If, as J. Dover Wilson claims, the sources of these editions were playhouse promptbooks, this evidence indicates that act divisions were not employed by Shakespeare's company.[9] But if the sources of at least some of these editions were Shakespeare's own manuscripts, then their lack of

---

approximations because some plays are of uncertain date or origin. Henry L. Snuggs contends that only 81 plays printed between 1591 and 1610 were definitely produced at the public theaters, but an even greater proportion of these than of those on Greg's list are undivided—only 10, in fact, are divided; see *Shakespeare and Five Acts* (New York: Vantage, 1960), p. 38.

8. *Act Division*, pp. 98–99.

9. "Textual Introduction," p. xxxvi.

division implies that Shakespeare did not even use acts as structural devices in the composing of his plays. And, according to Jewkes,

> the most likely copy from which a printer would work would be the original author's copy, still in the possession of the company, but not used, once the scribal copy which served as prompt-book had been made. Only if a play were being printed long after it had ceased to be a part of an active repertory would the prompt-book be likely to be sent to the printer's. (*Act Division*, p. 13)

Although most of the plays in the First Folio are divided, the research of textual scholars has cast doubt on the authorial origin of most of these divisions. Many of these texts do seem to derive from promptbooks—which would have acquired divisions after the practice of act intervals spread to the public theaters.[10] Some, particularly those transcribed by Ralph Crane, show traces of literary interpolation. In a few the division is clearly inept.[11] A large number of the Folio texts are, in fact, based on the more authoritative but undivided quartos. The most reliable text of nearly every Shakespearean play is an undivided quarto, an undivided text in the Folio, or a divided text that shows signs of interpolation.[12]

If the theaters for which he wrote did not, in fact, employ act intervals, would Shakespeare have felt compelled nevertheless

10. Unlike the printers of the quartos, the editors of the Folio would have had easy access to promptbooks as they were shareholders of the King's Men.

11. Some examples of clumsy act divisions in the Folio will be discussed later in this chapter.

12. See Wilson, "Textual Introduction"; E. K. Chambers, *William Shakespeare* (Oxford: Clarendon Press, 1930), 1: 199–201, 307, 328, 335, 358, etc.; Snuggs, *Five Acts*, pp. 52–55; Jewkes, *Act Division*, pp. 36–40. Without the aid of modern textual analysis, Samuel Johnson asserted that the division of Shakespeare's plays into acts was an arbitrary imposition of editors; see the preface to Johnson's *Plays of William Shakespeare* (1765) in *Samuel Johnson on Shakespeare*, ed. W. K. Wimsatt, Jr. (New York: Hill and Wang, 1960), p. 64.

consistently to adopt a structure of five units? Just as Shakespeare did not need to divide his plays for theatrical reasons, he did not need to divide his plays to make them presentable as literature because he apparently made no effort to present them in literary form. Unlike Jonson, he did not oversee the publication of his dramatic works.

That one of his plays, *Henry V*, is clearly divided into five acts by choral monologues does not suggest that the remaining are implicitly so divided. On the contrary, if the choruses in *Henry V* were removed, even its five-act structure would not be very discernible. Shakespeare evidently had difficulty conforming his imagination to the arbitrary restrictions of such a structure and perhaps felt the need in his experiment with act divisions to call explicit attention to those divisions.[13]

T. W. Baldwin, the most insistent defender of the theory that Shakespeare conformed to the five-act convention, admits that the public stage for which Shakespeare wrote did not have act intervals but argues that an act is a "unit of thought," not necessarily a stage unit,[14] and hence "the structural, rhetorical act division of the composing dramatist has no necessary connection with stage observance of acts."[15] Yet Baldwin devotes surprisingly little space in *William Shakespeare's Five-Act Structure*[16] to demonstrations that even the few individual plays he examines reveal five units of thought. He devotes most of this enormous book to discussions of Terence's five-act structure,

13. The presence of the choruses in *Henry V* also seems to confirm the other evidence that the public theater did not have act intervals. If the public theaters did not have act intervals, the only way a playwright could call attention to act divisions would be by means of a device such as the choral monologue.

14. *On Act and Scene Division in the Shakespeare First Folio* (Carbondale: Southern Illinois Univ. Press, 1965), p. ix.

15. *On the Compositional Genetics of "The Comedy of Errors"* (Urbana: Univ. of Illinois Press, 1965), pp. 85–86.

16. (Urbana: Univ. of Illinois Press, 1947).

medieval and Renaissance commentaries on Terence and their role in the sixteenth-century grammar school curriculum, and act division in sixteenth-century academic drama, in order to give the impression that the five-act structure was an inescapable method of construction for a dramatist of Shakespeare's generation. In another book on the same topic he flatly declares that "by the last fifteen or twenty years of the sixteenth century, it was assumed that any respectable dramatist writing in the current style would write in acts."[17] In order to reach this conclusion, he is forced to discount or ignore the following details: (1) the greatest playwright of all time may not have conformed to what a "respectable dramatist writing in the current style" would do; (2) Shakespeare was exposed to a native dramatic tradition that completely ignored classical conventions, including the five-act convention;[18] the theater for which he wrote had closer ties to this tradition than to the tradition of academic drama; (3) very little documentary evidence exists concerning Shakespeare's education and dramatic apprenticeship.

Like Baldwin, Clifford Leech contends that even though no theatrical imperative required five acts, a psychological imperative did or, rather, sometimes did: "When Shakespeare began to write, a dramatist in the public theatre would commonly, though not necessarily always, think in terms of a five-Act structure, whether or not the Acts were separated by intervals or by Chorus-speeches, dumb-shows and the like." Leech supports this contention by summarizing the action of several Shakespearean plays which, in his view, exhibit a five-part pattern. *Twelfth Night*, he argues, displays a "high degree of conformity" to such

17. *Act and Scene Division*, p. 7.
18. The classical dramatists themselves frequently violated the five-act convention—perhaps because they were unaware of its existence. See Snuggs, *Five Acts*, chap. 1, "The Origin of the Five-Act Convention"; and Philip Whaley Harsh, "Note on Division into Act and Scenes," in *An Anthology of Roman Drama* (New York: Rinehart, 1960), p. xxxi.

a pattern. Yet, as Leech himself admits, "We must, I think, recognise that no obvious demarcation-line exists between Acts II and III. . . . Acts II and III tend to flow together: without reference to the Folio text, we could not easily decide where one should end and the other begin." In *Titus Andronicus*, "the five-unit structure is apparent, despite the omission of Act-headings in the Quartos." [19] But there is at least one fly in this ointment, too: "It has been argued by Sir Walter Greg that the Act-division in the Folio *Titus* is not the author's because at the end of Act I Aaron the Moor remains on the stage and is the first speaker in Act II." [20] Leech points out that no cleared stage occurs at the Folio division between Acts II and III of *King John* because Constance remains onstage and that two of the traditional act divisions in *A Midsummer Night's Dream* occur at points when characters remain onstage. In other words, Leech tries to explain away one example of an improbable act division by citing other examples of equally improbable act divisions.

Problems also arise in applying the pattern to *Othello* and *Hamlet*. In *Othello* "Acts III and IV are run closely together"; "there is no new development of action in Act IV." Leech says in regard to *Hamlet*, "But if we may freely admit that the place of the break between Acts III and IV is by no means clear, we can at least see that Shakespeare was in no doubt as to the breaks after Acts I, II, and IV" ("Five-Act Structure," pp. 259, 260, 261). The impression left by Leech is that, if Shakespeare was indeed striving for a clearly delineated five-part structure, he consistently bungled the job.

Leech makes what is perhaps his most telling admission after presenting his version of the five-part structure of yet another

19. "Shakespeare's Use of a Five-Act Structure," *Die Neueren Sprachen* 6 (Jan. 1957): 256, 252, 253, 257.

20. Ibid., p. 257. The passages by Greg to which Leech refers are on p. 205 and in n. 7 of *The Shakespeare First Folio: Its Bibliographical and Textual History* (London: Oxford Univ. Press, 1955).

play: "*Macbeth*, however, is a highly complicated play in that its deepest effect on us is in opposition to that suggested by its Act structure" (ibid., p. 259). He does not argue that the act structure is somehow ironic but simply concedes that it does not reflect the deepest issues of the play. That the act structure does not reflect the deepest issues of the play suggests, however, that the act structure is not the structure of the play and that focusing our attention on it would not help and may hinder a full understanding of the play.

I am not arguing that Leech's structural analyses are necessarily invalid; but his analysis in each case is so generalized and subject to qualification by Leech himself that the structure he arrives at for a given play is unconvincing as *the* structure of the play. Looked at from a different perspective, the same play Leech divides into five sections could, with equal plausibility, be divided into two, three, four, six, or more sections. (That an apple pie—to use a homely metaphor—can be divided into five pieces does not mean that an apple pie has a five-part structure.) Indeed, other critics have argued that either most of the plays or a particular play can be divided in one of these alternative ways. Emrys Jones, for example, maintains that Shakespeare's plays generally exhibit a two-part structure.[21] Don M. Ricks finds a four-part structure in *Henry VI, Part One*.[22]

Although A. C. Bradley refers to acts to locate dramatic events for his reader, he does not equate acts with structural divisions of the plays. In fact, he argues that Shakespearean tragedies exhibit a basic three-part rather than a five-part structure: "As a Shakespearean tragedy represents a conflict which terminates in a catastrophe, any such tragedy may roughly be

21. See *Scenic Form in Shakespeare* (Oxford: Clarendon Press, 1971), especially chap. 3, "The Two-Part Structure."

22. See *Shakespeare's Emergent Form: A Study of the Structures of the "Henry VI" Plays*, Utah State University Monograph Series 15, no. 1 (Logan: Utah State Univ. Press, 1968): 62.

divided into three parts": the Exposition, the Conflict, and the
Catastrophe.[23] He later notes that a Crisis generally occurs near
the middle of a play "and *where it is well marked* it has the
effect, as to construction, of dividing the play into five parts
instead of three; these parts showing (1) a situation not yet one of
conflict (2) the rise and development of the conflict . . . (3) the
Crisis (4) the decline . . . (5) the Catastrophe" (ibid., p. 50; my
emphasis). But even this structure is not reflected by traditional
act divisions. The well-marked crisis serves to divide the middle
part of the play, the Conflict, into three parts, and the Conflict
comprises not only the second, third, and fourth acts but "usually a part of the First and a part of the Fifth" (ibid., p. 41).

Even Bradley's more flexible pattern cannot be applied successfully to some of the tragedies, however. His attempt to fit
*King Lear* into the pattern leads him to the assertion that "the
right way to look at the matter, *from the point of view of construction*, is to regard Goneril, Regan, and Edmund as the leading characters" (ibid., p. 51; Bradley's emphasis). The italics
indicate that Bradley himself realizes that from any other point
of view the assertion could not be defended. (Compare Leech's
admission that the structure he imposed on *Macbeth* does not
reflect the deepest issues of *Macbeth*.) That the principle of construction Bradley finds in *Lear* distorts the play suggests that
*Lear* is not, in fact, constructed along the lines he proposes.

Acknowledging the intractability of the play, Bradley concludes that its structure is flawed and that "the principal structural weakness . . . arises chiefly from the double action"
(ibid., p. 205). Bradley is wrong, I think, about the structural
weakness of *Lear*, but he has put his finger on one reason why
the structure of at least some of Shakespeare's plays is not re-
ducible to a linear pattern of five acts or three parts or four
parts. A number of Shakespeare's plays incorporate multiple

23. *Shakespearean Tragedy* (1904; rpt. Cleveland: World Publishing Co.,
1955), p. 41.

plots which at any particular point are at quite different stages of development. Even plays without a full-fledged subplot often involve separate lines of action or distinct sets of characters between which groups only occasional contact is made. The attempt to reduce the structure of one of these plays with interwoven strands to a simple linear pattern involving a small number of divisions is bound to distort or oversimplify that structure.

Instead of trying to force the nine scenes of *Love's Labor's Lost* into a five-act structure, for example, it might be better to start an analysis of the play's structure by examining the pattern formed by those nine scenes. The construction of this early play is based on a fairly simple alternation of scenes. The odd-numbered scenes focus on the noble characters and the even-numbered on the comic subplot. The first scene introduces both plots and the ninth concludes both, but even in these scenes the major focus is on the main plot. Of nine important noble characters, Berowne is the only one to appear in an even-numbered scene. Of seven important characters in the subplot, none appears in scene 3 (II.i), only Costard appears in scene 5 (IV.i), and the only low characters to appear even briefly in the long scene 7 (IV.iii) are Costard and Jaquenetta. A full analysis of the play's structure would have to examine the development of each plot and the relationships between the two plots but could not ignore the clear pattern of alternating scenes established by Shakespeare.

With a few exceptions the traditional divisions of Shakespeare's plays are those established by W. G. Clark and W. A. Wright in the 1863 Cambridge edition. The bibliographic revolution that took place in the early years of the twentieth century swept away nearly all other editorial encrustations, but somehow the act divisions, which did not begin appearing in editions of Shakespeare's works until after his death, maintained a special sacrosanct status. Encased in brackets and perhaps dismissed in a "Note on the Text," they have, nevertheless, been retained and continue to misguide the reader about the structure of the plays.

Scene divisions, on the other hand, cannot be dismissed as editorial encrustations. According to G. K. Hunter, another adherent to the five-act theory, "The Shakespearean quartos (both 'good' and 'bad') provide a record of entries and exits, and no more. All clear-cut separation of scene from scene, and, of course, enumeration of scenes, is editorial in exactly the same way as is the act-division."[24] But if a "scene" is defined as a portion of a play during which the stage is continuously occupied, then Elizabethan plays are indisputably divided into separate scenes because they contain breaks during which the stage is empty. No play by Shakespeare contains fewer than eight such cleared stages. Such breaks did apparently have a recognized significance for the Elizabethan theater. In the surviving playhouse "plots," which were plot summaries used backstage, scenes are invariably divided from one another by ruled lines.[25] Rather than attempting to mask the break between scenes, Shakespeare frequently calls attention to it. According to A. C. Bradley, 291 of 748 scenes in his plays end with a rhyming couplet.[26] According to Bernard Beckerman, of 336 scenes in plays written by Shakespeare for performance at the Globe Theatre, 192 end with explicit exit lines and 74 end with implicit exit lines.[27] New scenes are often heralded by music or other offstage sounds that call attention to the break in continuity.

24. "Were There Act-Pauses on Shakespeare's Stage?" in *English Renaissance Drama: Essays in Honor of Madeleine Doran and Marc Eccles*, ed. Standish Henning, Robert Kimbrough, and Richard Knowles (Carbondale: Southern Illinois Univ. Press, 1976), p. 22.

25. See W. W. Greg, *Dramatic Documents from the Elizabethan Playhouses* (Oxford: Clarendon Press, 1931), vol. 2: *Reproductions and Transcripts*.

26. "Scene-Endings in Shakespeare and in *The Two Noble Kinsmen*," in *A Miscellany* (London: Macmillan, 1929), p. 218.

27. *Shakespeare at the Globe*, p. 107.

The real issue is not whether or not scenes existed but whether or not they are significant units of dramatic structure as well as of theatrical presentation. J. Dover Wilson dismisses the importance of such units by maintaining that the divisions between scenes "were theatrical and not literary in character— that is to say they occurred when one group of players left the stage to make room for another, even when the action was continuous and the *mise en scène* unaltered. In a word the rules across the 'plot' were *exeunt omnes* lines."[28] He implies that, though a theatrical division occurs at any point when all the characters leave the stage, such a division has no "literary" importance if the following scene is set in the same locale without any lapse in time. But, as has been frequently observed, many scenes in Shakespeare's plays are unlocalized, some change location in midscene,[29] and in many scenes time is unspecified or telescoped. Thus, it would hardly seem that changes in time or location are reliable criteria for even literary divisions of the plays. In any event, how can "action" in the dramatic sense of the word be "continuous" when all the characters onstage leave and are replaced by an entirely different set of characters? G. E. Bentley's remark that Shakespeare "wrote a drama of persons not . . . of places"[30] is more than a charming metaphor. The entrance or exit of an important character is far more important to the *dramatic* structure of the action than a lapse in time or a change in location. If this is so, then the complete change in characters that occurs at the break between scenes will usually be an even more important element in the dramatic structure, even if the new scene does not involve a change in location or a lapse in time.

28. *The Two Gentlemen of Verona* (1921), in *The New Cambridge Shakespeare* series, p. 78.
29. See, e.g., *Julius Caesar*, III.i.
30. *Shakespeare and His Theatre* (Lincoln: Univ. of Nebraska Press, 1964), p. 57.

That the break between scenes is a meaningful division within
a play is demonstrated by the following comparison between two
similar incidents in *The Comedy of Errors*. Very soon after Antipholus of Ephesus leaves the stage in the custody of Pinch during the mayhem in the next-to-last scene (IV.iv), Antipholus of
Syracuse enters. An appearance by one of the brothers has
never before been followed later in the same scene by the other's
appearance.[31] Thus, at the height of the confusion, the solu-
tion—that is, a face-to-face encounter between the twins—
seems closer than it ever has. And yet, at one earlier point the
brothers presumably came even closer to meeting. At the beginning of Act III, scene ii, the Syracusan Antipholus enters with
Luciana just after his Ephesian twin left with other characters to
end the previous scene; no time has elapsed, and no change of
location has occurred. While thirteen lines separate the exit of
one brother from the entrance of the other in Act IV, scene iv,
no lines intervene here. In actual clock time the Antipholi miss
each other in the earlier case by only a second or less, while
about a half minute must separate them in the later case. Yet I
am sure that the audience's sense that the brothers nearly ran
into one another is much stronger in the next-to-last scene than
at the beginning of Act III, scene ii. It is our automatic tendency
to compartmentalize two scenes, rather than the conscious deduction that such an encounter could not occur at the earlier
point, that is the key to this difference in our responses to the
two incidents.

Because act divisions lack authority and serve to obscure the
actual structure of the plays whereas scene divisions are legitimate dramatic units and were recognized as such in the Elizabethan theater, I propose that the present division of Shake-

31. Antipholus of Syracuse appears in I.ii, II.ii, III.ii, and IV.iii; his twin
of Ephesus in III.i and IV.i. After narrowly missing one another in IV.iv, they
finally meet in V.i.

speare's plays into acts and scenes be replaced by the division of the plays simply into scenes numbered sequentially. Furthermore, some existing scene divisions should be eliminated and others added at appropriate points because the criterion for scene division discussed earlier in this chapter has never been applied consistently by editors. The continuity of a play is not broken and hence a scene division does not occur unless the stage is cleared of all living characters. In a very few cases all the characters onstage exit and a new set of characters enter, but a break in continuity is avoided because at least one of the exiting characters notices the approach of the entering characters.[32] That Shakespeare created such tenuous liaisons, apparently to avoid a break in continuity, seems to indicate the seriousness with which he regarded such breaks.

A scene in which a character falls asleep or becomes unconscious does not end even if all other characters leave the stage. Such situations are not uncommon in Shakespeare's plays. In Act IV, scene ii, of *Cymbeline*, for example, Imogen does not regain consciousness until after the other characters have left. I doubt if any editor has ever suggested that their departure and her subsequent awakening mark a scenic break.[33] But in apparent desperation about how to divide *A Midsummer Night's Dream* into five acts—only eight times during the play is the stage clear of characters—the Folio editors twice resorted to the insertion of act divisions at points when the stage is still occupied by sleeping characters. These divisions were apparently inserted only because of the need for act divisions and certainly do not reflect a convention that a scene division occurs whenever the stage

32. See, e.g., *Measure for Measure*, I.ii.115–19. The edition of Shakespeare's plays cited in this study is *The Complete Signet Classic Shakespeare*, Sylvan Barnet, gen. ed. (New York: Harcourt, 1972).

33. A cleared stage does, however, occur earlier in IV.ii (at l. 100), which thus is not a single scene but comprises two scenes.

becomes clear of all conscious characters. The Folio editors did not insert scene divisions at other such points even in *A Midsummer Night's Dream*.[34]

The continuity of a play *is* broken when the stage has been cleared of all living characters, and thus a scene division occurs if only a corpse (even though represented by an actor) remains onstage. In the midst of *Titus Andronicus*, Act II, scene iii, for example, the stage is entirely cleared of living characters. After Demetrius and Chiron murder Bassanius and drag Lavinia away, Tamora delivers what sounds like a scene-ending soliloquy:

> Ne'er let my heart know merry cheer indeed
> Till all the Andronici be made away.
> Now will I hence to seek my lovely Moor,
> And let my spleenful sons this trull deflower.
>
> (ll. 188–91)

Her exit marks the end of one dramatic movement, and the subsequent entrance of Aaron with Quintus and Martius marks the beginning of another, in which Quintus and Martius are falsely accused of Bassanius's murder. Though left onstage after Tamora's exit, the corpse of Bassanius is not even visible to an audience because it has been deposited in a pit. Though the location has not changed and though Bassanius's body will subsequently be discovered, the dramatic continuity has been broken, and this fact should be acknowledged by a scene division. In order to enhance a theatrical effect that occurs in *Henry IV, Part One*, Act V, scene iv, Shakespeare even makes use of an audience's unconscious tendency to assume a scene has ended when the stage has been cleared of living characters. During the course of this battle scene, Douglas exits, after having apparently killed Falstaff, and Hal mortally wounds Hotspur. After Hotspur dies, Hal, seemingly the only living character onstage, delivers epitaphs of sorts, first for Percy and then for Falstaff.

---

34. See, e.g., II.ii.26; II.ii.34; II.ii.65; II.ii.83; and IV.i.103.

When Hal exits and the stage has presumably been emptied of living characters, an audience would automatically assume that one continuous dramatic movement has ended, that the scene is over and a new scene will now begin with the entrance of new characters—we probably are tempted to look toward the stage doors to see who will enter. But, instead, one of the corpses rises from the dead. In order to create the stunning effect of Falstaff's resurrection, Shakespeare has led us to believe Falstaff is dead, and this effect is enhanced by our further erroneous assumption that the scene has ended. And the return to life of the seemingly deceased Falstaff extends the life of the seemingly defunct scene.

The results of my application of these principles to the division of Shakespeare's plays are presented in the appendix, which provides a correlation of the resulting scene divisions in each play with the traditional act and scene divisions.[35] I will henceforth locate passages in the plays by reference to the divisions presented in the appendix. (For the convenience of the reader, however, I will continue to provide the traditional designations as well.) According to the traditional system, for example, the passage in which Cassius exclaims, "How many ages hence / Shall this our lofty scene be acted over / In states unborn and accents yet unknown!" would be cited as *Julius Caesar*, III.i.111–13. According to the system I am proposing the same passage would be cited as 8.111–13, that is, lines 111–13 of scene 8.

In a number of plays, including half of the comedies, the locations of divisions under the system I have proposed are the same as under the traditional system. Most of the discrepancies

35. Because plays involving collaboration raise special problems that are outside the scope of this study, I have excluded from my analysis three plays on which Shakespeare is thought by most scholars to have collaborated with another author. Those plays are *The Two Noble Kinsmen*, *Pericles*, and *Henry VIII*. Scenic divisions of these plays, however, are provided in the appendix.

between the two systems involve episodes without dialogue that
depict processions of various types or sorties during battles.
These deserve to be counted as scenes when they are preceded
and followed by a cleared stage and are thus separated from
prior and subsequent action.[36] The current practice of including
such scenes in the stage directions opening the following scene
obscures the break in continuity that has occurred. Even if represented in the text by the single word "*Excursions*," such an
episode may, in fact, occupy more stage time than a short scene
with dialogue and in the theater would be visually striking. Although the main function of most scenes without dialogue is simply to be emblematic of a battle or of the leading of forces to a
battle, significant action does take place in a few. Richard III
meets his death in a scene without dialogue, for example.[37] A
less climactic but yet important development occurs in what I
argue is the twenty-third scene of *King Lear*. This episode consists of a procession, preceded and followed by a cleared stage,
that is represented in print by the following terse stage direction
(at the beginning of what is traditionally designated as Act V,
scene ii): "*Enter, with drum and colors*, Lear, Cordelia, *and*
Soldiers, *over the stage*; *and exeunt*." In his previous appearance
onstage Lear had only begun to recover from the disorders that
had wracked his mind and body. But by the time this scene
occurs, he has revived enough to lead an army into battle; he
has revived enough to assume the kingly role he abdicated in his
first appearance in the play. Only six lines after the departure of
the military procession, Edgar announces Lear's defeat in battle.
Our tendency to compartmentalize two scenes (two episodes di-

36. Not all excursions are separate scenes. If, for example, characters
already onstage become involved in or witness a sortie, the sortie does not
constitute an independent scene; see, e.g., *Henry VI, Part Three*, scene 29
[V.iv], s.d. after l. 82).

37. For a discussion of this scene (*Richard III*, 28 [V.v, opening s.d.]), see
chapter 3.

vided by a cleared stage) allows us to accept the rapidity (in clock time) of this reversal. Yet the image of the revived Lear is still in our minds and intensifies our shock at Edgar's news.

Scene divisions do not necessarily correspond to breaks between narrative episodes. On the one hand, two or more seemingly unrelated episodes are sometimes united in the same scene. On the other hand, some narrative episodes are divided into two or more separate scenic units. An individual Shakespearean scene, nevertheless, almost always displays a distinct and coherent internal dramatic structure.

A particularly striking example of a scene that incorporates disparate elements yet possesses internal artistic coherence occurs in *King Lear*. After Kent has quarreled with Oswald and been placed in the stocks by order of Cornwall, he falls asleep. Edgar enters, delivers a soliloquy in which he describes his intention to disguise himself as Poor Tom, and leaves without ever acknowledging Kent's presence. Lear, the Fool, and a Gentleman then enter; Kent awakens and hails them; and a series of incidents involving various sets of characters ensues without a break. Because the stage has not been cleared since Kent's quarrel with Oswald, the Folio editors, in this case with full justification, regarded the entire sequence as one scene (II.ii).

On the apparent assumption that Edgar delivers his soliloquy in a different fictive location than that in which Kent is sleeping, however, most editors since Pope have made Edgar's soliloquy into a separate scene (II.iii) and have therefore been compelled to label the resumption of the action involving Kent as II.iv.[38] But in the first place, as I have argued, character continuity, not location, is the determining factor in scenic division. If two sets of characters occupy the stage at the same time they belong to the same *dramatic scene* even if they are unaware of one an-

38. See Horace Howard Furness, ed., *A New Variorum Edition of Shakespeare: King Lear* (1880; rpt. New York: Dover, 1963), p. 135n.

other's presence and, furthermore, even if they are in separate
fictive locations. Elsewhere in Shakespeare's plays, characters
who do not interact directly or who are even in separate locations, such as Richard and Richmond at their respective tents
before the Battle of Bosworth Field in *Richard III*, are nevertheless unquestionably in the same scene.[39] Furthermore, division
of the passage in *Lear* according to the tradition established by
Pope creates an awkward situation, like those created by the act
divisions in *A Midsummer Night's Dream*, in which a character
falls asleep in one scene and, without ever having left the stage,
wakes up in a later scene.

More importantly, the division of this sequence of episodes in
*Lear* into three scenes obscures the structure of this part of the
play. The segments that straddle Edgar's soliloquy are unified by
more than the mere presence of Kent. The scene begins with a
quarrel between Lear's representative, Kent, and a lowly representative of one of his malevolent daughters, proceeds to a confrontation mainly between Kent and Cornwall, the husband of
the other of those daughters, and eventually escalates to a direct
confrontation between Lear himself and both those daughters.
The effect of this progression would be greatly diminished if it
did not all take place within one continuous scene. That one
scene (scene 7 according to the system I have proposed) covers
an entire day—it begins with the words "Good dawning to thee"
and ends as "the night comes on" (7.494 [II.iv.297])—might
appall a neoclassical critic but is not an argument that it therefore needs to be broken into separate scenes. It is merely one of
many examples of Shakespeare's ability to telescope time.

39. The scene in which Richard and Richmond appear at their separate
tents, however, is not coextensive with the traditional division V.iii. A cleared
stage occurs after line 18 of this "scene" and another after line 271. But no
cleared stage occurs between lines 19 and 271, and for most of these 253 lines
(which compose scene 24 of the play) both Richard and Richmond are onstage
in separate fictive locations.

Although the clear progression of this scene is not interrupted by a cleared stage, it *is* interrupted by Edgar's soliloquy. And Shakespeare could have avoided this seemingly awkward interruption by placing Edgar's soliloquy before the entrance of Kent and Oswald. It would then have obviously qualified as a separate scene, would not have interrupted the action of the following scene, and would not have created a problem for editors.

The complete lack of direct interaction between Edgar and the only other character onstage does give the soliloquy an unusual independence from the scene in which it is found. Yet during the course of Edgar's soliloquy a viewer unfamiliar with the play could not be sure that no interaction would occur. Until Edgar's exit, such a viewer might reasonably expect that interaction *will* occur, might occasionally glance at Kent to see if he has awakened. Even a viewer familiar with the play probably does not entirely forget about the presence of Kent. Shakespeare perhaps chose to incorporate two lines of action in the same scene for the sake of the implicit comparison thus established between those lines of action and, in particular, between the two characters who share the stage but do not directly interact. Kent has been unjustly rejected by Lear, has disguised himself, and now suffers ignominy in the stocks; Edgar has been unjustly rejected by his father and in this soliloquy reveals his intention to disguise himself ignominiously as Poor Tom. Edgar's soliloquy thus serves to unite more closely the main plot and the subplot, which, as many commentators have noted, parallel one another in various ways. The comparison between Edgar and Kent, implicitly established by their counterpoised presence on the stage at the same time, would have been far less forceful had Edgar's soliloquy preceded the entrance of Kent and Oswald and thus been separated from Kent's humiliation by 153 lines.

Placed where it is, Edgar's soliloquy serves other purposes as well. Although the audience remains aware of Kent's presence, Edgar does become the center of attention; and this diversion,

however brief, makes the passage of time that occurs in the line
of action involving Kent more dramatically persuasive. Edgar's
soliloquy bears somewhat the same relationship to the scene in
which it occurs as one of the "mirror-scenes" described by Hereward T. Price bears to the play in which it is found.[40] Like those
scenes, it does not advance the action of the larger unit but does
focus some of the themes of that unit and hence, like those
scenes, "may be said to mirror" the larger whole. Nearly every
word of the soliloquy is echoed or brought to life in the surrounding scene. For example, Edgar says, "Edgar I nothing am"
(7.197 [II.iii.21]), and Lear later tells Regan, "Thy sister's
naught" (7.328 [II.iv.131]); Edgar plans to disguise himself as
a madman, and Cornwall earlier asks if Kent is "mad" (7
[II.ii].87); Edgar is forced to imitate "Bedlam beggars" (7.190
[II.iii.14]), and Lear at one point does bitterly mimic a beggar:
"On my knees I beg / That you'll vouchsafe me raiment, bed,
and food" (7.349–50 [II.iv.152–53]). Our imaginations are
stimulated, as they otherwise might not have been, by the incor-
poration of disparate narrative elements in the same continuous
scene. Only after Edgar's departure does an audience realize
that his soliloquy constituted a kind of scene within a scene.
Shakespeare tries to have it both ways and succeeds.

An example of a narrative episode divided into separate scenic units is that of Hamlet's first encounter with the Ghost,
which is interrupted by a cleared stage. Though the *narrative*
action is continuous according to Dover Wilson's criteria, the
cleared stage marks the end of one *dramatic* movement and the
beginning of another. And while the two resultant scenes (I.iv
and v) are obviously linked, each has an independent dramatic
structure.

40. See Hereward T. Price, "Mirror-Scenes in Shakespeare," in *Joseph
Quincy Adams Memorial Studies*, ed. James G. McManaway, Giles E. Dawson,
and Edwin E. Willoughby (Washington, D.C.: Folger Shakespeare Library,
1948), pp. 101–13.

Scene 4 (I.iv) is located, as the first scene of the play had been, on the battlements of Elsinore, and Hamlet's opening comment to Horatio and Marcellus—"The air bites shrewdly; it is very cold" (l. 1)—recalls Francisco's comment in the earlier scene: "'Tis bitter cold, / And I am sick at heart" (1 [I.i].8–9). The connection is strengthened by our awareness that Hamlet, too, is "sick at heart." Even the time of the two scenes is virtually identical:

*Bernardo.* 'Tis now struck twelve.

(1.7)

*Horatio.*          I think it lacks of twelve.
*Marcellus.* No, it is struck.

(4.3–4)

The men confronted in the earlier scene first by the cold and darkness and then by the portentous appearance of the Ghost display mutual respect and comradeship toward one another. An image of mutual respect and friendship is again created at the beginning of scene 4, especially between Hamlet and Horatio, and is implicitly contrasted with the "swagg'ring" (l. 9) revels of the King and his cronies, revels of which Hamlet disapproves.

When the Ghost enters, Hamlet's initial reactions are not unlike Horatio's reactions when confronted by the Ghost in the earlier scene. Both address it directly and vigorously and repeatedly ask it to explain its equivocal appearance. Each admits his fear, but each risks confronting it:

*Horatio.* I'll cross it, though it blast me.

(1.127)

*Hamlet.* I do not set my life at a pin's fee.
. . . I'll follow it.

(4.65, 68)

Horatio was the spokesman for the group of three mortal men to whom the Ghost appeared in scene 1. Though Hamlet clearly

has a special relationship to this ghost of his father, his first long
speech to the Ghost is still primarily that of a representative of
the group of men confronted by the supernatural. This speech
ends:

> What may this mean
> That thou, dead corse, again in complete steel,
> Revisits thus the glimpses of the moon,
> Making night hideous, and we fools of nature
> So horridly to shake our disposition
> With thoughts beyond the reaches of our souls?
> Say, why is this? Wherefore? What should we do?
>
> (ll. 51–57)

But when the Ghost beckons Hamlet and Hamlet decides to
follow it, the similarity with the opening scene is replaced by a
contrast. In that scene the men finally threaten the Ghost with
weapons. In this it is Hamlet who threatens his companions, and
his words call attention to the irony: "Unhand me, gentlemen. / By heaven, I'll make a ghost of him that lets me!"
(ll. 84–85). He frees himself and follows the Ghost.

Though the narrative incident of the encounter with the Ghost
continues in the next scene, scene 4 clearly has a self-contained
dramatic structure. The emotional pitch of the scene sharply
rises at the entrance of the Ghost, rises to the point of crisis
when the Ghost beckons Hamlet, and reaches a climactic peak
when Hamlet violently disengages himself from his comrades.
The Ghost has still not spoken, still not revealed the import of
its appearance, but a decisive dramatic event has occurred.
Hamlet, whose isolation from the court of Claudius was dramatized in an earlier scene and was reasserted by his remarks early
in this scene, has now forcibly isolated himself even from those
companions, including Horatio, whose comradeship has been
set against the vulgarity of the court.

After this climax and the exit of the supernatural figure and the protagonist of the play occurs a final segment, a brief coda, which lowers the emotional pitch and provides a sense of closure. Horatio and Marcellus, who were the two principal speakers in the last segment of the opening scene after the departure of the Ghost, this time are left onstage to consider not only the behavior of the Ghost but that of Hamlet. Horatio's first comment after the exit of those two figures concerns the latter: "He waxes desperate with imagination" (l. 87). Although Marcellus then urges immediate pursuit ("Let's follow. 'Tis not fit thus to obey him," l. 88) and Horatio vigorously assents ("Have after!" l. 89), the latter delays their departure momentarily by asking a question ("To what issue will this come?" l. 89). That Marcellus's response ("Something is rotten in the state of Denmark," l. 90) and Horatio's further comment ("Heaven will direct it," l. 91) do delay their pursuit is indicated by Marcellus's negation of still further talk and his repetition of his earlier behest: "Nay, let's follow him" (l. 91). Though impassioned, this hurried commentary and speculation by secondary characters represent a falling off from the emotional peak of Hamlet's threat and his violent disengagement from his comrades and round off this scene, this distinct unit of the play. The exchange between Horatio and Marcellus gives the actors playing Hamlet and the Ghost time to breathe before their return to the stage. But it also gives the audience time to breathe before a new dramatic movement, a new rise in intensity, begins.

After a cleared stage a new dramatic movement does begin. The dialogue between Hamlet and the Ghost rises in intensity as the Ghost reveals in stages the dreadful purport of its visit. It first mentions "revenge" in line 7 of scene 5 (I.v) but does not mention "murder" until line 25 and does not identify the murderer until line 40. After filling in the ghastly details of the murder and enjoining Hamlet to take action against Claudius but not against Gertrude, the Ghost leaves.

The rest of the scene, first in Hamlet's soliloquy and then in

his words and actions after the entrance of Horatio and Marcellus, dramatizes Hamlet's frenzied, nearly hysterical, reaction
to the Ghost's revelation. Shakespeare handles magnificently the
dramatic problem posed by the rejoining of Hamlet and his companions. The reestablishing of Hamlet's contact with his companions and his swearing them to secrecy might easily have nul-
lified our sense of his isolation, so emphatically established in
the preceding scene. Shakespeare solves the problem by distancing Hamlet from those companions through his manic behavior and the ironic tone of his remarks to them. Hamlet even
parodies the obviously inappropriate conventions of mundane
social intercourse:

> I hold it fit that we shake hands and part:
> You, as your business and desire shall point you,
> For every man hath business and desire
> Such as it is, and for my poor part,
> Look you, I'll go pray.
>
> (5.128–32)

Hamlet's distance from his companions is also maintained by his
refusal to divulge even to Horatio the Ghost's revelation: "For
your desire to know what is between us, / O'ermaster't as you
may" (ll. 139–40).[41]

Hamlet's isolation has thus been forcefully reasserted. And
our sense of that isolation is hardly lessened later by Hamlet's
calmer and more sincere expressions of friendship. He drops his
antic disposition and sarcasm to tell his closest friend, "There
are more things in heaven and earth, Horatio, / Than are dreamt
of in your philosophy" (ll. 166–67). But he still does not say
what those "things" are, just as the Ghost refrained from telling
Hamlet the "secrets" of its "prison house" (l. 14). Hamlet is
almost as isolated from even his closest comrade as the Ghost is

---

41. The coldness of this refusal becomes cruel perversity if the actor playing Hamlet extends the pause at the end of the first line.

from the human being closest to it. Eventually, Hamlet does renew his intimacy with and reveal his secrets to Horatio, but at this early turning point of the play Shakespeare clearly wants to dramatize Hamlet's isolation.

The ending of this scene, like that of the previous one, creates a firm impression of dramatic closure before the stage is cleared. After the bizarre swearing ceremony is finally over, Hamlet begins the last speech of the scene by telling the Ghost—whose commands ("Swear") have punctuated that ceremony—"Rest, rest, perturbèd spirit" (l. 182). Hamlet, too, has been perturbed, but he has now calmed down and speaks without irony to his companions:

> So, gentlemen,
> With all my love I do commend me to you,
> And what so poor a man as Hamlet is
> May do t'express his love and friending to you,
> God willing, shall not lack. Let us go in together,
> And still your fingers on your lips, I pray.[42]
>
> (ll. 182–87)

But, as at the end of the preceding scene, the departure of the characters is momentarily delayed. Hamlet briefly gives vent to his emotions: "The time is out of joint. O cursèd spite, / That ever I was born to set it right!" (ll. 188–89). This outburst confirms Hamlet's reestablishment of intimacy with his companions. It expresses genuine emotion rather than an antic disposition and discloses more of the nature of the Ghost's revelation

42. The contrast between Hamlet's address to his companions as they are about to leave the stage together and his earlier speech in which he parodies conventional leave-taking is heightened by verbal echoes: "Why, right, you are in the right; / And so, . . ." (ll. 126–27); "Rest, rest, perturbèd spirit. So, gentlemen" (l. 182); ". . . and for my own poor part" (l. 131); "And what so poor a man as Hamlet is" (l. 184); "Look you, I'll go pray" (l. 132); "And still your fingers on your lips, I pray" (l. 187). But the echoes cut both ways. At the very moment that Hamlet reestablishes an intimacy of sorts with his comrades we are reminded that he has been and still is isolated from them.

than Hamlet has so far disclosed. Yet at the same time the couplet reaffirms Hamlet's isolation—he possesses knowledge his
friends do not share and shoulders alone a terrible, unspecified
responsibility. As has often been observed, the phrase "cursèd
spite," like the phrase "perturbèd spirit," applies equally well to
Hamlet and to the Ghost. That Hamlet can be described by
terms equally applicable to the Ghost is another indication of the
distance that has opened up between Hamlet and his comrades.
Furthermore, Hamlet's outburst, which delays the departure of
the three men in this scene, specifically and ironically recalls
the exchange between Marcellus and Horatio, which delayed
their departure in the earlier scene:

> *Marcellus*. Something is rotten in the state of Denmark.
> *Horatio*. Heaven will direct it.
>
> (4.90–91)

Marcellus did not know and still does not know what that "something" is, whereas Hamlet now does know why "the time is out of
joint." Horatio was confident that heaven will direct the course
of events, whereas Hamlet is in anguish that the burden of set-
ting right that course has been placed on him.[43]

Just as Marcellus finally cut off further talk and repeated his
injunction to pursue Hamlet ("Nay, let's follow him") at the end
of the previous scene, Hamlet cuts off his own outburst and
repeats his invitation to his companions ("Nay, come, let's go
together," l. 190). But even though Horatio and Marcellus "follow" their comrade at the end of scene 4, even though they
eventually rejoin him and "go together" with him at the end of

43. This irony is ultimately mitigated, however, for Hamlet eventually not
only places his trust in Horatio but late in the play even comes to share
Horatio's belief concerning the direction of human affairs: "Our indiscretion
sometime serves us well / When our deep plots do pall, and that should learn
us / There's a divinity that shapes our ends, / Rough-hew them how we will"
(20 [V.ii].8–11).

scene 5, Hamlet, who broke away from his comrades near the
end of the first of these scenes, is still very much alone at the
end of the second. The single narrative episode of Hamlet's confrontation with the Ghost is thus divided into two companion
scenes, two distinct dramatic movements, each with its own exposition, rising action, climax, and denouement.

Although the arguments I have presented in this chapter to
demonstrate that the scene is the basic unit of Shakespeare's
dramatic structure conflict with the five-act theory of that structure, they support and are supported by an alternative view of
Elizabethan and Shakespearean dramatic construction. In *Endeavors of Art: A Study of Form in Elizabethan Drama*, Madeleine Doran applies an observation made by the art critic
Heinrich Wölfflin to English Renaissance drama:

> One of the chief points of difference between renaissance and
> baroque painting he finds in the "multiple unity" of the former,
> the "unified unity" of the latter. He means that renaissance art
> "achieves its unity by making the parts independent as free
> members, and that the baroque abolishes the uniform indepen-
> dence of the parts in favour of a more unified total motive. In the
> former case, co-ordination of the accents; in the latter, subor-
> dination." Now multiplicity is one of the first things that strikes
> us as characteristic of sixteenth century literary art. [44]

Doran goes on to delineate the "multiplicity of detail," the "co-
piousness" of Elizabethan, particularly Shakespearean, drama,
especially in contrast with more economical classical drama.
But one implication of Wölfflin's observation is not explored by
Doran. If, as I have maintained, scenes are the major structural

44. (Madison: Univ. of Wisconsin Press, 1954), p. 6. The first proposition
by Wölfflin that Doran discusses occurs in chapter 4 of *Principles of Art History*, translated from the 7th German edition (1929) by M. D. Hottinger (New
York, 1932). The extended passage she quotes is found on p. 159 of the same
book.

divisions of Shakespeare's plays, then they would seem to be the specific "parts" of a play made "independent as free members" through which a play "achieves its unity."

The scene was an ideal structural unit for a drama that achieved its unity through multiplicity. A scene can focus on a single character in private or on a public event involving a score of characters; a scene can contain a long series of incidents and run for hundreds of lines or can be limited to a single incident without any dialogue at all. The way in which unity was achieved through such a flexible multiple-purpose structural unit is suggested by Empson's remark, cited at the beginning of this chapter. The "system of 'construction by scenes'" employed by Elizabethan dramatists, particularly Shakespeare, "clearly makes the scenes . . . stand out as objects in themselves, to be compared even when they are not connected," and such comparisons serve to unify a play. Though the present study will focus on the structure of individual scenes, many examples will be discussed of scenes within particular plays that are "compared even when they are not connected." A number of critics besides Empson, including Hereward T. Price, Marco Mincoff, Bernard Beckerman, Emrys Jones, and Mark Rose, have stressed the importance of scenes as structural elements in Shakespeare's plays. But none has conducted the comprehensive and systematic investigation of the internal structure of scenes that is attempted in the present study.[45]

45. Jones, *Scenic Form*, and Mark Rose, *Shakespearean Design* (Cambridge: Belknap Press of Harvard Univ. Press, 1972), both contain useful analyses of individual scenes, but only a small part of each book focuses on the internal structure of scenes, and both obscure the variety of structures employed by Shakespeare. Rose, for example, argues that most scenes have the design of either a triptych or a diptych. Not only is this an oversimplification, but Rose's governing metaphor obscures the crucial difference between a static, atemporal art form and the dynamic, temporal medium of drama. Jones, on the other hand, excludes the comedies, the largest group of plays in the canon, from his analysis.

Just as the complete change in characters that occurs at the break between scenes is an important element in the dramatic structure of a play as a whole, entrances or exits of characters are significant elements of the internal dramatic structure of a scene. Almost any change in the composition of the group of characters onstage is bound to change the nature and direction of the dramatic development of the scene. The character does not have to be an important figure himself to effect such a change of the tone or direction of a scene. A messenger who enters with momentous news, for example, will alter the tenor of the conversation of more important characters already onstage. The interval between one entrance or exit and the next such change has for a long time been recognized as an important structural unit in classical French drama, and the term *scène* has been applied to it. (To avoid confusion such intervals will be referred to in the present study simply as "segments" of a scene.) Act divisions in the classical French theater usually occur, in turn, at those points when the stage is entirely cleared of characters and, in this respect, correspond to scene divisions in Shakespearean drama. Though there are many more scenes in a given play by Shakespeare than acts in a French play, the scene is nevertheless the largest structural subdivision that is unquestionably to be found in every play by Shakespeare, and the *liaison des scènes* within an act in the French theater corresponds to the continuity within a Shakespearean scene.

A number of Shakespearean scenes contain only one segment; that is, only a single character or a single unchanging group of characters appears in each of these scenes. Such "unitary" scenes will be discussed in chapters 2, 3, and 4. Scenes that comprise two segments will be discussed in chapter 5, and multipartite scenes, which comprise a longer series of character groupings, are the focus of chapter 6.

# Two ✖ Solo Scenes

In chapter 1 I attempted to demonstrate not only that the scene is a basic unit within the overall dramatic construction of a Shakespearean play but that individual scenes possess their own recognizable internal structure. Some scenes are long and intricately constructed, while others are brief and not at all complex in structure. The most simply structured scenes are generally those in which no important characters enter or leave after the start of the scene and no minor characters enter with news that changes the course of the action. Because these scenes contain only a single unchanging group of characters, they may be termed "unitary scenes." The simplest scenes of all are those in which a single player enters, delivers a speech, and leaves without making contact with another player. Such scenes are infrequent in Shakespearean drama. *Antony and Cleopatra* with 45 scenes (42, according to the traditional system of division), many of them very short, contains none. Of 780 scenes in 35 plays, only 30 are solo scenes, and 12 of these are formal choruses.[1]

Those choruses consist of four prologues, six midplay choruses, and two epilogues. *Henry V* with a prologue, an epilogue,

---

1. These and all subsequent computations are based on the system of scenic division presented in chapter 1 and in the appendix, rather than on the traditional system of division. A precedent for the classification of formal choruses as "scenes" was established in the First Folio, whose editors labeled the speech of "Time, the Chorus" in *The Winter's Tale* as "Scena Prima" of "Actus Quartus."

and four midplay choruses contains half of the total. Just as one type of image will appear sporadically throughout Shakespeare's work but repeatedly in a given play, so too a particular device of scenic construction that appears intermittently throughout the canon will occur repeatedly in one or two particular plays. The choral scene is such a device. Except for *Henry V*, only two plays, *Romeo and Juliet* and *Henry IV*, *Part Two*, have as many as two such scenes.

Some choral scenes, like the Prologue to *Troilus and Cressida* and scene 28 (V.Chorus) of *Henry V*, provide information about events not dramatized. Some—notably the Prologue to *Henry V*—ask the indulgence of the audience for the limitations of stage performance. A few, such as the two in *Romeo and Juliet*, summarize or comment on the forthcoming or preceding action. Some provide details of atmosphere or mood:

> Now entertain conjecture of a time
> When creeping murmur and the poring dark
> Fills the wide vessel of the universe.
> From camp to camp, through the foul womb of night,
> The hum of either army stilly sounds.
>
> (*Henry V*, 18 [IV.Chorus].1–5)

Most choral scenes serve more than one of these functions. The two personifications who deliver choral monologues—Rumor in the Prologue or Induction to *Henry IV*, *Part Two* and Time in *The Winter's Tale* (9 [IV.i])—provide self-characterization as well as exposition. The two choral epilogues do not have much in common. The Epilogue to *Henry V*, one of three choral scenes in sonnet form, again raises the issue of theatrical limitations ("In little room confining mighty men," l. 3) that is a prominent theme of earlier choruses in the play. The speech also praises Henry V, refers to the subsequent reign of his son, and asks for the audience's approval of the performance. By contrast, the Epilogue to *Henry IV*, *Part Two*, the only choral scene in prose,

is quite informal.[2] It is so disjointed that many scholars believe
it is a composite of separate epilogues for different occasions; it
is usually omitted in modern performances of the play.[3]

A number of Shakespearean plays have epilogues delivered
by an actor who has played a leading role during the performance. But only one of these monologues, that "spoken by Prospero," actually constitutes an independent scene. After participating in the final merrymaking in *As You Like It*, Rosalind
remains onstage to deliver the epilogue. No cleared stage occurs
before the actor playing the King of France delivers the epilogue
to *All's Well That Ends Well*. Pandarus enters the final scene of
*Troilus and Cressida* just in time to be cursed by Troilus who
then leaves with all the other characters before Pandarus addresses the audience.[4] The other fairies leave Puck onstage to

2. The only choral scenes (besides the two epilogues) that are not in blank
verse are the two in *Romeo and Juliet*, which are in sonnet form, and Time's
speech in couplets in *The Winter's Tale*.

3. Both Norman N. Holland, Jr., editor of the Signet edition, and A. R.
Humphreys, editor of the Arden edition, argue that the speech is a composite
of separate epilogues. See *The Complete Signet Classic Shakespeare*, p. 722n.;
and *The Second Part of King Henry IV* (Cambridge: Harvard Univ. Press,
1966), p. 186n. In any case, this Epilogue has fewer resemblances to the
Epilogue of *Henry V*, delivered by a chorus, than to some of the monologues
delivered by characters who step out of their roles to speak informally to the
audience at the end of the final scene. These resemblances led Martin Holmes
to the intriguing but highly conjectural conclusion that the Epilogue to *Henry
IV, Part Two* was spoken by William Kempe, who played Falstaff in the play;
see *Shakespeare and His Players* (New York: Scribner's, 1972), pp. 46–50.

4. Troilus's final long speech in the play resembles the concluding speech
of other plays and may have constituted the original ending of the play. But—
whether or not the Pandarus section was added by Shakespeare in a revised
version of the play—as R. A. Foakes points out, the existing double ending is
appropriate to a play which, throughout, maintains an ambivalence of tone.
Foakes argues that these endings are not opposed but complementary and
together establish an "'open' ending"; see *"Troilus and Cressida* Recon-
sidered," *University of Toronto Quarterly* 32 (Jan. 1963): 142–54. In any case,
the text in its present form does not end with Troilus's speech, and no scene
break occurs to separate Pandarus's epilogue from the rest of the final scene.

present the epilogue to *A Midsummer Night's Dream*, and Feste remains after the final scene of *Twelfth Night* to sing the closing song.[5] Although it can constitute an independent scene, an epilogue, like a soliloquy, may also be merely an element in a longer, continuous scene. But Prospero almost certainly leaves the stage and then returns to deliver the speech that in the Folio is given the formal title, "Epilogue spoken by Prospero." This title is preceded by Prospero's request to the other characters onstage at that point, "Please you, draw near," and by the stage direction *"Exeunt omnes."*

Some critics regard this epilogue as merely a plea for applause.[6] Hallett Smith, for instance, argues that it "has the same function of distancing as the epilogue to *As You Like It*."[7] The

5. The existing stage directions before Feste's song and Puck's speech are ambiguously incomplete, but it is unlikely that either performer exits and then reenters. The direction before the final song in *Twelfth Night* is *"Exeunt. Clown sings"* (after l. 389 of scene 19 [V.i]). In Shakespearean stage directions *"Exeunt"* indicates that more than one character exits but not necessarily that all the characters onstage exit. As a result, *"Exeunt"* is often followed by a qualification. (See, for example, the stage direction following line 145 of *Richard III*, scene 6 [II.ii]—*"Exeunt. Manet* Buckingham *and* Richard.") The direction "Clown *sings*" is almost certainly just such a qualification, merely a clipped form of *"Manet* Clown, *who sings."* This interpretation is far more likely than the alternative, that *"Exeunt.* Clown *sings"* should be interpreted to mean *"Exeunt omnes. Reenter* Clown, *who sings."* Similarly, the simple *"Exeunt"* preceding Puck's final speech probably means *"Exeunt. Manet* Puck" rather than *"Exeunt omnes. Reenter* Puck." (Compare the simple stage direction *"Exeunt"* after line 254 of *Hamlet*, scene 2 [I.ii], at which point Horatio, Marcellus, and Bernardo exit, but Hamlet remains onstage.) The song at the end of *Love's Labor's Lost* is certainly not separated from the rest of the final scene by a cleared stage and is even incorporated into the fictional world of the play. Armado introduces it by asking the King, "Most esteemed greatness, will you hear the dialogue that the two learned men have compiled in praise of the owl and the cuckoo?" (9 [V.ii].882–85).

6. A few believe it to be spurious. See, e.g., Stanley Edgar Hyman, *Iago: Some Approaches to the Illusion of His Motivation* (New York: Atheneum, 1970), p. 85.

7. *Shakespeare's Romances: A Study of Some Ways of the Imagination* (San Marino, Calif.: Huntington Library, 1972), p. 138. Theodore Spencer sim-

latter speech does seem to have such a function. After a very
tenuous maintenance of his fictional role in the opening words—
"It is not the fashion to see the lady the epilogue" (23.199–200
[Epilogue.1–2])—the boy actor playing Rosalind completely
drops the pose and engages in banter: "If I were a woman, I
would kiss as many of you as had beards that pleased me, com-
plexions that liked me, and breaths that I defied not" (23.214–
17). Although the performer is still in the costume of Rosalind,
he has clearly divested himself of his role and has stepped out of
the fictional world of the play. One could not mistake even the
opening words of the epilogue for a speech by the dramatic character Rosalind.

But the situation in *The Tempest* is quite different. After a
cleared stage, the actor playing Prospero, still in costume, enters and begins a speech that an audience would at first be unable to distinguish from a soliloquy:

> Now my charms are all o'erthrown,
> And what strength I have's my own,
> Which is most faint.
>
> (10 [Epilogue].1–3)

Though Prospero has vowed to break his staff and drown his
book, he retained his magic powers at least until the final line of
the previous scene, when he set Ariel free. The opening lines of
his seeming soliloquy, then, provide confirmation that he has
lived up to his vow; we are now seeing what we have not seen
before—Prospero no longer a magician. And although the actor
then proceeds to address the audience directly, he also stead-
fastly maintains his fictional role as Prospero throughout the remainder of the speech:

---

ilarly dismisses the speech as "merely a prayer to the audience"; see "Shake-
speare's Last Plays," *Shakespeare and the Nature of Man* (New York: Mac-
Millan, 1942), rpt. in *Twentieth Century Interpretations of "The Tempest,"* ed.
Hallett Smith (Englewood Cliffs, N.J.: Prentice-Hall, 1969), p. 45, n. 2.

. . . Now 'tis true
I must be here confined by you,
Or sent to Naples. Let me not,
Since I have my dukedom got
And pardoned the deceiver, dwell
In this bare island by your spell;
But release me from my bands
With the help of your good hands.
Gentle breath of yours my sails
Must fill, or else my project fails,
Which was to please. Now I want
Spirits to enforce, art to enchant;
And my ending is despair
Unless I be relieved by prayer,
Which pierces so that it assaults
Mercy itself and frees all faults.
As you from crimes would pardoned be,
Let your indulgence set me free.[8]

(10.3–20)

Smith disparages the views of "allegorical and Christian interpreters of this epilogue" (*Shakespeare's Romances*, p. 138). Yet it is possible to cast a cold eye on such interpretations and still see that the speech in a partly witty, partly serious way alludes to major themes of the play and extends the context of those themes to include the audience. We are given power, or told that we have power, not simply over an actor but over a

8. The adroit ambivalence of the speech is present even in the opening lines. They can be translated into a conventional announcement by the actor that he has abandoned his role. But unlike the opening of the epilogue to *All's Well That Ends Well*—"The king's a beggar, now the play is done" (23.334 [Epilogue.1])—the opening of the Epilogue to *The Tempest* also represents a plausible utterance by a dramatic character. Indeed, many critics discuss the speech as a whole in much the same way one would discuss any other speech by a dramatic character; see, e.g., D'Orsay W. Pearson, "'Unless I Be Relieved by Prayer': *The Tempest* in Perspective," *Shakespeare Studies* 7 (1974): 278.

dramatic character. According to Robert Egan, "rather than stepping out of his dramatic context to address us in our own sphere of reality, Prospero offers to bring us into the world of the play."[9] And Prospero asks us to do for him what he has just done for Ariel. Indeed, if we deny him prayer and leave him "here confined," we would be associating ourselves with the "damned witch Sycorax," who "did confine" Ariel in a pine on the island (2 [I.ii].264, 275). Prospero asks us to do for him what he had earlier done for Alonso and his companions. They were "confined together," and Ariel told Prospero, "They cannot budge till your release" (9 [V.i].7, 11). Now Prospero asks us, "But release me from my bands." Prospero told Alonso, "I do forgive / Thy rankest fault—all of them" (9.131–32), and now, in seeking to be freed of "all faults" himself, he explicitly recalls his own act of forgiveness ("Since I have my dukedom got / And pardoned the deceiver"). On the one hand, the speech is certainly a clever means of inducing our applause, if such means were necessary. On the other, it is a plea to recognize the play's themes and to imitate a character, or at least to identify imaginatively with a character, who has shown mercy in the course of the play.

Surprisingly few main characters have solo scenes. None of Hamlet's soliloquies constitutes an independent scene. The only character in *Othello* with a solo scene is the Herald who paraphrases the document he carries (5 [II.ii]). *Richard III* is the only Shakespearean play that opens with a soliloquy by a major character, and this soliloquy, like a prologue, sets the scene and foreshadows the ensuing action. But unlike a prologue delivered by a chorus, this speech leads without a break into the first interaction between characters. The only plot Richard describes

9. *Drama within Drama: Shakespeare's Sense of His Art in "King Lear," "The Winter's Tale," and "The Tempest"* (New York: Columbia Univ. Press, 1975), p. 117. Karol Berger explores some of the "metatheatrical" implications of the epilogue in "Prospero's Art," *Shakespeare Studies* 10 (1977): 211–39.

in detail is the one against his brother Clarence, and at the conclusion of that description, Clarence enters. Each of Richard's subsequent soliloquies is also part of a longer scene. Yet the lowly Scrivener in the same play has a scene all to himself in which he comments on the Hastings indictment he is carrying (14 [III.vi]). In *Julius Caesar* Brutus, Antony, Cassius, and Caesar deliver soliloquies, but only that of Artemidorus, in which he reads aloud the letter he is carrying, comprises a separate scene (6 [II.iii]). Although delivered by dramatic characters, the detached soliloquies of the Herald, the Scrivener, and Artemidorus resemble that other group of solo scenes, the choral monologues. These three characters comment on rather than actively participate in the action. Artemidorus is the most active of the three, but his later attempt to deliver his letter of warning to Caesar is quickly rebuffed. The document each of these characters carries is a physical prop that tends to obscure his essentially choral function. The only remaining example of this type of scene involves a slight variation. In his brief solo scene near the end of *Timon of Athens* (19 [V.iii]), the Soldier does not read a document that he carries with him but rather reads Timon's self-composed epitaph that he finds onstage.

Two other minor characters have solo scenes according to the criteria established for scene divisions in chapter 1. At the beginning of the traditional division IV.v of *Coriolanus*, a servant enters alone, cries out, "Wine, wine, wine! What service is here! I think our fellows are asleep," and presumably exits, although no such stage direction is provided. Another servant then enters, speaks a few words as he crosses the stage ("Where's Cotus? My master calls for him. Cotus!"), and exits. No apparent contact occurs either between the two servants or between the second and Coriolanus, who subsequently enters. Although the time and location of the action are continuous from the entrance of the First Servingman until after Coriolanus's entrance and although each servingman is onstage only briefly, the recog-

nition that the two servants' passages are separate scenes illumi-
nates the structure of the play, at least the structure of that part
of the play from the traditional division III.i to the scene in
which Coriolanus meets Aufidius.

Scene 14 (III.i) contains a significant turning point—the tribunes have finally secured the upper hand in their struggle to
dispose of Coriolanus, are finally confident enough to accuse
him of treason and to call for his death. In scene 23 (IV.v.5–
end) the banished Coriolanus finally joins the enemies of Rome.
That Coriolanus should join the Volscians is both ironic and,
after his rejection by the Romans, dramatically inevitable. The
structure of the sequence of scenes between 15 (III.ii) and 23
serves to maintain suspense by postponing the inevitable. Coriolanus's irrevocable break with the Romans, for example, does
not occur until scene 16 (III.iii); in scene 15 he agrees to answer
the charges against him "mildly . . . Mildly!" (l. 145). But his
reluctance to do so and the general presentation of his character so far inspire little confidence that he will abide by this re-
solve. In the previous scene Menenius accurately observed,
"His heart's his mouth: / What his breast forges, that his tongue
must vent" (14 [III.i].256–57). And this observation is echoed
early in scene 16 by one of the tribunes:

> . . . Being once chafed, he cannot
> Be reined again to temperance; then he speaks
> What's in his heart, and that is there which looks
> With us to break his neck.
>
> (16.27–30)

Scene 15, then, merely postpones the inevitable banishment.

Similarly, the increasing frequency of cleared stages, of interruptions in the continuity of the action, after the initial confident
show of force by the tribunes in their struggle against Coriolanus
postpones the ironic inevitability of his joining the enemies of
Rome. Scene 16 is by far the longest (335 lines) in the play. The

next six scenes are progressively shorter: first come two scenes of less than half the length of 16 (145 and 144 lines); then three much shorter scenes (58, 53, and 52 lines); and then one scene of only 26 lines. The dwindling process continues with the two solo scenes of the servants, the first of which contains thirteen words and the second, eight. This progression of shorter and shorter scenes thus continues right up to the point at which Coriolanus steps into the house of his archenemy. The more and more frequent cleared stages—interruptions in the continuity— occur in a performance of the play whether or not the two servants' brief passages are regarded as separate scenes. But if they are not so indicated in a text of the play, the progression will be obscured for the reader.

The first scene in this sequence, 14, began with a question by Coriolanus, still a stalwart defender of Rome, "Tullus Aufidius then hath made new head?" (that is, "Is it true that Tullus Aufidius has raised a new army?"); scene 23 begins with Coriolanus entering the house of Tullus Aufidius in order to join that army. This irony would also be obscured if Coriolanus's entry were not recognized as the beginning of a new scene.

Despite their extreme brevity and seeming lack of substance, the two servants' solo scenes (21 [IV.v.1–2] and 22 [IV.v.3–4]) also serve other functions. Each of the two scenes ironically echoes scene 20. The words of the First Servingman ("What service is here!"), as has frequently been pointed out,[10] establish a light dramatic irony since, in the concluding line of the previous scene, Coriolanus declared, "I'll do his [Aufidius's] country service" (20 [IV.iv].26). A service wholly unexpected and far more momentous than the kind sought by the First Servingman is about to be offered. The Second Servingman's even shorter speech also contains a suggestive echo of scene 20, and

10. See, e.g., the footnote to this line in the Arden edition of *Coriolanus*, ed. J. P. Brockbank (London: Methuen, 1976).

only twenty lines intervene between the two passages. Seeking
his archenemy, Coriolanus asks a Citizen "Where great Aufidius
lies" (20.8). Before the actual confrontation between the two
warriors occurs, however, we see another character in search of
his peer—the Second Servingman is seeking his fellow servant
("Where's Cotus?"). Ironic similarities between the actions of
low characters and those of their betters occur in many Elizabethan plays, even in ones, like *Coriolanus*, without extended
subplots involving the low characters.

Furthermore, the two scenes form a balanced pair. Both are
solo scenes, and both are very short. They involve similar actions, carry similar ironic echoes of scene 20, and even employ
similar series of grammatical constructions. As with many pairs
of parallel scenes in Shakespeare's plays, the second is shorter,
a condensed version, as it were, of the first. I realize that I have
placed a heavy burden on two seemingly negligible and straight-
forward passages. But the functions claimed for these scenes
resemble functions served by many other scenes in Shakespeare's
plays. Even if the initial motive for his decision to include these
scenes was to avoid an immediate reentry by Coriolanus, he was
not incapable of turning a necessity to advantage.

One of the instances in which a major character does have a
solo scene occurs in *Timon of Athens*. Scene 13 (IV.i) of that play
consists exclusively of Timon's soliloquy. But that Timon should
have no contact with other characters either before or after this
soliloquy is appropriate because Timon here renounces human
fellowship. After cursing the people of Athens, one and all, he
declares,

> Timon will to the woods, where he shall find
> Th'unkindest beast more kinder than mankind.

> (13.35–36)

As I argued in chapter 1, Edgar's "Poor Tom" soliloquy in *King
Lear* does not qualify as an independent scene. At the same

time, however, it exhibits an unusual independence from the
scene in which it occurs and is virtually a scene within a
scene—Shakespeare tries to have it both ways and succeeds.
Like Timon, Edgar discusses his outcast state. Unjustly sus-
pected of plotting against his father, Edgar has had to flee the
society of men under even greater compulsion than Timon, and
while Timon merely declares a preference for the company of
beasts to that of men, Edgar is forced to assume a beastlike
existence himself:

> . . . Whiles I may 'scape,
> I will preserve myself; and am bethought
> To take the basest and most poorest shape
> That ever penury, in contempt of man,
> Brought near to beast.
>
> (7.181–85 [II.iii.5–9])

In a solo scene in *King John*, Arthur, like Edgar, is in the act of
escaping and seeks anonymity in a lowly disguise, and like both
Edgar and Timon, he is emphatically and explicitly a lone
outcast:

> There's few or none do know me; if they did,
> This ship-boy's semblance hath disguised me quite.[11]
>
> (11 [IV.iii].3–4)

Although many of Shakespeare's main characters are meta-
phorically alienated from society or even banished, Shakespeare
reserves solo scenes to emphasize the more literal and complete
alienation of Arthur and Timon and gives Edgar a kind of solo
scene within a scene for much the same purpose.

In two battle sequences, however, main characters have brief

11. Like several of the other solo scenes I have discussed and will be
discussing, this one is not a separate scene according to the conventional
division of the play. But Arthur dies at the end of his soliloquy, and the stage is
temporarily cleared of living characters. The rationale for a scene division in
such cases is presented in chapter 1.

solo scenes. In each case the character enters, expresses the violent single-mindedness with which he is seeking single combat with a particular opponent, and exits to continue the search. The following speech comprises the entire solo scene in which a finally aroused Achilles seeks the slayer of his beloved Patroclus:

> Where is this Hector?
> Come, come, thou boy-queller, show thy face;
> Know what it is to meet Achilles angry.
> Hector, where's Hector? I will none but Hector.[12]
>
> (*Troilus and Cressida*, 21.1–4 [V.v.44–47])

12. Neither the 1609 Quarto nor the 1623 Folio text of *Troilus and Cressida* has satisfactory stage directions in the vicinity of this passage. At a point (l. 44 of V.v of the Signet edition) just before Achilles' entrance, four characters— Diomedes, Agamemnon, Nestor, and Ulysses—are onstage. At the end of a half-line speech by Nestor occurs the stage direction "*Exit*" and then the stage direction "*Enter* Achilles." At the conclusion of Achilles' speech occurs the stage direction "*Exit*." According to the stage directions, then, Diomedes, Ulysses, and Agamemnon remain onstage during and after Achilles' speech. But after the entry of Ajax and his delivery of one line occurs the contradictory stage direction "*Enter* Diomed" (in the Folio; "*Enter* Diom." in the Quarto). And the exchange between Diomedes and Ajax as well as the ensuing action make Ulysses' and Agamemnon's continued silent presence onstage extremely unlikely. So Diomedes, Ulysses, and Agamemnon almost certainly exit—and a cleared stage is created—before Ajax's entrance. The conventional division recognizes this cleared stage by beginning V.vi with Ajax's entry. Presumably either the "*Exit*" after Nestor's speech or the "*Exit*" after Achilles' speech should have been an "*Exeunt*"—but which one? Either Diomedes, Agamemnon, and Ulysses remain to observe Achilles search for Hector as they and Nestor have just observed Ajax search for Troilus; or they exit with Nestor. The second possibility is far more likely. If they remain to see Achilles finally aroused—an arousal for which they have been struggling the entire play— why does none of them comment on it? Why would Nestor exit alone? Furthermore, if the four exit together, the first "*Exit*" would merely have to be emended to "*Exeunt*" whereas, if the three remain, the "*Exit*" after Achilles' speech would have to be more elaborately emended to "*Exit, followed by* Agamemnon, Diomedes, *and* Ulysses" or "*Exeunt, severally*," since a simple "*Exeunt*" would imply that Achilles, whose speech nowhere acknowledges the presence of the others, joins them as he leaves the stage. Hence, Achilles'

This scene has striking similarities to that in which Macduff searches for Macbeth.[13] Near the beginning of his speech, Macduff, echoing Achilles, demands, "Tyrant, show thy face!" (*Macbeth*, 28.1 [V.vii.14]). He alludes to the helpless victims for whom he wants vengeance—"my wife and children's ghosts" (28.3 [V.iii.16])—whereas Achilles probably exaggerates the helplessness of the victim for whom he seeks revenge (see l. 2, above). Like Achilles, Macduff explicitly declares that he will not fight with any other combatant:

> . . . Either thou, Macbeth,
> Or else my sword, with an unbattered edge,
> I sheathe again undeeded.
>
> 　　　　　　　(*Macbeth*, 28.5–7 [V.vii.18–20])

A solo scene in each of these cases seems an appropriate way to set off a solitary character's intense and private quest after a personal enemy in the midst of general warfare.

In his solo scene in *As You Like It*, Orlando, like Macduff and Achilles, is thinking about one person to the exclusion of all others, but in this case that person is the woman he loves. Again like the two warriors, he is single-mindedly pursuing a personal mission, but his mission is to publicize the name and virtues of Rosalind throughout the forest. Like Artemidorus in *Julius Caesar*, the Scrivener in *Richard III*, and the Herald in *Othello*, he carries a document that is the chief subject of his soliloquy. In

---

speech is probably preceded and followed by a cleared stage and thereby constitutes a solo scene. See *The First Folio of Shakespeare*, "prepared by Charlton Hinman" (1623; facsimile rpt. New York: Norton, 1968), p. 614; and *Troilus and Cressida: First Quarto, 1609*, Shakespeare Quartos in Collotype Facsimile, no. 8 (London: The Shakespeare Association, and Sidgwick and Jackson, 1952), n. pag.

13. Scene 28 of *Macbeth* is part of the conventional division V.vii, but, according to the unambiguous stage directions, is preceded and followed by a stage cleared of living characters and is further set off by "*Alarums*" both before Macduff enters and after he leaves.

this case the document deals with love rather than public affairs.

In a markedly different context, then, Orlando's solo scene does have curious resemblances to others, but its propriety and effectiveness as a solo scene derive chiefly from the unique circumstances in which it occurs. Orlando has obviously just come from composing his verses and is explicitly on his way to carve Rosalind's name "on every tree" (12 [III.ii].9). The charming and almost pathetic tenor of his soliloquy would be dampened if he had an encounter with another character immediately before or after it. That he should be able to express his love in an elaborate poem consisting of two quatrains and a final couplet when totally alone enhances the irony that in Rosalind's presence he had been comically tongue-tied.

The scene is also very brief (ten lines) and avoids the danger inherent in a solo scene: that, as a segment isolated from other incidents by cleared stages and involving only one character, it will become static and undramatic. Any soliloquy can easily become static; but there is a genuine difference between a soliloquy delivered by a character who has just had or who immediately enters into interactions with other characters and one delivered by a character who comes onstage alone immediately before delivering it and then goes offstage immediately afterward.

The few remaining solo scenes in the canon, all of which involve important characters, are much longer and do not completely avoid the inherent danger of such scenes. One seems to have been intended, like those of Achilles and Macduff, to set off a character's intense personal concerns in the midst of a battle. In *Henry VI, Part Two*, scene 26 (V.ii.31–65), Young Clifford enters after the stage has been cleared of all other living characters, makes a highly rhetorical comment on war, then notices the body of his dead father, and expresses his emotions at length. But the scene has dramatic weaknesses. In the first place, there is hardly any difference in the attitudes Clifford expresses or in the overcharged rhetoric he uses before and after his discovery of his father's body. After the discovery he claims, "Even at this sight / My heart is turned to stone" (26.19–20 [V.ii.49–50]) and "Henceforth I will not have to do with pity" (26.26 [V.ii.56]), but the earlier part of his speech hardly indicates a heart susceptible to pity:

> . . . O war, thou son of hell,
> Whom angry heavens do make their minister,
> Throw in the frozen bosoms of our part
> Hot coals of vengeance!
>
> (26.3–6 [V.ii.33–36])

In the second place, unlike Achilles and Macduff who forcefully express their virulence in a brief space (four lines and ten lines, respectively), Clifford expounds at length (thirty-five lines). Thus, despite its bloodthirstiness, Clifford's two-part soliloquy with its formalized rhetoric is a long, static interruption of the turmoil of the battle sequence, especially since it is preceded and followed by a cleared stage. But *Henry VI, Part Two* is a very early Shakespearean play—it may even be the earliest.

The only solo scene in an early comedy is the soliloquy by Proteus that comprises scene 9 (II.vi) of *The Two Gentlemen of Verona*. It is a tour de force of euphuistic rhetoric, much as Clifford's soliloquy is a tour de force of Marlovian bombast. Proteus's opening lines are representative:

> To leave my Julia shall I be forsworn;
> To love fair Sylvia shall I be forsworn;
> To wrong my friend, I shall be much forsworn;
> And ev'n that pow'r which gave me first my oath
> Provokes me to this threefold perjury:
> Love bade me swear, and love bids me forswear.
>
> (ll. 1–6)

And Proteus continues in this vein even longer—the entire speech is forty-three lines—than Clifford does in his. But one of the most striking features of *The Two Gentlemen of Verona*,

Shakespeare's first foray into full-fledged romantic comedy, is the large percentage of scenes in which three or fewer characters appear. None of the first six scenes, and only one of the first ten, involves more than three characters. In this context it is almost more surprising that the play contains only one solo scene than that it does contain one. In other words, even in a play in which Shakespeare seems to have explored the possibilities of small-scale, private scenes, he still tended to avoid the solo scene.

Significantly, after these two very early experiments Shakespeare did not again include a long solo scene in any play until very late in his career. The first such scene after that in *The Two Gentlemen of Verona* is the soliloquy by Timon of Athens that has already been mentioned. Although a clear function is served by the detachment of this soliloquy from other incidents, its extreme length (forty-one lines) does nearly turn it into a set piece.

All four of the remaining solo scenes occur in one play, *Cymbeline*, and all four are long and involve major characters. Once again, a device that appears very sporadically throughout the canon is used repeatedly in a single play—no other Shakespearean work has more than one solo scene involving a major character. No other play except *Henry V* has more than two solo scenes of any type.[14]

Of the four solo scenes in *Cymbeline* two belong to Posthumus. Posthumus completely disappears from the play for the thirteen scenes between 11 (II.v) and 25 (V.i). As if to compensate for his absence, the last scene before his disappearance and the scene in which he reappears are wholly his. A solo scene, of course, highlights a particular character even more than does an ordinary soliloquy, which is preceded or followed without an

---

14. Only two other plays, *Timon* and *Coriolanus*, have more than one non-choral solo scene, and they each have only two. Only three additional plays, *Romeo and Juliet*, *Henry IV, Part Two*, and *Troilus and Cressida*, have as many as two solo scenes of any type.

interruption by the soliloquizer's interaction with other characters. Posthumus's two unshared scenes are also linked in other
ways. In both he expresses a strong emotion concerning Imogen,
and in each case the emotion is generated by a deception. The
first, in which he vulgarly denounces Imogen, occurs just after
Iachimo has falsely convinced him of her infidelity. The second,
in which he idealizes her memory, occurs just after he wrongly
accepts the bloody handkerchief sent by Pisanio as proof that
she has been murdered at his command.

The remaining two solo scenes are also linked to one another;
this linkage is much more curious because one of these scenes
(17 [III.vi.1–27]) is Imogen's—the only one in the canon involving a woman—and the other (20 [IV.i]) belongs to Cloten.
Both characters are on solitary missions to Milford Haven; both
are in disguise; both refer to the directions received from Pisanio;
and both pull out their swords as they exit. The similarities are
made more noticeable by the proximity of the two monologues—
they are separated by only two short scenes. These similarities
ironically emphasize the contrasts. Imogen's speech reveals her
innocent resolution, her fortitude, and even her fair-mindedness
and sense of proportion:

> . . . Two beggars told me
> I could not miss my way. Will poor folks lie,
> That have afflictions on them, knowing 'tis
> A punishment or trial? Yes. No wonder,
> When rich ones scarce tell true. To lapse in fulness
> Is sorer than to lie for need.
>
> (17 [III.vi].8–13)

In Cloten's solo scene, he reveals his cowardly and monstrous
plan and exposes his brutishness. He also exposes his lack of a
sense of proportion or objectivity, a deficiency demonstrated not
only by his comparison of himself and Posthumus but by his
ludicrous anticipation of Cymbeline's reaction to the rape and

degradation of his daughter: Cymbeline "may haply be a little angry for my so rough usage; but my mother, having power of his testiness, shall turn all into my commendations" (20 [IV.i].19– 21). Furthermore, just as Imogen reveals her sharp insight and objectivity in considering that she might have been deceived by those giving her directions, Cloten reveals his lack of these qualities in presuming that Pisanio "dares not deceive" him (20.24–25).

The ending of Cloten's solo scene involves a slight awkward-ness. He draws his sword and declares, "This is the very de-scription of their meeting place, and the fellow dares not de-ceive me" (ll. 23–25), but then he inexplicably exits. Also disturbing is the awkwardness that results from the elevation of Posthumus's earlier soliloquy into a solo scene. In the preceding scene, after Iachimo has poisoned his mind against his wife in the presence of Philario, Posthumus exits. Then Philario and Iachimo have a very brief exchange (less than four full lines) and race after him. Posthumus reenters and delivers a speech of thirty-five lines and exits. The brief exchange between Iachimo and Philario prevents an immediate reentry but results in an awkward loose end. After at first expecting Philario and Iachimo to burst in upon Posthumus, the audience may begin to wonder what happened to them but is never informed. This loose end could easily have been avoided if Iachimo and Philario, rather than Posthumus, had exited after Iachimo's deception of Posthu-mus. Elsewhere in the canon, when a character delivers a solilo-quy after being informed of shattering news or after being de-ceived by other characters, that soliloquy is generally part of a longer scene. Usually the informers or deceivers simply exit; for example, after falsely arousing Othello's suspicions about Des-demona in scene 9 (III.iii) of *Othello*, Iago leaves the Moor, who then delivers an emotional soliloquy. But Shakespeare departs from his normal practice and creates a loose end apparently in order to give Posthumus a solo scene before his long absence from the play.

None of these four scenes completely escapes the solo scene's potential for becoming undramatic. The longer a solo scene is, the greater the risk, and all four are long by Shakespearean standards for such scenes: Posthumus's occupy 35 and 33 lines of verse; Imogen's, 27 lines; and Cloten's, 240 words of prose (25 lines in the Signet edition). Thus, 120 lines of the play are given over to segments that lack character interaction and that are separated, not without awkwardness in two of the four cases, from other incidents. The solo scene's tendency to become static makes it unsuitable for extended emotional display, and for most of his career Shakespeare avoided the temptation to use it for this purpose. The success of most such scenes in the canon is not unrelated to their brevity. Early in his career, Shakespeare had tried to use solo scenes for emotional display in the cases of Clifford and Proteus, but the results were not entirely satisfactory. Nor are the solo scenes in *Cymbeline*, despite their reflections on one another, as effective as some of the others discussed in this chapter.

The solo scene can be an effective device in certain unique situations and also has a very limited number of general functions—for choral or quasichoral commentary or for highlighting a main character's physical isolation from other men or his quest after a particular personal enemy in the midst of a battle. But Shakespeare's clear preference to incorporate soliloquies in larger scenes rather than to isolate them is also consistent with a general feature of his dramatic technique. Each of his scenes has a double structure. On the one hand, it has its own self-contained structure, a unity not always of incident or even of place or time; on the other hand, it is part of the overall structure of the play. Shakespeare commonly satisfies the latter of these structural demands by incorporating various strands of the action in the same scene. These superficially diverse elements, however, are welded by theme, imagery, ironic juxtaposition, formal patterning, or other means into a coherent scenic unit. How Shakespeare manages to create unified scenes out of a series of diverse incidents will be the concern of a later chapter.

# Three ✠ Duets

A second type of unitary scene is the "duet," in which two characters enter simultaneously, interact, and leave simultaneously. (Although any dialogue between two characters could be called a duet, I will use the term in a narrow sense to refer to an entire *scene* that consists only of a single segment involving two characters.) The two characters either enter together, in which case the scene begins *in medias res*, or enter separately but simultaneously and meet onstage. Similarly, they either separate as they leave the stage or exit in one another's company. Although there are two possible ways to open and two possible ways to close such a scene, Shakespeare clearly preferred the economy and naturalness of opening and closing scenes in midconversation, thereby eliminating greetings and farewells, concentrating on only the most significant or relevant parts of an encounter, and creating a sense of continuity between offstage and onstage action. Of forty-two unitary duets in the canon,[1] three-fourths

---

1. This figure does not include a small number of scenes that involve only a minor departure from the definition. The second scene (I.ii) of *The Merchant of Venice*, for example, consists of a long dialogue between Portia and Nerissa, at the end of which a servingman enters to announce that the suitors presently in Belmont are about to leave and that another, the Prince of Morocco, is about to arrive. After having conversed for 120 lines, the two women leave almost immediately after the servant's entrance. In this particular case, the news brought by the entering character is not startling or portentous. The servant's entrance does not change the tenor of the scene or turn it in a new direction but merely gives a sense of closure to the conversation between Portia and Nerissa.

begin *in medias res*. In about one-half, the two characters both enter and leave together, whereas in only four such scenes do we see the entire encounter from the meeting to the separation of the two characters.

Duets occur more frequently in Shakespeare's plays than solo scenes. Yet one-third of the plays in the canon have none at all; only a handful have as many as three; and only *King Lear*, with five, has more than three. After discussing the typical contexts in which Shakespeare uses this kind of scene, I shall explore its unique frequency in that one masterpiece.

Rather surprisingly, none of Shakespeare's love "scenes" actually constitutes a scene detached from other episodes. In every case, either another character is onstage with the lovers or the dialogue is only part of a larger scene in which other characters appear or in which one of the lovers is alone to deliver a soliloquy. King Henry's wooing of Katherine near the close of *Henry V*, for example, not only occurs with Katherine's waiting woman Alice onstage but is preceded by and followed by public episodes without intervening cleared stages. The placement of the wooing episode in this larger context is appropriate because Henry's courtship of the princess of France is both a private and a political act.[2]

Those most famous lovers, Romeo and Juliet, whose love is crossed by both the stars and social circumstances, never have a scene all to themselves—we are never allowed to forget the circumstances that threaten their relationship. Their very first words to one another in the play, at the Capulet ball, immediately follow a conversation between Tybalt and Capulet in which the former vents his outrage at Romeo's presence and promises revenge. The exchange of devotion between the two lovers in the misnamed "balcony *scene*" is not only punctuated by the Nurse's offstage calls to Juliet but is preceded without an

---

2. This scene will be discussed in greater detail in chapter 6.

intervening cleared stage by Romeo's eavesdropping on Mercutio and Benvolio, who are searching for him. Mercutio's cynical and sarcastic remarks about Romeo as a lover and about love in general provide an ironic perspective on the dialogue between Romeo and Juliet in the same scene, especially since Mercutio still believes Romeo to be in love with Rosaline.[3] The irony is emphasized by a verbal echo. As Mercutio and Benvolio enter, Romeo overhears the latter call out, "Romeo! My cousin Romeo! Romeo!" (7 [II.i].3). After observing Juliet come onto the balcony and sigh, "Ay me!" (7.67 [II.ii.25]), Romeo eavesdrops on her soliloquy, which begins "O Romeo, Romeo! Wherefore art thou Romeo?" (l. 75). The prolonged leave-taking of the two lovers in scene 16 (III.v), which occurs on the morning after the consummation of their marriage, is jarringly interrupted by the entrance of the Nurse, who warns of the approach of Lady Capulet, and is succeeded without an intervening cleared stage by Juliet's dialogue with her mother, who promises revenge on Romeo for having killed Tybalt and announces the following Thursday as the date of Juliet's wedding to Paris. After her father enters, later in the scene, Juliet's supplications and the Nurse's intervention only stir Capulet to anger. (The only other times in the play that Romeo and Juliet are onstage together occur in scene 11 [II.vi], during which they are chaperoned by the Friar, and in scene 23 [V.iii], the final scene.)

Of those dialogues that do constitute independent scenes, only nine occur between members of opposite sexes. Five involve a noblewoman and a servant.[4] Two occur in history plays

3. A traditional scene division (II.ii) occurs after the exit of Benvolio and Mercutio even though Romeo remains onstage. The placement of this division was perhaps an attempt to isolate the love dialogue from the preceding episode, an isolation that, I am trying to show, Shakespeare sought to prevent.

4. The Countess in *All's Well That Ends Well* has one such scene (5 [II.ii]) with her Clown and one (12 [III.iv]) with her Steward. Oswald has one such scene (3 [I.iii]) in *King Lear* with Goneril and one (19 [IV.v]) with Regan. Imogen and Pisanio share a scene (15 [III.iv]) in *Cymbeline*.

between related nobles: Queen Elizabeth and her brother, Lord
Rivers, in *Henry VI, Part Three* (20 [IV.iv]) and Gaunt and his
sister-in-law, the Duchess of Gloucester, in *Richard II* (2 [I.ii]).
In both cases the women grieve over the fate of their husbands—the Duchess over the murder of Woodstock and the
Queen over the capture of Edward IV, which she considers tan-
tamount to death:

> *Queen Elizabeth.* Why, brother Rivers, are you yet to learn
>    What late misfortune is befall'n King Edward?
> *Rivers.* What, loss of some pitched battle against Warwick?
> *Queen Elizabeth.* No, but the loss of his own royal person.
> *Rivers.* Then is my sovereign slain?
> *Queen Elizabeth.* Ay, almost slain, for he is taken prisoner.
>
>                                            (ll. 2–7)

In another duet the male character does refer to the woman's
"charms" and calls her an "enchantress." But, despite the presence of sexual innuendos, the scene in which York and Joan of
Arc trade insults after he has captured her in battle can hardly
be considered a love scene.[5]

The only remaining duet between a man and a woman occurs

---

5. *Henry VI, Part One*, scene 40 (V.iii.30–44). This scene may not, in
fact, be a duet. The stage directions in *Henry VI, Part One* are notoriously
confused or inadequate. After Pucelle exits in the middle of the traditional
division V.iii occurs the following stage direction: "*Excursions.* Burgundy *and*
York *fight hand to hand. French fly.*" Then occurs the passage in which only
York and Pucelle speak. This passage ends with the direction "*Exeunt*," and
then Suffolk enters with Margaret. The stage is presumably cleared before the
duologue between York and Pucelle—York must capture her offstage and return with her—and is certainly cleared afterward. The duologue thus constitutes a separate scene. The only issue in doubt is whether the pair of antagonists are alone. At one point in the duologue York says: "See, how the ugly
witch doth bend her brows, / As if, with Circe, she would change my shape!"
(40.5–6 [V.iii.34–35]). The chief function of the speech is to taunt Pucelle,
and she does respond to the taunt ("Changed to a worser shape thou canst not
be" [40.7]). The seeming direction of York's remark to a third party may simply be a rhetorical device, but it may, in fact, be directed at a soldier guarding
Pucelle. But no third character speaks or is mentioned in a stage direction.

between a husband and wife whose marriage was not a love match. In scene 16 (III.iv) of *Antony and Cleopatra*, Antony and Octavia discuss not their mutual devotion but the mutual antagonism of Antony and Caesar and the conflicting loyalties of Octavia. Antony twice mentions Octavia's "love," but in each case he allows her to determine the object of that love:

> Let your best love draw to that point which seeks
> Best to preserve it.
>
> (ll. 21–22)

> When it appears to you where this begins,
> Turn your displeasure that way, for our faults
> Can never be so equal that your love
> Can equally move with them.
>
> (ll. 33–36)

Although he seems considerate in asking her to make up her own mind in choosing between her brother and himself, his detachment suggests that her choice is almost a matter of indifference to him. Furthermore, in forcing her to choose he suggests his real attitude toward her hope to reconcile the two men in her life. This exchange is only a love scene in the sense that it portrays Octavia's unrequited and divided love.

Several duets do focus on the loving relationship and loyal devotion between the two characters, but each of these scenes involves two men. The earliest scene of this type, between Talbot and his son in *Henry VI, Part One*, contains the kind of doggerel that provides fodder for disintegrationists:

> *Talbot.* Thou never hadst renown, nor canst not lose it.
> *John.* Yes, your renownèd name: shall flight abuse it?[6]
>
> (30 [IV.v].40–41)

6. Once again, the stage directions in this play are ambiguous. The duet between Talbot and John is followed by the direction "*Exit. Alarum: excursions, wherein* Talbot's Son *is hemmed about, and* Talbot *rescues him.*" This implies that John remains on stage after the duet. Yet Talbot's final words to his son ("Come, side by side together live and die") so strongly suggest that they

Most of the scene is in similarly clumsy couplets and much of it
in similarly clumsy stichomythia. On the other hand, the theme
of mutual devotion between an older and younger man that
emerges in this scene is not un-Shakespearean. The final
speeches of the two characters contain the following expressions
of this theme:

> *John.* No more can I be severed from your side
>     Than can yourself yourself in twain divide. . . .
> *Talbot.* Come, side by side together live and die.
>
> (ll. 48–49, 54)

The final speeches of the first of two duets between Orlando and
his fatherly servant Adam in *As You Like It* contain the following
similar declarations:

> *Orlando.* But come thy ways, we'll go along together. . . .
> *Adam.* Master, go on, and I will follow thee
>     To the last gasp with truth and loyalty.
>
> (6 [II.iii].66, 69–70)

Despite the markedly dissimilar circumstances, the two scenes
contain further parallels. In both cases the older man urges the
younger to flee danger, and the younger resists to avoid baseness:

> *John.* And shall I fly? . . .
>     The world will say, he is not Talbot's blood,
>     That basely fled when noble Talbot stood.
>
> (30.13, 16–17)

> *Orlando.* What, wouldst thou have me go and beg my food,
>     Or with a base and boist'rous sword enforce
>     A thievish living on the common road?
>
> (6.31–33)

---

leave together that the conventional division at this point seems justified. The
direction *"Exit"* sometimes occurs when clearly more than one character exits,
and Shakespeare did not always avoid immediate reentries.

A contrast between the two scenes is that the first is principally a demonstration of the younger man's courage and devotion to his father, whereas the second is primarily a demonstration of Adam's fatherly devotion to Orlando, at whose disposal he places his savings and his service. Orlando, however, has an opportunity to demonstrate his steadfastness in a second duet with Adam in which he promises, "If this uncouth forest yield anything savage, I will either be food for it or bring it for food to thee" (9 [II.vi].6–7). Although Orlando uses a mildly comic tone to cheer up the despairing Adam, the sentiment resembles that of John's assertion, "For live I will not, if my father die" (30.51).

The two scenes in *As You Like It* form a balanced pair. Both portray the devotion between the two men; one emphasizes Adam's sacrifice and the other, Orlando's. The connection between the two scenes is enhanced by their structural similarity—they are the only duets in the play. One of the ways Shakespeare binds a play together, in fact, is to establish both thematic and structural connections between scenes in different parts of the play.

Another duet whose chief focus is on the mutual devotion between two men is scene 13 (III.iii) of *Twelfth Night*, between Sebastian and Antonio.[7] Like the first scene between Orlando

---

7. Sebastian and Antonio are also the only characters to appear in an earlier scene (6 [II.i]), but that episode does not have a unitary structure because Antonio remains onstage to deliver a short but significant soliloquy after Sebastian departs. Other unitary scenes in which the friendship or mutual respect of the two men onstage is a prominent element include those between the Bastard and Hubert (*King John*, 18 [V.vi]), between Polixenes and Camillo (*The Winter's Tale*, 10 [IV.ii]), and that between Nicanor and Adrian (*Coriolanus*, 19 [IV.iii]). Though in the course of their duet in *The Two Gentlemen of Verona* (8 [II.v]), Speed and Launce insult and mock one another, their raillery is conducted in the spirit of good fellowship and they seem to have genuine affection for one another. The friendship of Bassanio and Antonio is a major topic of a duet in *The Merchant of Venice*, not between these characters

and Adam, it shows mainly the concern and sacrifice of the
older man for the younger. Antonio places himself in great danger in order to accompany Sebastian and places his purse at
Sebastian's disposal. One duet does contain an extended expression of heterosexual love, but only one of the lovers is present.
Julia explains her love for and admiration of Proteus to Lucetta,
her waiting woman, in *The Two Gentlemen of Verona*, scene 10
(II.vii). On the other hand, the scene actually portrays the mutual affection of the two women.

Shakespeare was nearly as reluctant to present a confrontation between two antagonists as a separate, independent scene
as he was to detach a love "scene" from other episodes. There
are, in fact, only three such scenes in the canon. One is the
scene between York and Pucelle. The remaining two are battle
scenes and are the only duets in Shakespearean drama without
dialogue. Talbot pursues the Dauphin across the stage in scene
8 (I.v, opening s.d.) of *Henry VI, Part One*. A much more decisive action occurs in scene 28 (V.v, opening s.d.) of *Richard
III*: "*Alarum. Enter* Richard *and* Richmond; *they fight*; Richard
*is slain*." (Richmond presumably exits upon slaying Richard, for
the next stage direction begins, "*Retreat and flourish. Enter*
Richmond.") That these episodes contain no dialogue does not
disqualify them as separate scenes. In each case, two characters
enter, an emblematic or decisive action takes place, and the
stage then becomes clear of living characters. In the second of
the two cases, Richmond's exit and immediate reentry could
have been avoided if Richmond were simply to remain onstage

---

but between Salerio and Solanio (11 [II.viii]). Similarly, in the duet that opens
*The Winter's Tale*, Camillo and Archidamus discuss the "rooted . . . affection"
(ll. 25–26) between Leontes and Polixenes. All of these male friendships are
unquestionably attractive except, curiously, the last one in the canon. The
comradeship of Nicanor and Adrian is of dubious attractiveness because it is
based on Nicanor's collaboration with the Volscian enemies of his own people.

to be joined by Stanley and the other nobles who enter at this point for the final episode. But, in the first place, an error of omission (that of Richmond's exit) is more likely than an error of commission (that of Richmond's subsequent entrance). In the second place, although Shakespeare apparently made an effort to avoid immediate reentry, he was willing to violate this "rule," if necessary, to achieve a more important dramatic goal. In this case that goal seems obvious. Richmond's exit and reentrance create the stunning theatrical effect of giving the stage, however briefly, to the dead body of the title character. The play, one should recall, is the only one in the canon that opens with a soliloquy by the protagonist (or by any nonchoral character for that matter). Richard holds forth mainly about himself for the first forty-one lines of the play. Very near the end of the play Richard once again holds the stage alone, yet he is now speechless. Other characters then enter to deliver the final forty-one lines of the play over his corpse. A clearly ironic symmetry is thus established between the opening and closing episodes.

But if duets are not used by Shakespeare for such prime dramatic situations as encounters between lovers or antagonists, what kinds of situations do they present? One large group of duets involves two courtiers or gentlemen who confer about public affairs. Such scenes thus tend to include exposition and choral commentary among their prominent functions. In the first scene of *The Winter's Tale*, the only play that opens with a duet,[8] Camillo and Archidamus discuss the current visit of Polixenes to Leontes and the history of the friendship between these kings.

8. The duet between the Archbishop of Canterbury and the Bishop of Ely (*Henry V*, 2 [I.i]) is preceded by a choral scene. Although the two Gentlemen whose dialogue opens *Cymbeline* exit at the approach of the Queen, Posthumus, and Imogen, a break in continuity is avoided because the exiting characters see the other characters enter and it is their approach that prompts the two Gentlemen to depart.

Although Camillo later emerges as a major character and Archidamus never again speaks in the play,[9] they have approximately equal dramatic as well as social status in this scene.

Despite its brevity and despite its obviously expository function, the scene does have other functions and does have an interesting dramatic structure. Most of the scene is an exchange of rather conventional courtesies and sanguine observations. Archidamus extravagantly praises the hospitality of Sicilia and disparages his own country's ability to provide comparably magnificent entertainment. Yet when Camillo introduces a note of extravagance into his praise of Prince Mamillius—"they that went on crutches ere he was born desire yet their life to see him a man" (ll. 42–44)—Archidamus introduces a note of reality which, following their previous remarks, sounds cynical:

> Would they else be content to die? (l. 45)

> If the King had no son, they would desire to live on crutches till he had one. (ll. 48–49)

And the suggestion that outwardly expressed sentiments conceal selfish motives undercuts not only the outwardly expressed courtesies with which the scene opened but the outward signs of indestructible friendship between Polixenes and Leontes that the two courtiers have just described. A mood is established and then unsettled. However slight, this shift foreshadows the much more violent shift that occurs in the next scene. The second scene begins with a parallel exchange of courtesies between the kings whose friendship is described in scene 1. By the end of scene 2 the mood of formal conviviality is completely shattered by Leontes' jealousy and its consequences.

If Archidamus's final speeches mark a turning point in the

---

9. Archidamus is not identified by name in the dialogue of the play; his name occurs only in the opening stage direction and speech prefixes of this scene and in "The Names of the Actors," which follows the Folio text of *The Winter's Tale*.

development of scene 1 for the playgoer or reader unfamiliar with the play, those speeches also contain in retrospect the climax of another development. That development consists of the progressive intensification of dramatic irony. The ironies become more and more painful as the scene proceeds. Archidamus opens the play by speculating on Camillo's possible future visit to Bohemia "on the like occasion" (l. 2). Camillo will, in fact, visit Bohemia, but much sooner than expected and in very dissimilar circumstances. Camillo's assertion that "Sicilia cannot show himself overkind to Bohemia" (ll. 23–24) becomes ironic because Sicilia can, and shortly does, show himself unkind to Bohemia.[10] A more forceful irony is contained in Archidamus's confident declaration: "I think there is not in the world either malice or matter to alter" the love between the two rulers (ll. 35–36). But the most painful irony of all occurs in Archidamus's final speech in which he speculates on how people would act "if the king had no son" (l. 48). This hypothetical situation actually comes about, and Mamillius, unlike Hermione and Perdita, is never resurrected or restored.

The duet in *Coriolanus* between a Roman and a Volsce (19 [IV.iii]) fulfills a similar variety of functions. Although we already possess most of the information exchanged, we do learn for the first time that the Volscians are preparing a new attack, and the two characters, who appear nowhere else in the play, supply choral commentary. E. A. J. Honigmann argues, however, that "the scene really exists to tell us that a Roman may choose to work for the Volscians, obliquely preparing us for Coriolanus' decision to do the same. More important, it suggests that a Roman and a Volsce who belong to the same social class may think and feel alike."[11] But the scene provides more than

10. Litotes, the rhetorical figure Camillo employs in this remark, easily lends itself to dramatic irony.
11. *Shakespeare: Seven Tragedies* (New York: Barnes and Noble, 1976), p. 183.

oblique preparation for the later action since it foreshadows in
various specific details the later encounter between Coriolanus
and Aufidius. Both encounters begin, for example, with a delay
in the identification of the Roman characters; Adrian does not at
first recognize Nicanor, nor does Aufidius recognize Coriolanus.
Both Nicanor and Coriolanus furnish hints rather than immediately identifying themselves and ask the same question:

> *Nicanor.* Know you me yet?
>
> (19 [IV.iii].5)
>
> *Coriolanus.* Know'st thou me yet?
>
> (23.63 [IV.v.67])

Adrian quickly guesses Nicanor's identity after being supplied
with the hint, "I am a Roman; and my services are, as you are,
against 'em" (19.4–5). Aufidius, however, is forced to ask for
his visitor's name six times (23.53, 54, 57, 59, 62, 64). That
Coriolanus unknowingly imitates the tactic of an almost negligible character, but without success, intensifies the inherent irony
of Aufidius's failure to recognize his archenemy. Not only does
Coriolanus finally have to supply his own name, but he has to
explain at length who he now is. Like Nicanor, he identifies
himself by describing his "services." He is no longer the doer of
"painful service" for Rome but is now the offerer of "revenge-
ful services" to benefit the Volscians (23.68, 89). Nicanor re-
sponded to Adrian's guess at his identity by saying "The same,
sir" (19.7). Coriolanus, however, is not the same man he once
was—"Only that name remains" (23.73) of his former identity.
Adrian tells Nicanor, "You will be welcome with this intelligence" (19.28), that is, that Coriolanus has been banished.
The banished Coriolanus himself receives a more explicit promise of reward and a more emphatic reception from Aufidius: "Let
me commend thee first to those that shall / Say yea to thy de-
sires. A thousand welcomes!" (23.144–45). Both Nicanor and
Coriolanus express joy when told that the Volscians are prepar-

ing a new attack on the Romans. Presumably because saluta-
tions were forestalled at the beginning of each encounter by the
delay in establishing the identity of the Roman character, each
episode ends with greetings:

> *Nicanor.* So, sir, heartily well met, and most glad of your
> company.
> *Adrian.* You take my part from me, sir. I have the most cause to
> be glad of yours.
> *Nicanor.* Well, let us go together. *Exeunt*
>
> (19.48–52)
>
> *Aufidius:* . . . A thousand welcomes!
> And more a friend than e'er an enemy;
> Yet, Marcius, that was much. Your hand: most welcome!
> *Exeunt*
>
> (23.145–47 [IV.v.149–51])

A striking metaphor introduced in the first of these scenes
reappears and is given new meaning in the second. Nicanor tells
Adrian, "I have heard it said the fittest time to corrupt a man's
wife is when she's fall'n out with her husband" (19.30–31). He
apparently means that Rome will more easily succumb now that
"she" has banished Coriolanus. But in the later scene it is Coriolanus who is placed in the feminine role after offering his services to Aufidius, who declares,

> I loved the maid I married; never man
> Sighed truer breath. But that I see thee here,
> Thou noble thing, more dances my rapt heart
> Than when I first my wedded mistress saw
> Bestride my threshold.
>
> (23.114–18 [IV.v.118–22])

And later in scene 23 the Third Servingman describes Aufidius's
offstage manner toward Coriolanus, "Our general himself makes
a mistress of him" (ll. 199–200). However incongruously, Coriolanus has become the wife who is betraying her husband. Al-

though Coriolanus's confrontation with Aufidius is part of a
larger scene, Shakespeare clearly meant to establish an ironic
parallel between that encounter and the earlier scene involving a
Roman who betrays his city by serving the enemy and a surprised and pleased Volscian.

Other duets between two courtiers or gentlemen include those
between the Bastard and Hubert (*King John,* 18 [V.vi]), Salerio
and Solanio (*The Merchant of Venice,* 11 [II.viii]), Cleomenes
and Dion (*The Winter's Tale,* 6 [III.i]), Kent and a Gentleman
(*King Lear,* 8 [III.i] and 17 [IV.iii]), Lennox and another Lord
(*Macbeth,* 17 [III.vi]), and Enobarbus and Eros (*Antony and
Cleopatra,* 17 [III.v]). Although, like the scene between Camillo
and Archidamus, these also serve a variety of other functions,
description of offstage action is a very prominent element in all.
Although half of them involve an important retainer (Camillo,
Kent, Enobarbus, and the Bastard), none of them portrays ac-
tion that significantly advances the plot.

About half of Shakespeare's duets involve a superior conferring with or giving instructions to a subordinate.[12] Some in this
group occur between a master and a servant. These range from
*Henry V,* scene 14 (III.iv), in which Princess Katherine learns
to pronounce English words "aussi droit que les natifs d'Angle-
terre" (ll. 37–38), at least according to Alice, the princess's old
attendant and language instructor; to the one in which an enraged Timon of Athens orders his perplexed steward to invite the
friends he denounces as "rascals" to a banquet.[13]

The remaining duets in this group involve a superior and his

12. Only one duet occurs between two servants (Speed and Launce; see
above, n.7).

13. *Timon of Athens,* 9.10 (III.iv.113). The rest include the two in *As You
Like It* between Orlando and Adam, the two in *All's Well That Ends Well* involving the Countess, the two in *King Lear* involving Oswald, the two brief ones in
*The Merry Wives of Windsor* (scene 2 [I.ii] between Evans and Simple, who is
actually Slender's servant, and scene 16 [IV.iii] between the Host and Bardolph, a servantlike employee of the Host in this play).

military, political, or ecclesiastical subordinate. Two of these share a number of unusual characteristics. In *Julius Caesar*, scene 14 (V.ii), Brutus sends Messala to the other wing of the army during the battle of Phillipi against Octavius: "Let them set on at once; for I perceive / But cold demeanor in Octavius' wing, / And sudden push gives them the overthrow" (ll. 3–5). Messala does not reply, and the scene contains only the six lines spoken by Brutus. A few moments later, Titinius blames the command given by Brutus in scene 14 for the decisive turn of the battle: "Brutus gave the word too early, / Who, having some advantage on Octavius, / Took it too eagerly" (15 [V.iii].5–7). Brutus's order was uncharacteristically impetuous, and its impetuosity was suggested by his fevered repetitiousness: "Ride, ride, Messala, ride. . . . Ride, ride, Messala" (ll. 1, 6).

In *Antony and Cleopatra*, scene 21 (III.ix), Antony gives Enobarbus orders for the disposition of the army at the outset of the Battle of Actium, again against Octavius. Enobarbus does not reply, and Antony has only four lines. Moments later, Scarus blames Antony for the loss of the sea battle. Showing uncharacteristic timidity, Antony committed a mistake—antithetical to that committed by Brutus in *Julius Caesar*—of retreating without reason. While the duet at the beginning of the battle did not portray his decision to retreat, it did suggest a fatal willingness to respond rather than to take the initiative:

> Set we our squadrons on yond side o' th'hill
> In eye of Caesar's battle; from which place
> We may the number of the ships behold,
> And so proceed accordingly.
>
> (scene 21 in its entirety)

Shakespeare sets up a clear contrast between Antony and Octavius by juxtaposing scene 21 with the previous one:

> *Caesar.* Taurus!
> *Taurus.* My Lord?

> *Caesar.* Strike not by land; keep whole, provoke not battle
> Till we have done at sea. Do not exceed
> The prescript of this scroll. Our fortune lies
> Upon this jump.
>
> (scene 20 [III.viii] in its entirety)

Caesar decisively takes both a risk and the initiative in a scene nearly as short and nearly as exclusively composed of his words. Another telling contrast between the two superficially similar scenes is that Antony and Enobarbus are alone on the stage, but Octavius and Taurus are accompanied by Octavius's "Army." This contrast adds potency to the words of Octavius and seems to deny it to Antony's.

Unlike the scenes between courtiers or gentlemen, which are often primarily discussions of offstage actions, many of the scenes between superiors and subordinates portray decisions being made or plots being laid. In addition to some of those already mentioned, duets in which decisive action takes place include the one in which Goneril gives Oswald the first overt orders in the campaign to humble and humiliate Lear (*King Lear*, 3 [I.iii]).

But many of these scenes, including the one just mentioned, are not so much depictions of actions as expressions of intention or explanations of motivations that one normally associates with soliloquies. In the third scene of *Lear*, for example, Goneril not only instructs Oswald to "Put on what weary negligence" he pleases (l. 13) but explains her justification for this order and alludes to her future course of action. That she should explain her motives and plans to a servant seems incongruous. This servant will later receive some individualizing touches from Shakespeare, but he does not appear before this scene and so at this point seems to be a very insignificant character. His entire verbal contribution to the scene consists of the following speeches: "Ay, madam"; "He's coming madam; I hear him"; "Well, madam" (ll. 3, 12, 22). Shakespeare could easily have included

Goneril's justifications in a soliloquy either after Oswald's exit or before his entrance. One reason Shakespeare did not open or close this scene with a soliloquy may have been to avoid two consecutive soliloquies—the preceding scene ends with a soliloquy by Edmund, and the succeeding scene begins with one by Kent. But two consecutive soliloquies do occur elsewhere in the canon. The juxtaposition of Edmund's soliloquy and Goneril's would not be so different, for example, from the juxtaposition of soliloquies by Macbeth and Lady Macbeth (*Macbeth*, 9–10 [II.i–ii]).

On the other hand, the scene as written has several dramatic advantages over an alternative in which Goneril's justifications were shifted to a soliloquy. The very incongruity of Goneril's disclosure to Oswald of her contempt for her father is vivid evidence of her filial disloyalty. Her declarations to an insignificant servant that her father, a king, is an "idle old man" and that "old fools are babes again" (*King Lear*, 3.17, 20) emphasize her irreverence more than her expression of these opinions in a soliloquy would have. A secondary dramatic function of the scene as written is to provide the first touches of Oswald's character. His easy and immediate acquiescence to Goneril's command that he be discourteous to Lear justifies Kent's later claim that he is a "superserviceable . . . rogue" (7 [II.ii].18).

Another scene in which the secondary character may initially seem superfluous is that between the Duke and Friar Thomas in *Measure for Measure* (3 [I.iii]). Friar Thomas does not appear elsewhere in the play, and his first two speeches seem to be those of a man who knows his place: "May your Grace speak of it?" (l. 6); "Gladly, my Lord" (l. 18). Less than six of the fifty-four lines of the scene are his. Most of the rest of the lines consist of the Duke's justifications for transferring power to Angelo while remaining in Vienna in disguise. These explanations of his motives, again, might have been given in a soliloquy. But the interaction between the Duke and the Friar gives us a per-

spective on those motives and on the Duke that would be missing from a soliloquy. In the first place, the Friar, unlike Oswald,
actually has the temerity to raise an objection to his superior's
plan:

> It rested in your grace
> To unloose this tied-up Justice when you pleased,
> And it in you more dreadful would have seemed
> Than in Lord Angelo.

> (ll. 31–34)

The Friar is suggesting, as tactfully as possible, that leaving the
revival of the enforcement of the laws to a surrogate is a derelic-
tion of duty. That the last two lines of the speech begin with
"and" is significant. In those lines the Friar is offering not the
reason why the Duke should have carried out the revival of enforcement himself but a *second* (and presumably less important)
reason. The first is that the responsibility, as well as the power,
for revived enforcement "rested" in the Duke himself.[14] Yet it is
the secondary point upon which the Duke leaps: "I do fear, too
dreadful" (l. 34). The Duke admits to having made a mistake in
the past—"'twas my fault to give the people scope" (l. 35)—but
now wants to evade the consequences of the correction of that
mistake:

> I have on Angelo imposed the office,
> Who may, in th'ambush of my name, strike home,
> And yet my nature never in the fight
> To do it slander.

> (ll. 40–43)

14. *The Oxford English Dictionary* actually cites these lines as one of the
earliest illustrations of the following denotation of the verb "to rest": "to lie *in*
or remain *with* one, as something to be accomplished or determined." But a
definition supplied by *Webster's New World Dictionary* (2nd College ed., 1970)
seems even more appropriate: "to be placed or imposed as a burden or
responsibility."

Almost as if he were afraid that the Friar might express dissatis-
faction with the prestidigitation by which no one will be held
responsible for the renewed strictness of the laws, the Duke
changes the subject to his current plans—not only has he set
Angelo up as a kind of scapegoat, but now the "Duke of dark
corners" plans to spy on him—and does not allow the Friar
another word in the scene. Perhaps realizing that his explanations have been unconvincing, the Duke promises, "Moe reasons for this action / At our more leisure shall I render you"
(ll. 48–49). He then claims to give "one" (l. 50), but he gives,
not a reason why he appointed a surrogate, but a reason why he
appointed this particular surrogate—because Angelo's innate
strictness will automatically lead him to apply the laws sternly.
The Duke evades the basic objection raised by Friar Thomas.
This evasion would not have been so evident if the Duke had
simply presented his justifications in a soliloquy.

In several of these duets, such as that between Polixenes and
Camillo (*The Winter's Tale*, 10 [IV.ii]), the subordinate character
plays a more obviously substantial role. During most of scene 5
(II.ii) of *All's Well That Ends Well* the Countess plays straight
man for her fool, the Clown Lavatch. But even here the Countess
ultimately defeats him at his own game. The Clown repeatedly
appends to his all-purpose answer—"O Lord, sir!"—a request
for further trial questions—"spare not me." The Countess finally devises a statement—"You were lately whipped, sir, as I
think" (l. 49)—that traps the fool. "Spare not me" could be
ludicrously interpreted as a request for unmerciful whipping.
Though the Clown scores a couple of palpable hits before the
scene ends, the Countess has proven herself no fool or, rather,
as good a one as Lavatch.

The typical depiction of a superior presenting his plan and
giving orders to his subordinate is reversed in scene 5 (II.ii) of
*Much Ado about Nothing*. The henchman Borachio explains the

plot he has devised and gives a long list of instructions to his master, Don John:

> Go you to the Prince your brother; spare not to tell him that he hath wronged his honor in marrying the renowned Claudio (whose estimation do you mightily hold up) to a contaminated stale. (ll. 21–24)

> Go then; find me a meet hour . . . ; tell them that . . . ; intend a kind of zeal. . . . Offer them instances . . . ; and bring them to see . . . (ll. 31–42)

And Don John responds, "I will put it in practice" (ll. 48–49). Shakespeare seems to have wanted to make Don John as disagreeable as possible and so has deprived him of the independence and inventiveness of some of his other villains. He depends on a henchman for his chief plot and accepts the henchman's commands. Not only is he vicious, but he lacks dignity and stature even among his cohorts. He is a worm.

As we have seen, a combination of thematic and narrative as well as structural similarities exists between various duets not only in the same play but in different plays and in quite different contexts. Shakespeare was not above borrowing even from himself. Two similar scenes that do not fall into the larger groups of duets are *The Merry Wives of Windsor*, scene 19 (IV.vi) and *All's Well That Ends Well*, scene 15 (III.vii). In both cases a young, attractive character who has met with an impediment to the consummation of his or her love enlists the aid of an older, sympathetic character who is financially insecure. Fenton gains the Host's help in his plot to elope with Anne Page, and Helena gains the Widow's in her plot to trick Bertram. The Host has just been robbed by the Germans and apparently faces financial ruin: "My mind is heavy; I will give over all" (*Merry Wives*, 19.1–2). The Widow, too, has fallen on hard times and lacks a dowry to make a suitable match for her daughter: "Though my estate be fall'n, I was well born" (*All's Well*, 15.4). And both

Fenton and Helena offer substantial rewards for assistance. Yet neither older character is mercenary; in both cases the younger character must convince the older of the justness of the plan despite its unconventionality. Fenton bases his case on the mutuality of love between himself and Anne; Helena, on the legality of her sleeping with her own husband. Both plots will be carried out "tonight" (*Merry Wives*, 19.19, and *All's Well*, 15.43). Both plots involve disguise and the substitution of one character for another. Helena will replace Diana at a tryst with Bertram. Slender and Doctor Caius, who each expect to elope with Anne, will each be deceived by the substitution of a boy dressed in the costume she had agreed to wear.

The younger character dominates each scene; the two scenes are of approximately the same length; and both are duets. While the scene in *All's Well That Ends Well*, which is generally considered to be the later play, may not have been directly patterned on the scene in *The Merry Wives of Windsor*, the similarities between the two scenes indicate not only that elements of plot, character, and theme recur in separate plays but that structural elements recur and may recur in conjunction with the recurrence of these other elements.

According to A. C. Bradley,

> the *peculiar* greatness of *King Lear*,—the immense scope of the work; the mass and variety of intense experience . . . ; the interpenetration of sublime imagination, piercing pathos, and humour . . . ; the vastness of the convulsion . . . ; the vagueness of the scene . . . ,—all this interferes with dramatic clearness.[15]

Bradley's charge that the play shows "structural weakness"[16] is not baseless. Yet Shakespeare has brought structure and unity to this immense and various play through a variety of techniques. Bradley himself points out the suggestive parallels between the

15. *Shakespearean Tragedy*, p. 200; Bradley's emphasis.
16. Ibid., p. 205. I have already discussed Bradley's charge in chapter 1.

main plot and the subplot. [17] Other critics have noted the unifying effects of recurring themes, image patterns, and verbal echoes. One further and more obviously structural contribution to the play's unity is the pattern of its scenes. The particular scenic pattern relevant to the present chapter is that of its duets; it has five, nearly twice as many as any other Shakespearean play.

Goneril and Oswald are the participants in the earliest of these duets (*King Lear*, 3 [I.iii]); Regan and Oswald are the participants in the final one (19 [IV.v]). Thus, the first in this series of similarly constructed scenes presents one of the two evil sisters and her servant, and the last presents the other villainous sister and the same servant. The middle duet of the five (12 [III.v]) brings together Cornwall and Edmund, the two major male villains of the play. The second (8 [III.i]) and the fourth (17 [IV.iii]) both portray the same sympathetic and well-meaning characters, Kent and the Gentleman. [18]

The last duet recalls and ironically reflects on the first in a number of ways. Both scenes open with a question asked by one of the sisters, and Oswald's response in both cases is "Ay, madam" (3.3 and 19.1). But whereas Oswald remained a yes-man in the earlier scene, in the second he repeatedly uses negatives and denies Regan's requests even after she attempts to bribe him ("I'll love thee much," 19.21). [19] One of his responses even seems to be an ironic, almost insolent, pun:

17. See ibid., pp. 210–11.

18. One other scene (24 [V.ii, except opening s.d.]) involves only two characters, Edgar and Gloucester, who enter together at the beginning and leave together at the end, but that scene is not a *unitary* scene because Edgar leaves Gloucester alone onstage and then returns with news of the defeat in battle of the forces of Lear and Cordelia. Unlike the entrance of the serving-man near the end of scene 2 of *The Merchant of Venice* (mentioned above, n. 1), Edgar's reentrance emphatically changes the tenor and direction of the scene. Scene 24 of *Lear* is discussed in detail in chapter 6.

19. Some productions have tried to exaggerate the baseness of the two sisters by having each of them in her scene with Oswald suggestively caress or leer at him. But the vileness of the two women needs no exaggeration.

*Regan.* . . . I know you are of her bosom.
*Oswald.* I, madam?

(19.26–27)

Oswald, who seemed to be merely a toady in the earlier scene, now shows signs of a genuine loyalty, however misplaced, which he will further exhibit in his dying speech.

More significantly, the first of these duets contains, as I have noted, the first overt order in the sisters' campaign to humble Lear, while the last contains the first outward expression of antagonism of one of the evil sisters for the other. In scene 3 Goneril complains of Lear's behavior and uses Oswald as an instrument to have the issue "come to question" (l. 14). In scene 19 Regan complains of Goneril's behavior toward Edmund and also uses Oswald to bring the issue into the open:

And when your mistress hears thus much from you,
I pray, desire her call her wisdom to her.

(ll. 34–35)

The sisters act in unison against their father, as Goneril notes in her scene with Oswald:

If he distaste it, let him to my sister,
Whose mind and mine I know in that are one.

(3.15–16)

But sisters that would destroy a father will not hesitate to turn on one another when a difference arises between them. Shakespeare connects the two conflicts by presenting the first stage of each in a duet.

The second and next-to-last duets are also connected in a variety of ways. Both open with a series of questions asked by Kent that prompt memorable descriptions by the Gentleman of offstage actions. In scene 8 (III.i) the latter gives a magnificent account of Lear in the storm. The mixture of pathos and violence depicted in that speech is balanced by the mixture of pathos and loveliness in the Gentleman's description in scene 17 (IV.iii) of the response of Lear's one faithful daughter to the news of her father's persecution. The portrait of a frantic Lear tearing his hair and "Contending with the fretful elements" (8.4) is balanced by the more delicate but no less moving struggle within Cordelia:

> . . . it seemed she was a queen
> Over her passion, who most rebel-like
> Sought to be king o'er her.

>                                             (17.15–17)

The Gentleman's description of Lear prepares us for the following scene, which actually shows us Lear in the storm; the Gentleman's description of Cordelia prepares us for the reappearance of the long-absent Cordelia in the next scene.

In the middle of both scenes the dramatic focus shifts from the Gentleman to Kent, but, in keeping with his reputation for plain speaking, Kent's descriptions of offstage developments are not as poetical as the Gentleman's. In the first scene Kent sends the Gentleman on the mission that eventually leads to the latter's description of Cordelia in the second scene, and Shakespeare thus establishes another link between the two scenes.

The central duet—the one between Cornwall and Edmund—most explicitly raises the theme of loyalty or devotion that is prominent in all five duets. In scene 3 Goneril demonstrates her disloyalty to her father; in scene 19 Regan demonstrates the lack of devotion between the two sisters, and Oswald demonstrates a perverse loyalty to his mistress. In contrast, the two scenes between Kent and the Gentleman present images of unselfish devotion. In the first the banished Kent and the anonymous Gentleman remain faithful to Lear despite his outcast state. Cordelia's devotion to her father despite his mistreatment of her is shown by her reaction, as described by the Gentleman in his second duet with Kent, to her father's sufferings. The depth of her emotions on hearing of them contrasts with the cold-bloodedness of her sister when she initiated those sufferings in scene 3.

In scene 12 (III.v) Edmund explicitly raises the issue of loyalty: "How, my lord, I may be censured, that nature thus gives way to loyalty, something fears me to think of" (ll. 3–5). The speech, of course, is patently insincere. The focus of the speech is not on the hypothetical struggle within him between the natural feelings of a son toward a father and political loyalty but on his fear of public censure.[20] Edmund, in fact, not only never possessed such natural feelings but does not really regard such feelings as natural at all. Edmund's one loyalty is, in fact, to Nature: "Thou, Nature, art my goddess; to thy law / My services are bound" (2 [I.ii].1–2). But this Nature is self-interest—to which loyalty, fraternal and filial, gives way.

Cornwall, for his part, seeks revenge on Gloucester for remaining loyal to Lear. In an aside Edmund hopes that a demonstration of that loyalty will further inflame Cornwall and provides a fleeting verbal picture of faithfulness that contrasts with his own "loyalty": "If I find him [Gloucester] comforting the king, it will stuff his [Cornwall's] suspicion more fully" (12.21–22).

This scene is a fascinating picture of two evil and self-interested men who are temporarily allied, each making, for the benefit of the other, a perfunctory claim for the morality of his actions. The language of morality is set on its head. Edmund twice calls his betrayal of his father "loyalty" (ll. 4, 23) and describes himself as "just" (l. 11). He calls his father's loyalty "treason" (l. 13), and Cornwall calls it "reprovable badness" (ll. 8–9). Fittingly, in the final speech of the scene the elder of these two

20. Compare Claudius's concern for outward appearance in his description of his supposed psychomachia, in which nature also loses: "Though yet of Hamlet our dear brother's death / The memory be green, and that it us *befitted* / To bear our hearts in grief"; "Yet so far hath discretion fought with nature / That we with wisest sorrow think on him / Together with remembrance of ourselves" (*Hamlet*, 2 [I.ii].1–3, 5–7; my emphasis).

villains symbolically adopts the younger: "I will lay trust upon thee, and thou shalt find a dearer father in my love" (ll. 25–26).

Yet the son outshines the father, for Edmund is the manipulator in the scene. His repeated allusions to the sacrifice he has made in informing on his father oblige Cornwall to grant him immediate compensation: "it hath made thee Earl of Gloucester" (ll. 18–19). Edmund's aside indicates that he has no more respect for his newfound father than for the old. He will "stuff" Cornwall's suspicion just as he stuffed that of the "credulous" Gloucester (2.183).

In scene 12 Edmund's "dearer father" bestows on him his natural father's position, and in the final duet Cornwall's widow expresses the desire to bestow Cornwall's position on him. Regan tells Oswald,

> My lord is dead; Edmund and I have talked;
> And more convenient is he for my hand
> Than for your lady's.

> (19.30–32)

Regan's loyalty to the memory of her dead husband is no stronger than her loyalty to her father or to her sister. Her grief is of shorter duration than Gertrude's, and her thoughts of remarriage are more o'erhasty. This o'erhastiness is strikingly represented by the abruptness of line 30.

The first duet between Kent and the Gentleman and that between Cornwall and Edmund both occur on the same night, the night of the storm. Near the end of the earlier scene Kent tells the Gentleman, "I will go seek the king" (8.50), and the Gentleman and he exit to search for Lear. Near the end of the later one, Cornwall instructs Edmund to "Seek out where thy father is, that he may be ready for our apprehension" (12.19–20). The two loyal retainers seek to bring comfort to the fallen King while the son seeks to catch the father "comforting the king" and bring him back to punishment.

Edmund's brief allusion in the midst of his betrayal of Gloucester to his father's devotion to Lear recalls the opening of the first
duet. At the outset of her scene of disloyalty to her father,
Goneril asks Oswald, "Did my father strike my gentleman for
chiding of his Fool?" (3.1). The first mention of the Fool in the
play is Goneril's complaint about Lear's defense of him. The two
self-interested and disloyal children present images of devotion
on the part of the fathers they are in the act of betraying. And
Goneril's reference in the first duet to Lear's solicitude for the
Fool is complemented by the image supplied in the second of the
Fool's devotion to Lear. After the Gentleman describes Lear in
the frightful storm, Kent asks, "But who is with him?" (8.15).
The Gentleman responds, "None but the Fool, who labors to
outjest / His heart-struck injuries" (ll. 16–17).

The structural similarity among these scenes and their symmetrical arrangement throughout the play call special attention
to the many other similarities and to the ironic contrasts among
them.[21] They not only reflect on one another but together almost
provide a skeleton of the play as a whole. Lear and Cordelia do
not appear in them, but Lear's sufferings and Cordelia's reactions to those sufferings are described. So is Lear's repentance.
Kent tells the Gentleman in scene 17:

A sovereign shame so elbows him: his own unkindness
That stripped her from his benediction, turned her
To foreign casualties, gave her dear rights
To his dog-hearted daughters: these things sting
His mind so venomously that burning shame
Detains him from Cordelia.

(ll. 44–49)

21. The effect of the structural similarity is enhanced by the simplicity of
that structure. In each case the theatergoer sees a scene, separated from other
episodes by cleared stages, in which two, and only two, characters interact
without interruption by any entrances or exits.

The Fool does not appear in these scenes, yet his relationship with Lear is encapsulated by brief remarks in the first two duets.

The duets in *King Lear* demonstrate the double structure described at the end of chapter 2. Each duet has a self-contained structure; but these similarly structured scenes as a group contribute in unexpected ways to the structure of the play as a whole.

# Four ⚔ Unitary Group Scenes

Shakespeare's plays contain a surprisingly large number of "unitary group scenes," that is, scenes in which three or more characters enter simultaneously at the beginning and leave simultaneously at the end and in which no other entrances or exits occur during the course of the scene. Approximately one-eighth of all the scenes in the canon are unitary group scenes.[1] Such scenes may involve any number of characters from three to, if not the "infinite numbers" prescribed by a stage direction in *Henry VI, Part Two* (after l. 32 of scene 13 [IV.ii]), as many as a theatrical company could afford or a stage could comfortably hold.

Although some group scenes seem virtually indistinguishable from solo scenes or unitary duets in the printed text since only one or two characters have speaking parts, the supernumeraries are not really supernumerary because they transform what otherwise would be a private occasion into a public one. Even though Viola and the Captain are the only speakers in the second scene (I.ii) of *Twelfth Night*, for example, the presence of other sailors onstage is important. If the scene had begun with the entrance of just a man and a woman, neither as yet identified, an audience might have leapt to irrelevant romantic conclusions unless the Captain were portrayed as an old man, which he is not in the existing scene.[2] More importantly, the

---

1. Of 780 scenes in 35 plays, 98 are unitary group scenes. One type of unitary group scene, the excursion or procession without dialogue—of which there are 25 in the canon—has already been discussed in chapter 1.

2. The Captain not only is not old but is presumably handsome. Viola tells

devotion Viola clearly inspires in the Captain is made to seem representative of similar feelings inspired in the others, particularly since she addresses her first two questions to the sailors in general, whom she calls "friends" (l. 1), rather than to the Captain in particular. Although none of those sailors speaks and although Viola eventually directs her remarks to the Captain in particular, the spirit of the scene has been established as one of comradeship rather than one of intimacy. In chapter 3, I noted the contrast between scenes 20 and 21 (III. viii and ix) of *Antony and Cleopatra*; the presence of Octavius's troops in scene 20 gives a potency to Octavius's commands, a potency that seems to be denied in the next scene to the commands of Antony, who is accompanied onstage by only a single subordinate.

As I also pointed out in the last chapter, although the two characters involved in a duet could either enter together or meet onstage and could leave either together or separately at the end of the scene, in a disproportionate number of cases the two characters enter together and leave together. Despite the even greater possibilities for divided entrances at the beginning and for divided exits at the end of a unitary group scene,[3] in most such scenes the entire group enters and leaves as a unit.

Although unitary group scenes are surprisingly common in Shakespeare's plays, only eleven of them are trios.[4] A third character immeasurably reduces the sense of intimacy possible with only two characters onstage, while on the other hand, three characters comprise too small a group to represent a public

---

him, "though that nature with a beauteous wall / Doth oft close in pollution, yet of thee / I will believe thou hast a mind that suits / With this thy fair and outward character" (2 [I.ii].48–51).

3. Two groups of several characters, or one group of several characters and a solitary character, or several groups of characters could enter or leave simultaneously.

4. The stage directions for five other scenes are sufficiently indefinite or ambiguous to permit the possibility that those scenes are trios, but in most of those cases the dramatic context suggests that a larger group is onstage.

gathering or even a full-fledged political faction. One trio does, however, depict a political coalition in an incipient stage: the Duke of York presents to Salisbury and Warwick his convoluted claim to the throne and obtains their support in the sixth scene (II.ii) of *Henry VI, Part Two*. But most of the trios in the canon depict either a private plot or a domestic conference; in six trios, two of the three characters are related. In scene 15 (III.iv) of *Romeo and Juliet*, for example, Capulet consults with his wife and Paris and decides, despite his earlier insistence upon Juliet's willing consent and despite the recent death of Tybalt, that Juliet shall marry Paris within the week. In scene 21 (V.ii) of *The Merry Wives of Windsor*, Page, Shallow, and Shallow's nephew Slender make their final preparations for the ill-conceived and fortunately thwarted elopement of Slender with Anne Page. Helena, the Widow, and the Widow's daughter Diana prepare in scene 19 (IV.iv) of *All's Well That Ends Well* for the second stage of Helena's elaborate plan to regain her husband. One trio actually portrays two members of a domestic circle dissuading the third from joining a military–political faction. The wavering Northumberland succumbs to the entreaties of his wife and daughter-in-law to abandon those in rebellion against Henry IV and to flee to Scotland (*Henry IV, Part Two*, scene 7 [II.iii]). Northumberland's willingness to flee is evident from his eventual surrender to Lady Percy's emotional but shaky argument that his failure to come to the aid of Hotspur will be redeemed by his failure to come to the aid of the remaining rebel lords.

Three trios depict the defeat or disintegration of a military force. That only three members of such a force appear together suggests in itself the crumbling of the army. The final rout of the Romans by the Britons in *Cymbeline* is dramatized by a very brief scene (30 [V.ii.14–end]) in which only Lucius, Iachimo, and Imogen (in disguise as Fidele) appear.[5] Lucius warns Fidele,

5. The stage becomes clear in the course of V.ii: Posthumus, Belarius,

Away, boy, from the troops, and save thyself,
For friends kill friends, and the disorder's such
As War were hoodwinked.

                                                    (30.1–3)

An audience's perception of the disorder, the breaking up, of the
Roman force is visually enhanced by the contrast between this
unitary trio and the unitary group scene without dialogue (26
[V.ii, opening s.d.]) that occurred only moments before and that
depicted an orderly procession of these characters accompanied
by "the Roman army." On the other hand, that Imogen does not
run off when sent by Lucius visually demonstrates the loyalty
of the boy "Fidele" for "his" master (a loyalty Lucius soon
overestimates).

The Romans, however, are the victors in the Battle of Corioles. Scene 10 (I.x) of *Coriolanus* depicts Aufidius, the leader
of the defeated Volscians, accompanied by "two or three soldiers." The ambiguity of the opening stage direction does not
affect the nature of the scene. Whether this particular scene is
presented as a unitary trio or a unitary quartet is unimportant.
What is important is that the leader of the Volscian army is
accompanied by *only* two or three soldiers, by only a small rem-
nant of that army. Again, this scene contrasts with an earlier
unitary group scene (2 [I.ii]), one in which Aufidius and the
Senators of Corioles discuss preparations for the defense of the
city. Despite Aufidius's deep concern, the Senators express confidence. Despite that confidence, the later unitary scene opens
with Aufidius's exclamation, "The town is ta'en!"

Scene 32 (IV.v) of *Antony and Cleopatra* does not occur immediately after a defeat in battle, but one of the themes of this
trio is the disintegration of Antony's forces. Antony and Eros,
one of his lieutenants, meet the Soldier whose advice to Antony

---

Guiderius, and Arviragus rescue Cymbeline and all "*exeunt. Then enter* Lucius, Iachimo, *and* Imogen" (s.d. after l. 13).

before the disastrous Battle of Actium to fight at land rather than
at sea was ignored. The Soldier now alludes to the consequences
of Antony's failure to follow that advice:

> Hadst thou done so,
> The kings that have revolted, and the soldier
> That has this morning left thee, would have still
> Followèd thy heels.

(ll. 3–6)

The soldier who has defected is Enobarbus, and his defection is
the subject of the remainder of the scene. That kings "have
revolted" from Antony is blunt evidence that his forces are dis-
integrating. But that Enobarbus has defected is, in dramatic
terms, more important evidence of that disintegration. We have
never seen those kings onstage, but we have frequently seen
Enobarbus as Antony's closest adviser and confidant.

Though unitary trios usually depict domestic conferences or private plots and only in special and appropriate contexts depict
members of an army, nearly half of all unitary group scenes
involving more than three characters portray the leaders of an
army or of a political faction. In many of these scenes the speaking characters are both military and political leaders and are
accompanied by nonspeaking followers, attendants, or soldiers.
One such scene is *Antony and Cleopatra*, scene 28 (IV.i). Caesar enters with Agrippa, Maecenas, and "his Army" and opens
the scene by expressing to his two lieutenants his anger at Antony's chiding letter and at Antony's mistreatment of Caesar's
messenger. Maecenas, the only other character to speak, urges
Octavius to take advantage of Antony's distracted state by attacking as soon as possible—"Give him no breath" (l. 8). Caesar accepts this advice and gives instructions to prepare for a
battle on the following day.

The two unitary group scenes (aside from "Excursions") in

*Henry VI, Part Three* both involve the leaders of a faction accompanied by followers and form a closely connected pair. Both
occur near the end of the play; the second is actually the final
scene. Both portray the Yorkist faction and, in fact, the same
three characters—Edward IV, Richard of Gloucester, and Clarence—are the only speakers in each. In the first (28 [V.iii]),
Edward exults over the Yorkist triumph at Barnet: "Thus far
our fortune keeps an upward course / And we are graced with
wreaths of victory" (ll. 1–2). But, employing meteorological imagery, he acknowledges a new threat posed by Queen Margaret's
forces:

> . . . in the midst of this bright-shining day
> I spy a black, suspicious, threat'ning cloud
> That will encounter with our glorious sun.
>
> (ll. 3–5)

Clarence responds to this danger with easy optimism, but, like
Maecenas in *Antony and Cleopatra*, scene 28, Richard advises
immediate action: "If she have time to breathe, be well as-
sured / Her faction will be full as strong as ours" (ll. 16–17).
Edward responds by ordering an advance at once to meet the
enemy at Tewksbury.

Scene 32 (V.vii) again opens with Edward's victorious exulta-
tion: "Once more we sit in England's royal throne / Repur-
chased with the blood of enemies" (ll. 1–2). But this time the
victory is unclouded by any apparent dangers. The irony is that
a much more insidious danger to Edward's line than that posed
by Margaret's army is actually onstage in the person of Richard.
Although Edward had used meteorological images in the earlier
scene, in this one he establishes a pattern of agricultural imagery: "What valiant foeman, like to autumn's corn, / Have we
mowed down in tops of all their pride!" (ll. 3–4). Ironically,
Edward is now at the top of his pride, and Richard announces in
an aside that he will "blast" the "harvest" (l. 21) of Edward's

heir. The threat in the earlier unitary group scene was external, recognized, and opposed—and, by being opposed, was ended. The threat here is within the Yorkist faction itself, unrecognized, and unmet by opposition.

In addition to numerous excursions and other scenes of purely physical action without dialogue, *Henry VI, Part One* contains three unitary group scenes. In the first, Charles the Dauphin, the Duke of Alençon, and Reignier (the Duke of Anjou) are accompanied onstage by their soldiers. These three leaders of the French forces express haughty confidence in themselves and denigrate the English will to fight:

> *Dauphin.* What towns of any moment but we have?
>    At pleasure here we lie near Orleans;
>    Otherwhiles the famished English, like pale ghosts,
>    Faintly besiege us one hour in a month.
> *Alençon.* They want their porridge and their fat bull-beeves:
>    Either they must be dieted like mules
>    And have their provender tied to their mouths,
>    Or piteous they will look, like drownèd mice.
> *Reignier.* Let's raise the siege; why live we idly here?
>
>                                        (2 [I.ii].5–13)

Their comments are immediately undercut by the following scene, an excursion without dialogue, in which the French "*are beaten back by the English with great loss*" (3, s.d. [I.ii, s.d. after l. 21]).

Immediately following the excursion, furthermore, the same three leaders enter again, this time unaccompanied by soldiers, and unintentionally parody the sentiments they expressed just before the battle. The Dauphin exited scene 2 with impressive bravado: "Him I forgive my death that killeth me / When he sees me go back one foot or fly" (2 [I.ii].20–21). But the emptiness of his bravado is exposed in the very next speech in the play, in which the Dauphin lamely defends his retreat:

. . . What men have I?
Dogs! cowards! dastards! I would ne'er have fled,
But that they left me 'midst my enemies.

$$(4.1-3 \text{ [I.ii.22-24]})$$

In the extended passage quoted above from scene 2, the French
commanders harped on the hunger of the English as a cause of
their vulnerability. In scene 4 the Dauphin cites the same condition as an element contributing to the English invincibility:

Let's leave this town, for they are harebrained slaves,
And hunger will enforce them to be more eager.

$$(4.16-17 \text{ [I.ii.37-38]})$$

Even the Frenchmen's similes uncomfortably reflect on their
prebattle opinions with unintended irony:

*Reignier.* The other lords, like lions wanting food,
  Do rush upon us as their hungry prey.

$$(4.6-7 \text{ [I.ii.27-28]})$$

The second unitary group scene in the play (10 [I.vi]) involves the same characters as the first with the addition of La
Pucelle, through whose leadership the French have managed to
secure Orleans. On the walls of the city Joan proclaims her own
accomplishment. The Dauphin extravagantly praises her and
promises extravagant demonstrations of his gratitude. Reignier
suggests public banquets in celebration. Once again, however,
the French leaders are made ridiculous by the immediately ensuing action. The English assault the city in the next scene, and
after an excursion in which *"The French leap o'er the walls in
their shirts"* (12, s.d. [II.i, s.d. after l. 38]), Alençon, Reignier,
and the Bastard of Orleans enter in dishabille to be shortly
joined by the Dauphin and Joan. As in the sequence following
the first unitary group scene, this latest reversal of the French
fortunes abounds with ironies. In scene 10 the Dauphin described Joan and catalogued the rewards he intended to bestow
on her:

Divinest creature, Astraea's daughter. . . .
France, triumph in thy glorious prophetess!

(ll. 4, 8)

. . . I will divide my crown with her,
And all the priests and friars in my realm
Shall in procession sing her endless praise.

(ll. 18–20)

The latter speech continued in the same vein for eleven more
lines, but the Dauphin's very next speech in the play, which
occurs after the debacle, opens with the question, "Is this thy
cunning, thou deceitful dame?" (13.12 [II.i.50]).

While in the first sequence the hunger suffered by the English
was changed from a source of celebration among the French
leaders to one of despair, in the second sequence the celebratory
feasting of the French ironically leads to their defeat. In scene
10 Reignier proposes, Alençon seconds, and the Dauphin confirms that the city shall "banquet royally, / After this golden day
of victory" (10 [I.vi].30–31). Early in the next scene Talbot
explains to Bedford and Burgundy,

This happy night the Frenchmen are secure,
Having all day caroused and banqueted;
Embrace we then this opportunity.

(11 [II.i].11–13)

Again, figurative language introduced in the unitary group
scene becomes ironic in retrospect. The Dauphin told Joan,
"Thy promises are like Adonis' garden / That one day bloomed
and fruitful were the next" (10.6–7). The speeding up of natural
processes has ironically been continued by the rapid decay of
those promises and of the Dauphin's own promises. In both unitary scenes, finally, the French presume supernatural support
for their cause:

*Dauphin.* Mars his true moving, even as in the heavens,
So in the earth, to this day is not known.

Late did he shine upon the English side;
Now we are victors; upon us he smiles.

(2.1–4)

*Reignier*. Dolphin, command the citizens make bonfires
. . . . . . . . . . . . . . . . . . . . . . . . . . . . . . . . . . . . . .
To celebrate the joy that God hath given us.

(10.12, 14)

The third unitary group scene occurs after the English have recaptured Rouen but this time portrays Talbot, the leader of the English forces, and Burgundy, who has allied himself with the English, accompanied by their troops. The opening two speeches, however, express disturbingly familiar sentiments:

*Talbot*. Lost, and recovered in a day again!
    This is a double honor, Burgundy;
    Yet heavens have glory for this victory!
*Burgundy*. Warlike and martial Talbot, Burgundy
    Enshrines thee in his heart and there erects
    Thy noble deeds as valor's monuments.

(24.1–6 [III.ii.115–20])

And these sentiments, like those of the French leaders in the two previous unitary scenes, are quickly undercut. In the very next scene Burgundy, moved by Pucelle's rhetoric, reverts to the French side. The Dauphin had promised to rear a "pyramis" to Joan in scene 10 (l. 21), only to declare her a "deceitful dame" in scene 13. Similarly, Burgundy's apostrophe to the absent Talbot in scene 25 (III.iii), "So farewell, Talbot; I'll no longer trust thee" (l. 84), marks his tearing down of the monuments he had erected in his heart in the preceding scene.

Burgundy's defection is significant militarily and is also significant thematically. When the English learn of Burgundy's reversion to the French side, Henry VI sends Talbot on a mission against Burgundy. That mission not only results in Talbot's death but exposes the fatal dissension among the English commanders themselves. And ironically, Gloucester's condemnation of Burgundy could be applied with as much justification to the nobles who fail to come to Talbot's aid:

> O monstrous treachery! can this be so,
> That in alliance, amity, and oaths,
> There should be found such false dissembling guile?
>
> (27 [IV.i].61–63)

The pattern formed by the three unitary group scenes in *Henry VI, Part One* is insistently ironic. The first two depict the French leaders anticipating or celebrating a victory over the English, and each is shortly followed by an ironic reversal of the French fortunes. But a second edge of Shakespeare's irony becomes apparent when Talbot and his ally exit with their forces after expressing sentiments that echo those of the French leaders in the two earlier, similarly constructed scenes. Our expectations of a reversal this time of the English fortunes should be raised and are quickly satisfied.

A set of unitary group scenes related to those involving military or political leaders are those involving political or military figures of intermediate rank. Such scenes are concentrated in the late tragedies. In *Macbeth*, scene 22 (V.ii), a group of Scottish thanes discuss Macbeth's increasing desperation and their plan to join their forces with the English army against him. As soldiers bear the body of a Parthian leader across the stage in scene 13 (III.i) of *Antony and Cleopatra*, Ventidius, a lieutenant of Antony and the conqueror of the Parthians, explains to his subordinate Silius the danger faced by any of Antony's officers whose exploits might appear to outshine those of Antony and who might thereby arouse Antony's ire.

Another set of scenes related to those in which leaders confer among themselves with followers onstage are those that are solely composed of a speech directed by a leader to his troops. The earliest, longest, and most famous of these scenes is Henry's oration to his soldiers during the attack on Harfleur in *Henry V* (10 [III.i]). In striking contrast to Henry's stirring oratory, Achilles' instructions to his Myrmidons in scene 23 (V.vii.1– 8) of *Troilus and Cressida* are laconic, cold-blooded, and ignoble.

Much of the humor of scene 23 (V.iv) of *The Merry Wives of Windsor* derives from its recalling such scenes of military exhortation. Addressing his troop of fairies in preparation for the Herne's Oak campaign against Falstaff, Evans, dressed as a satyr, urges them, "Be pold, I pray you. Follow me into the pit, and when I give the watch-'ords, do as I pid you" (ll. 2–3). "Into the pit" even sounds like a specific parody of "unto the breach," a phrase that had already been parodied twice in the scene following Henry's oration in *Henry V* itself—first by Bardolph's "On, on, on, on, on, to the breach" (11 [III.ii].1) and then by Fluellen's "Up to the breach, you dogs!" (l. 20).

In *Henry IV, Part Two*, scene 17 (V.iv), Doll Tearsheet and Hostess Quickly threaten and vilely abuse a Beadle who, accompanied by officers, is bringing them to court. The Hostess does make a brief and malapropian foray into stoicism—"Well, of sufferance comes ease" (l. 24)—but with a speed true to her name she reverts to vituperation by calling the Beadle a "starved bloodhound" (l. 26). This unitary group scene is one of a few in which a character or several characters are in custody and in transit.

Both the woman in custody and her custodians are far more civil in scene 19 (V.iii) of *The Two Gentlemen of Verona*. Silvia, a virtuous gentlewoman of Milan, has been apprehended by some unprofessionally courteous outlaws. They are conducting her to their captain, who, unbeknownst to Silvia, is her worthy admirer, Valentine. Unlike Doll and the Hostess in their reaction to their presumably deserved restraint, Silvia is truly stoic despite her hyperbole: "A thousand more mischances than this one / Have learned me how to brook this patiently" (ll. 3–4).

Two scenes in *Richard III* provide a contrast in attitude between the set of characters in custody in the first and the character under arrest in the second. The two scenes are clearly meant
to reflect on one another, and the connection between them is
intensified by the similarity in their structures as unitary group
scenes. In scene 11 (III.iii) Sir Richard Ratcliffe, aided by
Halberds, is conducting Rivers, Grey, and Vaughan to execution
at Pomfret. Though all three condemned men protest their fate,
their reactions are almost too neatly individualized. Rivers is
self-righteous: "Today shalt thou behold a subject die / For
truth, for duty, and for loyalty" (ll. 2–3). Grey is as abusive as
Doll and the Hostess: "A knot you are of damnèd blood-suckers"
(l. 5). And Vaughan is threatening: "You live that shall cry woe
for this hereafter" (l. 6).

Buckingham, who was instrumental in the arrest of the three
characters on their way to execution in scene 11, is on his own
way to execution in scene 21 (V.i). But his demeanor is in conspicuous contrast with that of the prisoners in the earlier scene,
particularly with the attitude struck by Rivers, the most voluble
of those prisoners. With arrogant assurance Rivers portrayed
himself as an about-to-be martyred saint, reminded an apparently forgetful and negligent God about justice, and offered an
unsaintlike prayer for the avenging of his own death by the
fulfillment of Margaret's remaining curses:

> . . . O, remember, God,
> To hear her prayer for them, as now for us!
> And for my sister and her princely sons,
> Be satisfied, dear God, with our true blood,
> Which, as thou know'st, unjustly must be spilt.
>
>                                   (11.18–22)

Although his execution is indeed unjust, Rivers manages to
squander our sympathies by his vengefulness and self-right-
eousness. Although he had been Richard's henchman, Buck-

ingham wins our sympathy by his candid self-appraisal, his humility before God, and his acknowledgment of the justness of his punishment:

> That high All-seer which I dallied with
> Hath turned my feignèd prayer on my head
> And given in earnest what I begged in jest.
> Thus doth he force the swords of wicked men
> To turn their own points in their masters' bosoms. . . .
> Come, lead me, officers to the block of shame;
> Wrong hath but wrong, and blame the due of blame.
>
> (21.20–24, 28–29)

Rivers had implicitly included Buckingham in his vengeful prayer. Buckingham explicitly apostrophizes Rivers, Grey, and Vaughan, but in self-abasement not in ire:

> Hastings, and Edward's children, Grey and Rivers,
> . . . . . . . . . . . . . . . . . . . . . . . . . . . . . . . . . . .
> Vaughan, and all that have miscarrièd
> By underhand corrupted foul injustice,
> If that your moody discontented souls
> Do through the clouds behold this present hour,
> Even for revenge mock my destruction!
>
> (ll. 3, 5–9)

They well might mock his destruction as his fate mimics theirs. The agent of Richard in their destruction has become Richard's victim in his turn. Yet there is less to mock in Buckingham's manner of meeting his fate than in their manner of meeting theirs. Buckingham deflects mockery in calling it down upon himself.

Several unitary group scenes qualify as "mirror-scenes," according to Hereward T. Price's description.[6] In fact, Price's primary example of a mirror-scene, *Titus Andronicus*, III.ii, is a

6. See Price, "Mirror-Scenes," pp. 101–13.

unitary group scene. This scene consists mainly of Titus's over-wrought expression of his grief and anger at the afflictions of his family. He entreats his brother Marcus, daughter Lavinia, and grandson Lucius to prepare themselves for taking revenge but does not discuss an actual plan. During the course of the scene Marcus kills a fly. At first Titus pities the "poor harmless" crea-ture (7 [III.ii].63). But after Marcus excuses his action by claim-ing the fly was black and ill favored like Aaron, Titus himself strikes at the dead insect. According to Price, this episode re-veals "the contradictory elements" in Titus's character of "ten-derness . . . and . . . unrelenting cruelty," and these opposites are the basis of the play's dramatic irony.[7] Price further argues that the scene as a whole

> has little or nothing to do with the plot: that is to say, if cut, it will not be missed. . . . On the other hand, it enlarges our knowledge of the problem which is the core of the work, and in this way *Titus* gains in depth and perspective. It brings every-thing into focus. The chief issues of *Titus* are there, and it may be said to mirror the play. ("Mirror-Scenes," p. 102)

Despite Price's overstatement of his case here—it is ques-tionable whether this scene "brings everything into focus" or "may be said to mirror the play"—he has usefully distinguished a significant type of scene that recurs in Shakespearean drama. During the course of his article Price relaxes his criteria to in-clude as "mirror-scenes" those that do not contribute to the plot but instead bring a character's personality or a theme into sharp focus.[8]

7. Ibid., p. 101.
8. Price's selection of the term "mirror-scenes" was perhaps unfortunate. In the first place, his relaxation of criteria seems to allow inclusion of scenes under this rubric that do not, in fact, mirror the play in any meaningful sense. Second, the term "mirror-scenes" is ambiguous because it could be applied even more appropriately to a pair of scenes in a play that mirror or reflect on one another in specific ways.

A scene not cited by Price but which possesses some of the important attributes of a mirror-scene is *Othello*, scene 8 (III.ii), given here in its entirety:

> *Enter* Othello, Iago, *and* Gentlemen.
> *Othello.* These letters give, Iago, to the pilot
> And by him do my duties to the Senate.
> That done, I will be walking on the works;
> Repair there to me.
> *Iago.*                    Well, my good lord, I'll do't.
> *Othello.* This fortification, gentlemen, shall we see't?
> *Gentlemen.* We'll wait upon your lordship. *Exeunt.*

Not surprisingly, this is the shortest scene in the play—even the Herald's solo scene is twice as long.[9] Were the playwright not Shakespeare, one might be tempted to regard this episode as inserted merely to separate a scene that concluded with the exit of Cassio and Emilia from one beginning with the entrance of those characters with Desdemona. It does not advance the plot; if cut, it would not be missed were not an immediate reentry of characters created. On the other hand, it brings, if not quite "everything," at least one paramount thing into focus. What the scene does, simply, is to provide one final, fleeting view of Othello in command—in command of Iago, in command of Cyprus, and in command of himself.

Before scene 8 we have seen Iago successfully turn Roderigo and Cassio into pawns. But we have also seen that Othello is no Roderigo or Cassio. He has been a poised and commanding figure in the early confrontation with Brabantio, in the scene in which Brabantio reviles him before the Duke, and in bringing to a halt the brawl manufactured by Iago. Scene 8 is the last we see of this poised and commanding figure until the very end of the play.

9. Only two other scenes in the play have fewer than 100 lines. The Herald's scene was discussed in chapter 2.

During the course of the next scene, which by contrast is the longest in the play, Othello loses command. He loses command of Iago because Iago has, in effect, gained control of him. Othello declares, "I am bound to thee forever" (9 [III.iii].213), and he is bound to Iago in a sense he does not intend. In allowing himself to come under Iago's control, Othello loses command of himself. Ironically, he tells Iago in scene 9, "Fear not my government" (l. 256), that is, his self-control. But he loses control of himself several times later in the scene: "O monstrous! monstrous!" (l.424); "I'll tear her all to pieces!" (l. 428); "O, blood, blood, blood!" (l. 448). And not much later in the play, his loss of control reaches the point of his actually falling into a trance. During the course of scene 9 Othello also renounces his military command:

> Farewell the plumed troops, and the big wars
> That makes ambition virtue! O, farewell!
> Farewell the neighing steed and the shrill trump,
> The spirit-stirring drum, th'ear-piercing fife,
> . . . . . . . . . . . . . . . . . . . . . . . . . . . . . . . . . .
> Farewell! Othello's occupation's gone!
>
> (ll. 346–49, 354)

Now that his occupation is gone he will no longer participate even in less stirring military functions like inspecting fortifications, as he was preparing to do in scene 8.

In a brief comment on the "fortifications" scene, Mark Rose has argued, furthermore, that an "Elizabethan sensibility, accustomed to thinking analogically, would have no difficulty relating this episode to the temptation scene, which reveals how inadequate Othello's personal fortifications are against Iago's siege."[10] An audience with such a sensibility might also relate scene 8 to the final scene. At the very end of the play Othello

10. *Shakespearean Design*, p. 75.

reenacts an incident in which he once smote a Turk who "tra-
duced the state" (15 [V.ii].353) and takes both parts, the Turk
and himself. The external fortifications against the Turks that he
went to inspect at the end of scene 8 provided defense neither
against Iago nor against a traducing Turk within himself.

A scene of the type represented by the "fly" episode in *Titus
Andronicus* and by the "fortifications" interlude in *Othello* does
not significantly advance the plot but instead focuses attention
on themes or characterization. For obvious reasons a unitary
structure is an appropriate form for such a scene. By being detached from other episodes and depicting only one character
or one unchanging set of characters, such a scene can effec-
tively provide a sharp focus on a specific theme or element of
characterization.

When Shakespeare includes two or more unitary group scenes in
a play, they are almost always clearly related to one another or
form a recognizable pattern. Earlier in this chapter, for example, significant connections were pointed out between the two
unitary group scenes in *Henry VI, Part Three*, between the two
in *Richard III*, and among the three in *Henry VI, Part One*.
Another example is provided by the two unitary group scenes in
*The Two Gentlemen of Verona*. In scene 13 (IV.i) Valentine is
unfortunately intercepted by outlaws but, fortunately, they give
him the option of becoming their leader rather than dying. In
scene 19 (V.iii) Silvia has been intercepted by the same band of
outlaws, but her seeming misfortune is seeming good fortune in
the eyes of the audience since the outlaws are bringing her to
Valentine. (This good fortune is ironically delayed, however, because Proteus "rescues" her from the outlaws.)

The two unitary group scenes in *The Merchant of Venice* also
form a balanced pair. In scene 4 (II.i) the Prince of Morocco
presents himself as a suitor to Portia, and she explains the story

of the caskets to him. In scene 10 (II. vii) Morocco chooses the wrong casket. The two principals are accompanied by their trains in both scenes but are the only ones to speak. The first opens with Morocco's request, "Mislike me not for my complexion," and the second ends with Portia's aside as he makes his exit: "Let all of his complexion choose me so" (10.79). The Prince extravagantly praises himself in scene 4, while Portia politely but coolly acknowledges his suit. After dismissing the leaden casket out of hand in scene 10, Morocco almost chooses the silver on the basis of his high self-estimation—"As much as I deserve? Why that's the lady!" (l. 31). But he goes on to praise Portia as extravagantly as he had praised himself in the earlier scene and finally chooses the golden casket on the basis of his association of Portia's high value with the high material value of gold. The connection between the scenes is not established by their similarity in structure; that similarity merely reinforces the connection.

The scenes in *Richard III* that depict characters on their way to execution and that, as we have seen, reflect upon one another are only two of five unitary group scenes in the play. The second of those two, Buckingham's, is also the first of a series of three consecutive unitary group scenes. Buckingham's last scene in the play is immediately followed by Richmond's first (22 [V.ii]). And Richmond's scene—in which he confers with Oxford, Blunt, and Herbert in the presence of soldiers as they proceed toward a confrontation with Richard's army—reflects on Buckingham's scene, just as Buckingham's had reflected on that of Rivers, Grey, and Vaughan. Whereas Buckingham was on his way to execution, Richmond, as Shakespeare's audience well knew, is on his way to kingship. Buckingham's stoic resignation is balanced by Richmond's confident hope. The contrast is epitomized by the ostentatiously rhetorical couplets that end the two scenes:

*Buckingham.* Come lead me, officers, to the block of shame;
Wrong hath but wrong, and blame the due of blame.

                                        (21 [V.i].28–29)

*Richmond.* True hope is swift and flies with swallow's wings;
Kings it makes gods, and meaner creatures kings.[11]

                                        (22.23–24)

Buckingham's penitence, his moral revulsion at his own past
crimes, which contrasted with Rivers's earlier self-righteous-
ness, is now counterpoised by Richmond's implied self-justification for his invasion. That self-justification is based not on extravagant claims of guiltlessness but on moral revulsion at
Richard's crimes.

Buckingham's reformation is convincing and attractive partly
because he neither transfers blame to Richard nor wishes revenge on his former confederate for betraying him. He refers to
that betrayal mainly to acknowledge the justness and fitness of
his own punishment rather than to vilify Richard. Richard's betrayal, nevertheless, is a major theme of his remarks. He refers
at length to the ironic fulfillment of the disingenuous prayer in
which he had earlier asked for retribution on himself if he ever
ceased to cherish Queen Elizabeth's family:

. . . God punish me
With hate in those where I expect most love!
When I have most need to employ a friend
And most assurèd that he is a friend,
Deep, hollow, treacherous, and full of guile
Be he unto me!

                                        (5 [II.i].34–39)

Buckingham also refers to the fulfillment of Margaret's prophecy
(which he quotes with understandable imprecision) that his

---

11. Richmond seems unaware of the irony of his hyperbole here. The only
"meaner creature" who will be made a king in the present circumstances will
be Richmond.

heart would be "split . . . with sorrow" by Richard (21.26). The abandonment and betrayal of Buckingham by this friend— who had once called him "My other self, my counsel's consistory, / My oracle, my prophet, my dear cousin" (6 [II.ii].151– 52)—is emphasized by the almost pathetic question with which Buckingham opens scene 21: "Will not King Richard let me speak with him?"

Again, the following scene provides a striking contrast. Richmond's opening line is "Fellows in arms and my most loving friends," and friendship is a major theme of the scene. The word "friends" occurs five times in twenty-four lines. Richmond's supporters are "loving friends" and "courageous friends" (l. 14), whereas Richard, according to Blunt, "hath no friends but what are friends for fear, / Which in his dearest need will fly from him" (ll. 20–21). The preceding scene emphasized the abandonment of the friendless Buckingham by Richard. And characters in the current scene plausibly predict that Richard will imminently be abandoned by his seeming friends.

After Richmond leaves accompanied by three prominent supporters of his faction and by his soldiers, Richard III enters, also accompanied by three prominent adherents and by soldiers.[12] The precise visual and structural similarities between these two juxtaposed unitary group scenes provide, once again, the ground for a series of contrasts. The assurance and optimism expressed in scene 22 contrast with the hollow cheer and the fatalism displayed by Richard and his adherents in scene 23 (V.iii.1–18). Very early in the latter scene Richard asks, "My Lord of Surrey, why look you so sad?" (l. 2). Surrey's response is unconvincing: "My heart is ten times lighter than my looks"

12. The latter scene comprises the first eighteen lines of the traditional division V.iii. During the segment, Richard's soldiers erect a tent that remains onstage; but all the characters leave the stage at the end of the segment, as indicated by the explicit stage direction "*Exeunt*," by the later direction "*Enter* Richard, Ratcliffe, Norfolk, *and* Catesby" at V.iii.46, and by the couplet that concludes the segment.

(l. 3). Richard and Norfolk then exchange comments that express grim fortitude rather than confidence:

> *Richard.* Norfolk, we must have knocks; ha, must we not?
> *Norfolk.* We must both give and take, my loving lord.
>
> (ll. 5–6)

Seemingly trying to break the mood, Richard gives a vigorous command, but quickly and almost absent-mindedly he falls into an expression of almost outright pessimism:

> Up with my tent! Here will I lie tonight;
> But where tomorrow? Well, all's one for that.
>
> (ll. 7–8)

In his last speech, Richard finally tries to suggest reasons for expecting a victory, but his arguments are ironically undercut by our recollection of specific comments made near the end of the previous scene. Richard claims a numerical superiority of forces. Oxford's claim in scene 22 that "Every man's conscience is a thousand men / To fight against this guilty homicide" (ll. 17–18) is certainly hyperbolic and seems complacent or naive. But Herbert's and Blunt's plausible predictions of massive desertions among Richard's forces redeem Oxford's contention and are still in our minds during the next scene. We are therefore prepared to regard Richard's claim of numerical superiority as mere prevarication or self-deception.

The patent flimsiness of Richard's next argument almost turns him into a pathetic figure:

> Besides, the king's name is a tower of strength,
> Which they upon the adverse faction want.
>
> (23.12–13)

Richard III is beginning to sound like Richard II (that is, the Richard II Shakespeare will later create). Richard's appeal to the king's name echoes phrases used by Richmond in the previous scene:

In God's name cheerly on, courageous friends,
To reap the harvest of perpetual peace
By this one bloody trial of sharp war.

(22.14–16)

. . . Then in God's name march!

(l. 22)

Not only did Richmond refer to the name of the power above and behind any king, but his references were primarily expressions of allegiance rather than of idle dependency on the efficacy of a name.

The second of those references occurred near the beginning of the final speech of scene 22 and immediately preceded Richmond's description of "true hope." In the final speech of scene 23 Richard clutches at false hopes based on numerical superiority and the strength of the king's name. The ironic connection between the concluding speeches of the two antagonists is further enhanced by another verbal parallel. Richard's instruction to "survey the vantage of the ground" (23.15) recalls Richmond's declaration that the expected defections of Richard's troops are "All for our vantage" (22.22). No topographical advantage that Richard may discover could possibly counterbalance the disadvantage of a mutiny among his army.

In addition to the fatalism expressed by the characters themselves and the palpable weakness of Richard's sources of confidence, Shakespeare suggests the imminent doom overhanging the characters who appear in scene 23 by a visual reference to one of the still earlier unitary group scenes. Richard, Norfolk, and Surrey are accompanied by only one other recognizable character, Sir Richard Ratcliffe. The three noblemen on their way to execution in scene 11 were also accompanied by only one other recognizable character—Sir Richard Ratcliffe.

The final scene of *Richard III*, as one might expect a final scene of a Shakespearean play to do, ties together many images and themes that were introduced throughout the play. But it is also a unitary group scene and contains specific allusions to the earlier unitary group scenes. Richmond, Stanley, and "divers other lords" relish their triumph over Richard, who was slain by Richmond in the preceding scene and whose body has remained onstage. Richmond's opening line—"God and your arms be praised, victorious friends" (29 [V.v].1)—echoes his opening line in scene 22—"Fellows in arms and my most loving friends." Those "loving friends," whom later in that scene he called "courageous friends," are now "victorious friends." Richmond's description in scene 22 of Richard as "The wretched, bloody, and usurping boar" (l. 7) is echoed in scene 29 when Stanley calls Richard a "bloody wretch" (l. 5). In the earlier scene Richmond reported that he had received "Lines of fair comfort and encouragement" from Stanley (22.6); in the final scene Richmond receives the crown itself from Stanley.

The first two of the five unitary group scenes focused on imminent executions. The last focuses on the imminent marriage between Richmond and Elizabeth that will secure the general peace. The first two such scenes contain prominent references to earlier oaths. Grey and Rivers and, later, Buckingham acknowledge the fulfillment of Margaret's curses. Buckingham recalls his own earlier "feigned prayer" that God has ironically granted. In the concluding speech of the play Richmond alludes to the very different oath he has solemnly sworn:

> And then, as we have ta'en the sacrament,
> We will unite the White Rose and the Red.

(29.18–19)

In the first unitary group scene Rivers had actually prayed for the slaughter to continue—"O, remember, God, / To hear her prayer for them, as now for us!" (11 [III.iii].18–19). In the final scene Richmond repeatedly prays for the end of the slaughter and does so in the concluding couplet of the play:

Now civil wounds are stopped, peace lives again;
That she may long live here, God say amen.

(29.40–41)

Fittingly, the last word in the last scene of this play which has
dealt with the last stage of England's prolonged civil strife is
"amen."[13]

A Shakespearean play may contain parallels between units
both larger and smaller than individual scenes. In some plays,
like *King Lear*, broad similarities exist between the main plot
and a subplot. In some plays, particular incidents or sequences
of incidents even within a single plot will mirror one another.
According to A. C. Bradley, for example, as the final catastrophe of *Coriolanus* "approaches it is felt to be the more inevitable
because the steps which lead to it are made to repeat as exactly
as possible the steps which led to his exile."[14] Every play contains passages of dialogue that echo one another and images that
recur. That these forms of parallelism can undeniably be found
in the plays does not mean that the particular type of patterning
with which I am here concerned—patterns formed by scenes
with similar structures—is illusory or insignificant. This type of
patterning is simply one of several means by which Shakespeare
gives artistic order to his material.

Like those in *Richard III*, the four unitary group scenes in
*Macbeth* reflect on one another and are arranged in a recognizable pattern. The first is the very opening scene of the play.
Three Witches confer briefly to the accompaniment of "Thunder
and lightning."[15] Although it is the opening scene, it does not

13. That this is actually the third use of the word "amen" by Richmond in
the concluding scene further indicates the emphasis in the scene on the theme
that England's strife has been conclusively ended.

14. "*Coriolanus*: British Academy Lecture, 1912," in *A Miscellany* (London: Macmillan, 1929), p. 94.

15. Unlike most of the trios discussed earlier, this conference can hardly

really initiate the plot or even supply much exposition. Its chief function seems to be to establish an atmosphere of gloom and portentousness. The remaining three unitary group scenes all occur very near the end of the play, and all three depict leaders of the forces against Macbeth, who are shown in three distinct stages of preparation for the climactic battle. These scenes (22, 24, and 26 [V.ii, iv, and vi]) alternate with scenes of the besieged Macbeth inside Dunsinane Castle (23 and 25 [V.iii and v]).

In the opening scene the Witches discuss, somewhat enigmatically, the time and place of their next meeting, and one implies that the chief object of that meeting is a joint encounter with Macbeth: "There to meet with Macbeth" (l. 7). That encounter proves to be fateful for both Macbeth and Scotland. In the first of the three later unitary group scenes the Scottish thanes discuss plans to join Malcolm, Siward, Macduff, and their forces: "Near Birnam Wood / Shall we well meet them" (22.5–6). The chief object of this meeting is also a fateful encounter with Macbeth, a joint military venture to unseat him from his ill-gotten throne.

The introductory stage direction of the opening scene was "*Thunder and lightning*"; the introductory stage direction of all three later unitary group scenes is "*Drum and colors.*" Visual and sound effects emphasize the disturbance of nature that accompanies the Witches' anticipation of the encounter with Macbeth that will be a prelude to the disruption of the Scottish state. On the other hand, visual and sound effects associated with concerted human efforts accompany the preparations for the military encounter with Macbeth that will restore order in the Scottish state.

The three figures who share the opening scene are on speak-

be described as a domestic one. Indeed, although they are called the Weird Sisters, whether or not the Witches are actually related is a matter of doubt.

ing terms with Graymalkin and Paddock, communicate in enigmatic, formulaic utterances, and apparently thrive on thunder, lightning, rain, "fog and filthy air" (l. 11). Their association with evil magic and a threatening and malignant atmosphere is balanced by the therapeutic imagery used by the thanes in the first of the later unitary group scenes:

> *Caithness.* Meet we the med'cine of the sickly weal,
> And with him pour we, in our country's purge,
> Each drop of us.
> *Lennox.*         Or so much as it needs
> To dew the sovereign flower and drown the weeds.
>
>                                (22.27–30)

The second of the later unitary group scenes carries the contrast even further. Malcolm gives a command that results in the seemingly magical operation of bringing Birnam Wood to Dunsinane. But what might appear supernatural to an observer is actually produced by men working together. In the last two unitary group scenes, characters repeatedly emphasize that restoration of order in Scotland depends on concerted human effort. Macduff tells his comrades, "Put we on / Industrious soldiership" (24.15–16). The last unitary group scene opens with Malcolm's command to his soldiers to bring to an end the seemingly magical subterfuge: "Your leavy screens throw down, / And show like those you are" (26.1–2). And Siward declares, "Let us be beaten, if we cannot fight" (l. 8). The malign supernatural influence of the Witches is now balanced by human intervention which, in bringing Birnam Wood to Dunsinane, temporarily gives the appearance of being supernatural.[16] Thus, the set of

16. Although Birnam Wood's trip to Dunsinane is apparently foreseen by spirits summoned by the Witches, how much responsibility those spirits can take for the occurrence is a question not answered by the play. But the stage and seemingly the control of events in the later part of the play have been taken over by human characters.

three unitary group scenes near the end of *Macbeth* complement and ironically reflect upon the unitary group scene that strikingly opens the play.

The five unitary group scenes in *As You Like It*, like the five unitary duets in *King Lear*, are arranged in an overtly symmetrical pattern. The first, third, and fifth depict either Duke Senior and the lords attending on him in the Forest of Arden or those retainers by themselves. The second and fourth each shows the tyrannical Duke Frederick, exercising the power usurped from Duke Senior, with his attendant lords. The first of these unitary group scenes is the first scene set in the Forest of Arden and marks the first appearance of Duke Senior. The fourth marks the last appearance of Duke Frederick and is the last scene in the play not set in the forest. The five scenes are 4 (II.i), 5 (II.ii), 8 (II.v), 11 (III.i), and 18 (IV.ii).

The two unitary group scenes involving Duke Frederick (5 and 11) form a balanced pair. In the first, Frederick is wrongly led to suspect Orlando of complicity in the flight of Celia and Rosalind and sends for Orlando's brother Oliver. Frederick does not appear again until the fourth unitary group scene, in which he wrongly accuses Oliver of complicity in the flight of Orlando and threatens him. Frederick displays his peremptoriness and paranoia in both scenes. Not only do his opening lines in the two scenes convey these qualities, but the second opening clearly echoes the first:

Can it be possible that no man saw them?
It cannot be.

(5.1–2)

Not seen him since? Sir, sir, that cannot be.

(11.1)

Both scenes are quite short, comprising twenty-one and eighteen lines respectively. (As with most other paired scenes in the canon, the second is shorter than the first, in this case by only three lines.) Each scene concludes with Frederick's commands to his attendant lords. Those sets of commands again reveal Frederick's authoritarianism, and again the later speech contains an echo of the earlier: "Do this suddenly" (5.19); "Do this expediently" (11.18).

The three unitary group scenes set in Arden (4, 8, and 18) present a very different Duke and a court-in-exile very different from Frederick's court. Near the beginning of his first speech in the play, at the start of the first scene set in Arden, Duke Senior asks, "Are not these woods / More free from peril than the envious court?" (4.3–4). This scene is immediately followed by the first of the two unitary group scenes set in Frederick's court, and the two juxtaposed scenes depict the contrast implied by Duke Senior's rhetorical question. Duke Senior opens scene 4 by addressing his "co-mates and brothers-in-exile" (l. 1).[17] Ironically, his actual brother was the cause of that exile. But a further irony amounting to poetic justice is that that brother opens the very next scene by expressing his contrasting distrust of and isolation from those around him:

> Can it be possible that no man saw them?
> It cannot be; some villains of my court
> Are of consent and sufferance in this.

> (5.1–3)

That the contrast is one of character rather than of mere circumstances is obvious in itself but is supported by the fact that Duke Frederick's suspicions are groundless. No one besides the characters who have actually fled is in on the conspiracy.

Frederick is in power but is not in control of circumstances and displays arrogance, rigidity, and peremptoriness. Duke Senior is in exile but transcends his circumstances by his humility

---

17. Compare Richmond's opening line in *Richard III*, scene 22 (V.ii): "Fellows in arms and my most loving friends."

and by his suppleness and openness of mind. He humbly takes instruction from the conditions of forest life, even from the "winter's wind":

> . . . when it bites and blows upon my body
> Even till I shrink with cold, I smile and say,
> "This is no flattery; these are counselors
> That feelingly persuade me what I am."

> (4.8–11)

Intentionally and somewhat playfully paradoxical, he shows the suppleness of his mind in making the very hardships he suffers into virtues. He refers to his present existence as

> . . . adversity,
> Which like the toad, ugly and venomous,
> Wears yet a precious jewel in his head.

> (4.12–14)

The emphasis of this simile could easily have been reversed: though wearing a precious jewel in his head, the toad is ugly and venomous. Adversity is indeed sweeter to Duke Senior than prosperity is to Duke Frederick.

But the direct contrast between the two ducal brothers established by the juxtaposition of the first two unitary group scenes is extended in the remaining unitary group scenes into a broader contrast between the two courts, which reflect the personalities of the respective dukes. Duke Senior appears in only the first of the unitary group scenes set in Arden and is replaced by Jaques as the central character in the later two. He even shares prominence with Jaques in the first, since most of the scene is devoted to a discussion of that absent character.

Jaques's views are presented in absentia by the First Lord, who had eavesdropped on his private meditations. Curiously, the very first mention of Jaques in the play is the First Lord's declaration of Jaques's agreement with the Duke's reservation about killing deer: "Indeed, my lord, / The melancholy Jaques grieves at that" (4.25–26). After observing a wounded deer, Jaques complained, according to the First Lord, that the exiles are permitted

> To fright the animals and to kill them up
> In their assigned and native dwelling place.
>
> (ll. 62–63)

His objection thus echoes the Duke's statement of his aversion to killing the "native" deer "in their own confines" (ll. 23–24).

Jaques and the Duke share other characteristics as well. The Duke asks the First Lord, "Did he not moralize this spectacle" of a wounded deer (l. 44)? Jaques did, just as the Duke has moralized similar spectacles, has found "sermons in stones" (l. 17) and in other features of forest life. Jaques's moralizing took the form of a series of epigrams quoted verbatim by the First Lord, just as the Duke's moralizing about the wind took the form of his quotation of his own epigram (see ll. 8–11, quoted above). Duke Senior and Jaques even have similar tastes in figurative language. The former calls the deer "burghers of this desert city" (l. 23), and the latter is quoted as calling them "citizens" (l. 55).[18] Both perceive flaws and limitations in various modes of life. According to the First Lord, Jaques "pierceth through / The body of the country, city, court, / Yea, and of this our life" (ll. 58–60). The Duke found fault with the "envious court" (l. 4) and the "public haunt" (l. 15) of the city and in this scene and elsewhere in the play does acknowledge the priva-

---

18. Passages of the play outside the three Arden unitary group scenes also reveal similarities in the figurative language used by the two characters. Jaques's famous "All the world's a stage" speech is actually only an extension of a metaphor first presented by the Duke in the preceding speech: "Thou see'st we are not all alone unhappy: / This wide and universal theater / Presents more woeful pageants than the scene / Wherein we play in" (10 [II.vii].135–38).

tions of the country. Yet this last similarity only highlights a
fundamental difference between the two characters. The malcontent Jaques can perceive only deficiency and deformity,
whereas the Duke can find sweetness even in adversity.

The second unitary group scene set in Arden (8 [II.v]) com-
plements the first. It marks the first actual appearance of Jaques
in the play as the earlier one had marked the first appearance of
the Duke. Although the Duke does not appear in scene 8, his
point of view (like that of Jaques in scene 4) is represented in
absentia. The references in the song "Under the greenwood
tree" to the adverse conditions of life in Arden ("winter and
rough weather," 8.7, 42) recall the Duke's references to the
"seasons' difference, as the icy fang / And churlish chiding of
the winter's wind" (4.6–7). The song also recalls the Duke's
remarks in its endorsement of forest life despite such drawbacks
and in the contrast it implicitly makes between the forest and the
envious court ("Who doth ambition shun / . . . Come hither,"
8.36, 40). And the lines in the second stanza, which describe
the man suited for the forest life—"Seeking the food he eats, /
And pleased with what he gets" (8.38–39)—also describe Duke
Senior. Though reluctantly, he is ready to "go and kill . . . venison" (4.21), and he is "pleased with what he gets" even if what he
gets is adversity.

Jaques, on the other hand, proudly announces early in the
scene that he "can suck melancholy out of a song as a weasel
sucks eggs" (8.11–12). The contrast with the Duke's personality
is intensified since the particular song sung in this scene reflects
the Duke's sunnier attitude. And the climax of the scene comes
when Jaques presents his own malcontented views in the form of
a parody of that song, a parody in which he ridicules those who
value the forest life. Thus, scenes 4 and 8 develop a contrast
between the characters of Jaques and the Duke even though only
one of them appears in each scene.

Scene 8 also contains oblique reminders of the issue of killing

deer that was so prominent in the first unitary group scene. A
light, comic disparity exists between the reference in the song to
the forester "Seeking the food he eats" and the stage action. The
Duke's meal, which presumably contains venison, is set out
onstage during the scene, and the scene ends with Amiens's
comment, "I'll go seek the Duke. His banquet is prepared"
(ll. 58–59). In this case, the food is waiting, and the man must
be sought.

The issue of deer killing reaches a climax of sorts in the last
unitary group scene (18 [IV.ii]). It opens with Jaques's question,
"Which is he that killed the deer?" After the responsible Lord
identifies himself, Jaques says to the others: "Let's present him
to the Duke like a Roman conqueror; and it would do well to set
the deer's horns upon his head for a branch of victory. Have you
no song, forester, for this purpose?" (ll. 3–6). Is this the same
Jaques who was observed weeping over a wounded deer, who
regarded killing deer as a usurpation? He no more regards the
killer of a deer as a usurper than he regards him as a Roman
conqueror or, as the comic song that concludes the very brief
scene implies, as a cuckold. Jaques's concern for the deer really
was merely the product of one of his "sullen fits" (4.67), as the
Duke called them, just as the Duke's objection to deer killing,
rather than being a seriously held conviction, was apparently
the product of his inclination to sermonize playfully and somewhat sentimentally upon all aspects of forest life. On the other
hand, the proposal Jaques makes in scene 18 reminds us of the
camaraderie the Duke has established with his followers. Duke
Senior appears in only the first unitary group scene, but the
remaining ones reinforce our impression of some of his essential
characteristics.[19]

19. Marco Mincoff maintains that the last of these scenes is clumsy, devoid
of interest, and merely inserted as a "wedge scene" to separate the preceding
and subsequent episodes involving Rosalind; see "Plot Construction in Shakespeare," *Annuaire de l'Université de Sofia* 36 (1940–41): 39. To serve as a

The five unitary group scenes in the play thus dramatize the contrast between the two dukes and the two ducal courts. The atmosphere of Frederick's court is grim and constrained, whereas that of Duke Senior's court-in-exile is lively and free. The most conspicuous member of Duke Senior's entourage may boast of his melancholy, but he is never grim. Duke Frederick's lords feed his paranoia and act as his tools. Jaques is the very opposite of a toady. He has the temerity to criticize the Duke in front of the other lords and to avoid his company. Rather than taking affront at Jaques's carping and aloofness, Duke Senior— at the end of the first unitary group scene—actually goes in search of this malcontent in his retinue. Just as he had found sweetness even in the buffets of the winter wind, the Duke finds pleasure even in Jaques's contrariness:

> I love to cope him in these sullen fits,
> For then he's full of matter.

$$(4.67-68)$$

Jaques's invective may be "venomous" like the toad in one of the Duke's similes, but, at least to the Duke, he "wears yet a precious jewel in his head." Jaques serves as a foil for the Duke, but, perhaps more importantly, the license and encouragement given Jaques demonstrate the Duke's toleration and magnanimity. And these characteristics, along with the others I have mentioned, make Duke Senior's court-in-exile, as presented in the first, third, and last of the unitary group scenes, so different from the court, as presented in the second and fourth unitary group scenes, of his suspicious and ignoble brother.

The set of unitary scenes in *As You Like It* also illustrates a curious feature of Shakespeare's technique. Only one of the scenes, that in which Frederick threatens Oliver, presents a se-

---

"wedge scene" may be one of its functions, but, as I hope I have shown, the scene also serves larger structural and thematic purposes as well.

rious conflict between any of the characters onstage, and that conflict is not a very significant one in the play. Very few of the scenes that we have examined in this chapter, in fact, have presented serious discord between characters. Of the seventy-three unitary group scenes containing dialogue that occur in Shakespeare's plays, only ten directly present any significant conflict,[20] even though the very essence of drama, including comedy, is generally presumed to be conflict. Yet we have noticed that, in *As You Like It* and in other plays discussed earlier, although individual unitary group scenes do not portray dramatic conflict, sets of such scenes, sometimes even consecutive scenes, establish intense dramatic contrasts. Duke Senior and Duke Frederick never appear onstage together in *As You Like It*. But by presenting their differences in juxtaposed scenes and by presenting the differences between their courts in contrasting sets of unitary scenes, Shakespeare makes those differences dramatic. Direct confrontation between the two dukes does not take place on the stage, but the audience retains conflicting images of the two dukes and of their two courts. An audience at *Richard III*, similarly, is provided with conflicting images of Richmond and Richard and of their situations before their cli-

20. These include, in addition to Frederick's and Oliver's confrontation, the four scenes of characters in custody (although Buckingham is hardly in conflict with the Sheriff and Silvia's relations with the outlaws are courteous), Valentine's scene with the outlaws (although he is eventually chosen their leader during the scene), the twelfth scene (III.i) of *Cymbeline* in which Lucius demands tribute from Cymbeline, the opening scene of *The Comedy of Errors* (even though Egeon's relations with the Duke of Ephesus, who has reluctantly condemned him to death, are almost cordial), the second scene (I.ii) of *Cymbeline* and the last (32 [V.vii]) of *Henry VI, Part Three* (even though the conflict in each of these two scenes is expressed not openly but by one character in asides). Thus, even in some of those unitary group scenes in which greater conflict might have been expected, it is minimized. A few other scenes contain instances of trivial, subdued, or brief conflict. As I noted in chapter 3, Shakespeare's plays contain only one unitary duet with dialogue that depicts a confrontation between antagonists.

mactic scene of individual combat. This technique of indirect conflict is one means by which Shakespeare is able to reserve direct confrontation for climactic moments; he thereby gives these moments greater power and yet maintains dramatic impetus and dramatic interest throughout a play.

# Five ✖ Two-Part Scenes

In the preceding discussions of unitary scenes, I have attempted to show that Shakespeare treated individual scenes as independent structural units. This conclusion was supported by evidence that he repeatedly turned to a particular scenic structure for a certain limited number of dramatic functions and that within some plays a very strong linkage or pattern exists among scenes with the same structure. Although the plays contain an unexpectedly large proportion of unitary scenes, most scenes include at least one exit or entrance of one or more characters during the course of the scene and therefore include two or more distinct groupings of characters. The present chapter will focus on two-part scenes, that is, scenes in which the grouping of characters changes once during the course of the scene. Chapter 6 will deal with multipartite scenes, scenes that involve a longer series of character groupings. Both chapters will provide further evidence that scenes are significant units of Shakespeare's dramatic structure, that an individual scene possesses a clear internal coherence and a clear internal structure, and that that structure is closely tied to the succession of character groupings within the scene.

Critics have occasionally noted the internal coherence of particular scenes. In a discussion of the opening scene of *Hamlet*, for example, Marco Mincoff arrived at the conclusion that "the whole scene is almost a complete work of art in itself, with its introduction, climax, and resolution."[1] Not every scene in

1. "The Structural Pattern of Shakespeare's Tragedies," *Shakespeare Survey*

Shakespeare lives up to this standard, but nearly every scene
contains evidence of Shakespeare's effort to bind it as closely as
possible into a coherent artistic unit. Evidence was presented in
the opening chapter which indicated that even if a scene continues a narrative incident begun in the preceding scene and
follows without a break in the fictional time frame, each of the
two scenes possesses its own internal dramatic structure. On the
other hand, some scenes incorporate a series of incidents that
pertain to separate narrative strands. Scenes that may lack unity
of narrative action, however, are unified in other ways.

An example of a two-part scene that incorporates separate
narrative strands is the sixth scene (II.i) of *Hamlet*. In the first of
its two segments Polonius engages Reynaldo to spy on Laertes in
Paris and instructs him at length on a particular intelligence-
gathering technique. Polonius instructs Reynaldo to claim knowledge of Laertes' vices when talking with other Danes in Paris so
they will feel unconstrained in telling him of actual transgres-
sions they know Laertes to have committed. Reynaldo's exit is
immediately followed by the entrance of Ophelia. Greatly agi-
tated, she explains to her father that she has just been visited by
Hamlet who appeared "As if he had been loosèd out of hell / To
speak of horrors" (6.83–84). Assuming Hamlet's condition to be
"the very ecstasy of love" (l. 102), Polonius decides to inform
the King. Superficially, the two incidents are unrelated and
seem to be joined in the same scene simply because of the con-
venient presence of Polonius in both. Yet the scene is unified by
a series of parallels between the two segments. Not only does
Polonius appear in both segments, for example, but he displays
in two different contexts some of the same attributes of his char-

3 (1950): 58. See also T. S. Eliot's analysis of the same scene; he said that it
possesses a "musical design . . . which reinforces and is one with the dramatic movement"; *Poetry and Drama* (Cambridge: Harvard Univ. Press,
1951), p. 19.

acter. His instructions to Reynaldo, who never reappears in the play, foreshadow his conduct in the interview with Ophelia.

The mission on which he sends Reynaldo clearly shows his predilections for intrigue and for the manipulation of others. But his reaction to Ophelia's tidings also shows these instincts at work. He treats her news as intelligence that must be handled in the most politic manner:

> . . . Come, go we to the king.
> This must be known, which, being kept close, might move
> More grief to hide than hate to utter love.
>
> (ll. 117–19)

Informing the King in this case is the better part of discretion. Polonius considers, but rejects as a matter of political expediency, the possibility of keeping the whole matter secret. His contrived syntax almost manages to conceal that his real concern is not with Hamlet's welfare but with his own relations with Claudius. According to Roy Walker, Polonius calculates that, "if Hamlet is mad for Ophelia's love, Ophelia's market value soars, the King and Queen may even be glad, if the matter is properly put to them, to permit the marriage—and so his daughter becomes Queen of Denmark! What a superlative triumph to crown the career of the grand master of statesmanship!"[2] Whether or not Walker's supposition is correct, Polonius does react with a calculated formulation of strategy rather than with compassion. His "I am sorry" (l. 106) could not be more perfunctory. Its insincerity is further suggested when he introduces a later comment with the same words: "I am sorry that with better heed and judgment / I had not quoted him" (ll. 111–12). The real stimulus of whatever sorrow he feels is mainly disappointment at the failure of his own information gathering, with which he is so obsessed, and at the failure of his discernment, on which he so prides himself. In the opening section he initiates a surrep-

2. *The Time Is Out of Joint* (London: Andrew Dakers, 1948), p. 46.

titious and deceitful intrusion into the affairs of his son, an intrusion that even includes the blackening of his son's character. In the second part he continues his blundering intrusion into the relationship between his daughter and Hamlet, an intrusion he began in scene 3 (I.iii) when he instructed her to discontinue her relations with Hamlet.

The unfatherly plan presented by Polonius in the first segment to make his son a subject for surveillance foreshadows his treatment of his daughter as the subject of interrogation in the second. He asks her the accusatory question, "What, have you given him any hard words of late?" (l. 107). He has apparently forgotten that it was he, ironically, who instructed her to spurn Hamlet. Ophelia reminds him of his earlier instructions, just as Reynaldo reminded him of his own words when he lost his train of thought in the earlier segment. Neither reminder, however, weakens Polonius's pride in his own mental acuity.

Another of Polonius's obsessions revealed in the opening segment is his concern with what he considers the inevitable indiscretions of youth. He instructs Reynaldo to attribute falsely to Laertes

> . . . such wanton, wild, and usual slips
> As are companions noted and most known
> To youth and liberty.
>
> (ll. 22–24)

Reynaldo should make these slips

> . . . seem the taints of liberty,
> The flash and outbreak of a fiery mind,
> A savageness in unreclaimèd blood,
> Of general assault.
>
> (ll. 32–35)

Using very similar language in the second half of the scene, Polonius mistakenly ascribes Hamlet's condition to the madness of love,

Whose violent property fordoes itself
And leads the will to desperate undertakings
As oft as any passions under heaven
That does afflict our natures.

(ll. 103–06)

Shortly after he assigns Reynaldo the task of falsely attributing youthful indiscretions to Laertes, Polonius now falsely attributes Hamlet's behavior to another sort of youthful indiscretion. Further evidence that this preoccupation has colored his interpretation of Hamlet's behavior is that Polonius manages to drag a reference to it even into his explanation for his prior misjudgment of Hamlet:

. . . it is as proper to our age
To cast beyond ourselves in our opinions
As it is common for the younger sort
To lack discretion.

(ll. 114–17)

An important source of unity in some scenes, like scene 6 of *Hamlet*, is the development of one character. The more that character's actions in different segments reflect on one another, the greater the unity imparted by this particular technique. But the development of Polonius's character is not the only link between the two segments of scene 6 of *Hamlet*.

Reynaldo exits after receiving directions to spy on young Laertes and report his indiscretions to Polonius. The servant who has been turned into a spy is replaced onstage by the contrasting figure of the lovely and ingenuous Ophelia. What she immediately does is to report to her father the indiscreet behavior of young Hamlet. Confused and concerned about Hamlet, she has no ulterior motives of her own. But Polonius, as we have seen, treats her revelation as strategic intelligence. Ophelia has unwittingly become, like Reynaldo, an agent in Polonius's spy network and, subsequently, is drawn even deeper into her father's intelligence-gathering operations. The suggestive and rather distressing parallel between Ophelia and Reynaldo established by the coupling of their interviews with Polonius in scene 6 is later reinforced when Polonius gives her instructions in preparation for her conversation with Hamlet, which her father and Claudius intend to monitor surreptitiously.

Unlike the sixth scene of *Hamlet*, most two-part scenes deal with only a single dramatic issue or incident even though the confines of such a scene do not always allow an elaborate development of the incident with the inclusion of exposition, conflict, climax, and denouement. All two-part scenes are bound together to some extent by the continuous presence onstage throughout the scene of at least one of the characters. This particular bond in itself may not be very strong. In some scenes none of the continuing characters plays a prominent part in both segments; even when a continuing character does play a prominent part in both segments, his actions in one may not reflect as strongly on his actions in the other as do those of Polonius in the two parts of scene 6 of *Hamlet*. Nevertheless, most two-part scenes are firmly unified by either narrative or character development or both. Most scenes with only two character groupings, like most unitary scenes, are also quite short. Two-part scenes thus occupy an interim stage between unitary scenes, which have a simple structure, and multipartite scenes, which contain a longer series of character groupings. Just as certain unitary scenes have marked similarities in content and dramatic function, certain two-part scenes bear significant resemblances to one another. Some two-part scenes within a given play even reflect directly on one another or form a significant pattern, as do some unitary scenes.

In 36 of the 123 two-part scenes in the canon, several characters enter at the beginning, one or more of these eventually exit, and the remaining characters leave simultaneously at the end of the scene. In a few cases one or more of the characters who began the scene exit during its course, and the character or characters left onstage are immediately joined by another character or set of characters to form the second grouping. The sixth scene of *Hamlet* is an example of this type of scene. But nearly two-thirds (77) of the two-part scenes in Shakespeare are created simply by the entrance of a new character or set of characters. The entering character or characters may not be significant figures themselves but very often bear a message or information that significantly changes the course and tenor of the scene. Even when a message merely confirms expectations, it usually changes the tenor of the scene: speculation becomes certainty, hope becomes joy, fear becomes despair.

*King John* contains three consecutive two-part scenes during the battle sequence near the end of the play, and in each the direction of the scene is changed by a character who enters midway to deliver a message. During the brief dialogue that opens scene 15 (V.iii), Hubert tells the ailing King John that the battle is apparently going against John's forces. But a messenger shortly enters and informs the King that the enemy reinforcements have been shipwrecked and that the "French fight coldly and retire themselves" (l. 13).

At the start of the next scene, Salisbury, Pembroke, and Bigot, who have allied themselves with the French, are dismayed at the resistance shown by John's forces but are determined to continue the fight. They are joined by Count Melun, who reveals to the three English noblemen the Dauphin's plan to repay them for their support by cutting off their heads. The tenor of the scene certainly changes, because the Englishmen now shift their allegiance. Salisbury calls the revelation of the Dauphin's intended treachery "this most fair occasion" (16 [V.iv].51) and the anticipated reconciliation with John, "happy newness, that intends old right" (l. 61).

The third scene in this sequence takes place in the Dauphin's camp. Among his train, the Dauphin expresses haughty confidence about the outcome of the battle. But just as he declares that the French are "almost lords" of the field (17 [V.v].8), a messenger enters and announces the defection of the English lords and the shipwreck of the French reinforcements. Since the audience was informed of these facts in the two preceding scenes, the chief interest of the current situation for us lies in the contrast between the premature self-congratulation in which the Dauphin has just indulged and his stunned and disappointed reaction to these reversals:

> Ah, foul, shrewd news! Beshrew thy very heart!
> I did not think to be so sad tonight
> As this hath made me.
>
> (ll. 14–16)

These three consecutive scenes of reversals obviously reflect on one another. The first depicts the reaction in the English camp to unexpectedly favorable news; the last, the reaction in the French camp to unexpectedly unfavorable news; and the middle one actually portrays a group of characters switching allegiance from the French to the English camp. As one might highlight the development of one's argument by presenting a series of related ideas in parallel grammatical structure, Shakespeare here emphasizes his dramatic point by presenting a series of episodes in parallel scenic structure. This series of scenes lends support to Wolfgang Clemens's belief that "it would be worthwhile to enquire into the way in which the recurrence of scenes which display similarity of structure and theme serves the purpose of dramatic presentation."[3]

Some short two-part scenes, like some unitary scenes, focus on a character or theme rather than advance the plot and thus qualify as mirror scenes. In the tenth scene (III.iii) of *Julius*

3. *Shakespeare's Dramatic Art* (London: Methuen, 1972), p. 88.

*Caesar*, Cinna the Poet delivers a short soliloquy in which he mentions his forebodings; a group of plebeians then enters and eventually attacks him merely because his name is the same as that of one of the assassins of Caesar. This incident is not necessary to the plot as no important character is directly concerned. Cinna the Poet appears nowhere else in the play, and the plebeians are not individualized—the questions, commands, and threats of different plebeians echo one another. Like the "fly" scene in *Titus Andronicus*, this one would not be missed if it were cut. Citing it as a mirror scene, Hereward T. Price merely notes that the attack by the plebeians on Cinna serves "to show the brutal excesses inevitably following on Brutus's murder of Caesar" ("Mirror-Scenes," p. 108).

But this brief, self-contained two-part scene mirrors the play in other ways as well. The previous scene showed the power of words, particularly of words that become detached from their real meaning. Antony inflamed the plebeians against the conspirators by repeatedly calling the latter "honorable men." The power of words and the breakdown between the word and what it refers to are embodied in the next scene when the mob vents its fury on a man named "Cinna" even though he is not the right Cinna.

The plebeians commit a crime similar to the one they seek to revenge. Antony had accused the conspirators of murdering Caesar without just cause, and the plebeians murder Cinna without just cause. Cinna's opening soliloquy, furthermore, establishes specific ironic associations between him and Caesar:

> I dreamt tonight that I did feast with Caesar,
> And things unluckily charge my fantasy.
> I have no will to wander forth of doors,
> Yet something leads me forth.

If his dream is prophetic, then one interpretation is that he will feast with Caesar, "not where he eats, but where 'a is eaten," for

Caesar is dead. Caesar himself opened an earlier scene with a similar reference to an ominous dream:

> Nor heaven nor earth have been at peace tonight:
> Thrice hath Calpurnia in her sleep cried out,
> "Help, ho! They murder Caesar!"
>
> (5 [II.ii].1–3)

Cinna's premonitions about himself—"And things unluckily charge my fantasy"—resemble Calpurnia's premonitions about Caesar—"O Caesar, these things are beyond all use, / And I do fear them" (5.25–26). Cinna "had no will to wander forth," and neither did Caesar:

> . . . I will stay at home.
>
> (5.56)
>
> . . . I will not come today.
> Cannot, is false; and dare not, falser:
> I will not come today.
>
> (ll. 62–64)
>
> . . . go tell them Caesar will not come.
>
> (l. 68)
>
> The cause is in my will: I will not come.
>
> (l. 71)

These similarities only emphasize the ironic and grotesque contrasts between the two characters and the two situations. Caesar is the most powerful man in the world, whereas Cinna is not even Cinna the politician and conspirator but Cinna the Poet. The audience's sense of Caesar, however guilty, as a victim is now balanced by the image of Cinna as a wholly innocent victim. The brutality of Caesar's murder is now balanced by the brutality of Caesar's would-be avengers. Although it does not advance the plot, scene 10 provides a condensed, ironic parallel of an element of the main action.

This scene is one of many two-part scenes that, unlike most

unitary scenes, depict conflict. Usually, direct conflict occurs only in one of the two segments. In this particular case the conflict occurs in the second segment, but more typically it occurs in the first. One common type of two-part scene opens with the depiction of disagreement, tension, or outright physical conflict between two characters or two groups of characters; one of the two characters or one of the two parties leaves, and the remaining individual or group comments on the enemy or makes further plans.

Scene 16 (II.iv) of *Henry VI, Part One* opens with a dispute between Richard Plantagenet (who will later become the Duke of York) and Somerset over a legal issue never actually explained. They are accompanied onstage by Warwick, Suffolk, Vernon, and a Lawyer. Shakespeare's omission of any clarification of the legal issue in dispute suggests that it is not the real source of disagreement. What is dramatized instead of a debate over the issue itself is the personal animosity between Richard and Somerset and the enlisting of supporters by each.

Other details stress the unimportance of the actual issue. Near the beginning of the scene Plantagenet asks Suffolk to give his opinion, but Suffolk declines on the basis of his ignorance of and habitual disregard for legal processes. In a complementary exchange Somerset asks Warwick to give his judgment, but Warwick, too, pleads incompetence. A moment later Plantagenet and Somerset again seek support but this time introduce the element of personal and factional loyalty by asking the others to pluck a white or a red rose, which are the insignia, respectively, of the houses of York and Lancaster. Warwick now unhesitatingly picks a white flower and Suffolk a red one. The dramatically relevant question is whose side one is on rather than who is in the right.

Many of the speeches in the first part of the scene fall into an artificial pattern in which the disputants echo one another—for example:

> *Plantagenet.* The truth appears so naked on my side
>   That any purblind eye may find it out.
> *Somerset.* And on my side it is so well appareled,
>
> . . . . . . . . . . . . . . . . . . . . . . . . . . . . . . . . . .
>
>   That it will glimmer through a blind man's eye.
>
> (16.20–22, 24)

Somerset contradicts Richard but borrows Richard's vocabulary, syntax, and figurative language. These echoes help establish the fundamental similarity of Richard and Somerset despite their opposition. The egotism, self-interest, and contentiousness they share, rather than any substantive issue, are the causes of strife. After Vernon and the Lawyer pick white roses, the two principal antagonists trade a long series of insults and threats.

Somerset and his supporter, Suffolk, eventually leave; all the characters who remain are members of the Yorkist faction. As in many two-part scenes in which the second grouping is created by the departure of some of the characters who began the scene, the structure of this scene is that of action in the first part and commentary on that action in the second. Warwick predicts,

> . . . this brawl today,
> Grown to this faction in the Temple garden,
> Shall send, between the red rose and the white,
> A thousand souls to death and deadly night.
>
> (ll. 124–27)

And the scene ends with Richard's concurring prophecy: "This quarrel will drink blood another day" (l. 134). We recognize the accuracy of these forecasts but are horrified at the tone in which they are presented. These characters accept as a matter of fact that a thousand souls should die as a result of what has been depicted as a petty quarrel, as a clash of egos rather than of principles. As in many other cases, the commentary reveals as much about the commentators as about the subject of their commentary.

The ninth scene (III.i) of *Richard II* also depicts a bitter confrontation in the first of two segments and a forward-looking parley among members of a single faction in the second. In the opening segment Bolingbroke recounts to his followers the crimes of Bushy and Green, who stand before him as prisoners, and orders their execution. The two condemned men accept their fate but bitterly deny their guilt and are then led away. In the second segment, Bolingbroke issues new orders to his followers. Just as one source of the unity of scene 6 of *Hamlet* is the development in both segments of the same traits of Polonius's character, this scene in *Richard II* is unified by Bolingbroke's dominance in both segments and by his concern in both with securing his position.

But again like that scene in *Hamlet*, this is also unified by specific parallels between the two segments. Aside from their offenses against himself, the chief crime of which Bolingbroke accuses Bushy and Green in the opening segment is the alienation of King Richard from his Queen:

> You have in manner with your sinful hours
> Made a divorce betwixt his queen and him,
> Broke the possession of a royal bed,
> And stained the beauty of a fair queen's cheeks
> With tears, drawn from her eyes by your foul wrongs.
>
> (9.11–15)

Immediately after the departure of Bushy and Green, Bolingbroke reveals his desire to ingratiate himself with the Queen:

> Uncle, you say the queen is at your house;
> For God's sake, fairly let her be intreated.
> Tell her I send to her my kind commends;
> Take special care my greetings be delivered.
>
> (ll. 36–39)

This solicitude for the Queen is the main focus of the brief second segment of the scene and seems to represent a conscious

effort by Bolingbroke to contrast his own actions with those of
the men he condemned in the opening segment.[4] And this implicit concern to justify himself, furthermore, recalls Bolingbroke's similar concern in the opening segment, in which he told
Bushy and Green that he is recounting their crimes for the following reason: "to wash your blood / From off my hands, here in
the view of men" (ll. 5–6).

In a curious way, the last scene (23 [V.v]) of *Henry IV, Part
One* almost reenacts scene 9 of *Richard II*. Henry may now be
king, but he is still trying to establish the security of his position. In the first part of this scene, which occurs after the Battle
of Shrewsbury, Henry sentences to death Worcester and Vernon,
who stand before him as prisoners. He vigorously denounces
Worcester's crime of abusing his own kinsmen's trust and thereby
precipitating the battle needlessly. In a brief speech Worcester,
like Bushy and Green, accepts his fate but not his guilt. After
the two condemned men are led off, Henry is surrounded only by
his supporters and in the final speech of the play gives military
directives to his commanders. Bolingbroke's final words in scene
9 of *Richard II* were:

> . . . Come, lords, away
> To fight with Glendower and his complices;
> A while to work and after holiday.
>
> (ll. 42–44)

After declaring his intention "To fight with Glendower and the
Earl of March" in his last speech of *Henry IV, Part One*, Henry

---

4. Ironically, in a later scene, Northumberland, Bolingbroke's lieutenant
and the man who led Bushy and Green to their execution, interrupts the one
and only dialogue in the play between Richard and his Queen to enforce their
separation. Bolingbroke thus eventually commits, much more blatantly, the
very crime of which he had accused Bushy and Green in the first part of scene
9. The contrast he had attempted to establish in the second part of that scene
between himself and the men he had just condemned has been replaced by an
ironic similarity.

concludes the play with the words: "Let us not leave till all our own be won" (23.40, 44). The work goes on; holiday has not yet arrived. Henry presumably recalls the past but is still condemned, at least by Shakespeare, to repeat it. My point is not that Shakespeare expected an audience attending the later play to recall specific details of a scene in the earlier one. My point is simply that, in constructing the final scene of *Henry IV, Part One*, Shakespeare himself seems to have had in mind the ninth scene of *Richard II*. He returned to that scene not merely for individual elements but for the ordering of those elements and for the overall organization of the scene in the later play. Furthermore, that two scenes in two different plays display similar sequences of elements suggests, once again, that Shakespeare regarded individual scenes as distinct dramatic units.

Independently, each of these two-part scenes also exhibits an internal unity. As I have argued, the two segments of scene 9 of *Richard II* are unified in part by Bolingbroke's seeming effort in the second segment to establish a contrast between himself and the men he condemned in the first segment. The two segments of scene 23 of *Henry IV, Part One*, on the other hand, establish an implicit comparison between the King and Prince Hal. In the first segment Henry dispenses justice, condemns Worcester and Vernon to immediate execution. After those characters are led off, Henry's sternness is replaced by Hal's mercy. The main action of the second half of the scene is Hal's decision to grant clemency to Douglas, to release him without ransom. Whether or not Worcester, Vernon, and Douglas deserve their respective fates is, I think, less important than these final impressions of the King and the Prince. Insecure on his throne, the King is not inclined and perhaps cannot afford to grant mercy to his enemies. On the other hand, the son actually strengthens his own later hold on the crown by his clemency, which bolsters his reputation as a chivalrous and magnanimous leader. Even while participating in his father's efforts to divide and conquer internal

enemies, Hal, in showing mercy to Douglas the Scot, initiates
his campaign to unify through his personality the disparate elements of the British polity. Hal's clemency is perhaps as calculated and politic as Henry's severity.

In neither of the two scenes just discussed is the conflict between opponents in the opening segment very dramatic. It is
static, incapable of development, because it is already resolved.
Bushy, Green, Worcester, and Vernon are completely in Henry's
control. Their lives are about to end; their effective opposition to
Henry has already ended. The conflict between Henry and Worcester in the first part of the final scene of *Henry IV, Part One*
has less dramatic significance than the indirect comparison between Henry's stern justice in the first part and Hal's clemency
in the second.

Another two-part scene in which a direct conflict in the opening segment is outweighed in significance by an implicit comparison between the two segments is scene 15 (III.iii) of *The
Merchant of Venice*. The opening part of the scene is a confrontation between Antonio and his antagonist, Shylock, who are accompanied by Antonio's friend Solanio and by the Jailer. But the
confrontation is far from an equal exchange. Antonio's two
speeches are merely feeble requests to be heard and comprise a
total of less than two full lines. The remainder of the seventeen-
line segment is taken up by Shylock's ranting. We observe Antonio's meekness and mannerliness in the face of this onslaught,
but our attention is almost completely dominated by Shylock.
The focus of the segment is on the intensity and the obsessional
nature of Shylock's emotions. His verbal repetitiousness gives a
hysterical tinge to his obduracy. Five times he vows, "I'll have
my bond" (ll. 4, 12, 13) or "I will have my bond" (ll. 5, 17). He
repeatedly demands silence: "Tell me not of mercy" (l. 1);
"Speak not against my bond!" (l. 4); "I will not hear thee speak"
(l. 12); "speak no more" (l. 13); "I'll have no speaking" (l. 17).

After Shylock leaves, the scene focuses on the contrasting

personality of Antonio, with Solanio serving as his foil. Solanio immediately engages in invective against the departed Shylock: "It is the most impenetrable cur / That ever kept with men" (ll. 18–19). Rather than indulging in vituperation himself, Antonio gives his friend an extremely dispassionate explanation of Shylock's motives:

> He seeks my life. His reason well I know:
> I oft delivered from his forfeitures
> Many that have at times made moan to me.
> Therefore he hates me.

$$(ll. 21–24)$$

Antonio has almost contradicted Solanio by claiming that Shylock's motives are at least comprehensible and human. Solanio next engages in complacent optimism: "I am sure the duke / Will never grant this forfeiture to hold" (ll. 24–25). Antonio immediately and directly contradicts this assertion and then proceeds to explain calmly and dispassionately the political and economic limitations on the freedom of the Duke's actions in the matter. Antonio eventually does display some emotion in his final lines (though even here the grim facetiousness of the second quoted line suggests a degree of ironic detachment):

> These griefs and losses have so bated me
> That I shall hardly spare a pound of flesh
> Tomorrow to my bloody creditor.
> Well, jailer, on. Pray God Bassanio come
> To see me pay his debt, and then I care not!

$$(ll. 32–36)$$

But Antonio's melancholy resignation and his longing for a final reunion with the friend he loves could hardly be further from the emotions displayed by Shylock in the opening segment.

The effect of the scene as a whole is to establish Antonio's character as nearly the antithesis of Shylock's. Antonio's loving nature contrasts with Shylock's vengefulness; his self-sacrifice with Shylock's egocentrism; his calmness with Shylock's emotional volatility; his melancholy resignation with Shylock's hysterical willfulness; his dispassionate reasonableness with Shylock's unreasonable passion. These contrasts are enhanced by the verbal contrast between the expository mode of Antonio's speeches and the exclamatory mode of Shylock's. The direct conflict between Shylock and Antonio that occurs in the first half of the two-part scene is less striking, less dramatically significant, than the indirect conflict, the contrast between Shylock's character, which is the focus of the first part, and Antonio's character, which is the focus of the second.

In the opening segment of some two-part scenes, the audience is aware of an actual conflict between the motives of the characters, but no overt conflict occurs at all. An example of this variation is scene 10 (III.iii) of *King Lear*, which opens with a dialogue between Edmund and Gloucester, who is completely unaware of his son's treacherous nature. Gloucester even takes Edmund into his confidence by expressing sympathy for Lear, denigrating Cornwall, and revealing his intention to side with the invading forces against Cornwall. Edmund goes further than his father in condemning Cornwall's actions—"Most savage and unnatural" (l. 7)—and, ironically, Gloucester cautions his son to be prudent and circumspect. The audience knows that Edmund is as "savage and unnatural" as Cornwall and, having already deceived his father and betrayed his brother for his own advantage, is capable of betraying the father as well. No conflict between the characters occurs onstage in this segment, but an impression of conflict is certainly created in the minds of the audience. Left alone, Edmund fulfills our expectations by revealing his intention to inform on his father immediately. The twenty-five-line scene thus consists of two unequal parts. The first part is a twenty-line conversation in which Gloucester violates Cornwall's injunction not "to speak of" Lear (l. 5) and in which Edmund says only four words and is explicitly told to "say . . . nothing" (l. 8)—told so in the course of Gloucester's instructions on how Edmund can help keep Gloucester's merciful mission to Lear secret from Cornwall. The secónd part is a five-line soliloquy in which Edmund *does* speak, speaks of his intention to betray that secret. This structure, this pattern of silence and speech, is a map of the substance of the scene.

Our sense of the opposition between Edmund and his father is intensified by the detailed contrast between Gloucester's character as presented in the opening segment and Edmund's character as revealed in his closing soliloquy. Edmund contributes even less dialogue to the first segment of this scene than Antonio does to the first part of scene 15 of *The Merchant of Venice*. And the Edmund who appears in this segment is Edmund as Gloucester imagines him to be. The focus of the segment is on Gloucester's pathetically misplaced trust in Edmund, on his ironically misplaced concern for Edmund's welfare, and on his loyalty to his "old master" (l. 18) and consequent opposition to the "unnatural dealing" (l. 2) of Cornwall.

In the closing soliloquy Edmund appears in his true character, displays his untrustworthiness and his disregard for his father's welfare, and announces his intended collusion with Cornwall. Before exiting, Gloucester affirms his loyalty to Lear despite the personal risk this loyalty entails; after Gloucester's exit, Edmund affirms his readiness to betray both Lear and his own father for personal gain.

This two-part scene, then, is one of a number that highlight a comparison between a character featured in the opening segment and one featured in the closing segment. Also among this number is *The Merchant of Venice*, scene 15, in which Shylock is contrasted with Antonio. In scene 23 of *Henry IV, Part One*, Henry is counterpoised with Hal; Henry's severity in the opening segment contrasts with Hal's clemency in the second part, but a similarity may exist between the underlying motives of the two characters. Ophelia and Reynaldo are counterpoised in the

two segments of scene 6 of *Hamlet*; the striking contrast between
these characters is, as I have argued, undercut by an unexpected parallelism.

The scene just examined is also one of a set of two-part scenes
in which a character expresses sentiments to another character
or group of characters in the first part but then reveals in a
soliloquy quite different sentiments or ulterior motives con-
cealed from those characters. In the first segment of *Measure
for Measure*, scene 13 (IV.iv), Escalus and Angelo discuss the
Duke's letters of instructions concerning preparations for his return to Vienna. Angelo must conceal from Escalus his actual
thoughts and feelings. After Escalus departs, Angelo gives expression both to his sense of guilt over his recent deeds and to
his anxiety about exposure, an anxiety intensified by the imminent return of the Duke.

But Angelo is a less accomplished concealer of his actual
feelings than Edmund. The emotions he releases in his soliloquy
are not completely pent up during the earlier segment. Both he
and Escalus express puzzlement about the Duke's instructions.
But Escalus's comments are matter-of-fact, and he even defends
the rationality of a provision questioned by Angelo. Angelo's
much more extreme reaction reflects his incomplete suppression
of his anxiety. The Duke's letters, he claims, are written "in a
most uneven and distracted manner. His actions show much like
to madness; pray heaven his wisdom be not tainted" (ll. 3–5).
Forced to conceal his actual emotions, Angelo even seems un-
consciously to be projecting his sense of his own failings onto
the Duke. With a reputation for purity, he himself has become
"tainted." His uncontrollable lust for Isabella has driven him to
actions that show "much like to madness." With a reputation for
rectitude and for strict performance of his duties, Angelo has
become "uneven and distracted." He opens his soliloquy by
saying

This deed unshapes me quite, makes me unpregnant,
And dull to all proceedings.

(ll. 20–21)

Angelo's immoderate comment to Escalus must be almost as
puzzling to Escalus as the Duke's enigmatic instructions, but
Escalus is ignorant of the circumstances that have undermined
Angelo's composure. In this scene, unlike the tenth scene of
*King Lear*, the focus of both segments is on the psychological
stress experienced by the deceiver. Angelo reveals that stress
openly in the final soliloquy, but its effect on him is apparent to
us in the opening dialogue as well.

As is indicated by the two scenes just discussed, Shakespeare
found the soliloquy a particularly effective way to close a scene.
In fact, more two-part scenes end than begin with soliloquies,
even though, as was pointed out earlier, nearly two-thirds of all
two-part scenes include more characters in the second segment
than in the first. Of those two-part scenes in which new characters enter after the scene has begun, fewer than one-fifth (14 of
77) open with a soliloquy. On the other hand, of those scenes
with fewer characters in the second segment, over half end with
a soliloquy (20 of 36).

Some of these closing soliloquies consist of direct commentary on the action that took place in the opening segment. The
action that opens scene 28 (V.ii, third sentence of opening s.d.
to l. 10) of *Cymbeline* is a skirmish between Posthumus and
Iachimo, who are on opposing sides in the battle between the
Britons and the Romans.[5] Neither combatant speaks, and nei-

5. Scene 28 is part of the traditional division V.ii, during the course of
which the stage becomes cleared four times. The traditional division opens
with a stage direction describing two separate processions, after each of which
the stage is presumably cleared (scenes 26 and 27). Then Posthumus and
Iachimo enter and fight; Posthumus exits; Iachimo soliloquizes and exits
(scene 28). Then "*the battle continues*"; "Cymbeline *is taken*" by the Romans

ther recognizes the other. Posthumus finally disarms Iachimo
and exits. Wounded in pride more than in body, Iachimo then
comments on his defeat. This brief two-part scene contributes to
the partial restoration of our good opinion of both Posthumus and
Iachimo. In the first segment Posthumus displays his courage
and martial skill. Thus, he speedily fulfills the vow he made in
his last soliloquy (which was the last speech in the play before
his combat with Iachimo): "Let me make men know / More valor
in me than my habits show" (25 [V.i].29–30). Indeed, Iachimo's
commentary in the second segment of scene 28 provides vivid
testimony that Posthumus has been at least as good as his word;
Iachimo emphasizes the disparity between his opponent's lowly
appearance, appropriate to a "carl," a "drudge," or a "lout"
(28.4, 5, 9), and his opponent's soldiership which, if representative, would make the Britons "gods" (l. 10) in comparison with
the Romans. Posthumus's fulfillment of his recently made vow
suggests he may also have undergone the more general moral
regeneration implied by his further promise, made at the end of
the same recent soliloquy: "I will begin / The fashion, less without and more within" (25.32–33).

Although Iachimo's soliloquy in the second segment of scene
28 is partly an attempt to explain away his defeat, to salve his
wounded martial pride, that speech also suggests an incipient
moral regeneration. Like Posthumus, Iachimo seems to have
come to realize the superiority of inner worth to the outer trap-
pings of dignity: "Knighthoods and honors, borne / As I wear
mine, are titles but of scorn" (ll. 6–7). More importantly, in
commenting on his defeat, he acknowledges both his guilt and
his remorse:

---

(s.d. after l. 10), but Belarius, Guiderius, Arviragus, and later Posthumus
come to his rescue; all characters onstage eventually *"exeunt"* after line 13
(scene 29). *"Then enter* Lucius, Iachimo, *and* Imogen" (s.d. after l. 13), who
*"exeunt"* after five lines of dialogue (scene 30, discussed in chapter 4). The
departure of these characters concludes V.ii.

> The heaviness and guilt within my bosom
> Takes off my manhood. I have belied a lady,
> The princess of this country, and the air on't
> Revengingly enfeebles me.

(ll. 1–4)

Ironically, it is not the air but the lady's husband who, unknowingly, has revenged himself. In the first part of this two-part scene, Posthumus (though he does not speak a word) partially regains our favor by fulfilling the vow he made a few moments earlier and by defeating a villain; in the second part, that villain, in turn, partially redeems himself with a speech that foreshadows his later public admission of guilt and expression of remorse.

A pattern of action in the first segment and commentary on that action in the second is not restricted to scenes that end with a soliloquy. At least one scene already discussed has this structure. After the bickering and the plucking of roses in the first part of scene 16 (II.iv) of *Henry VI, Part One*, the Lancastrians leave, and the Yorkists remain to comment on the incident.

More common than scenes in which the second segment is devoted to commentary on the action of the first are scenes in which a character who departs at the end of the opening segment is the subject of commentary in the second. Most of scene 23 (IV.iv, except opening *"Excursions"*) of *Henry V* portrays Pistol's extortion of a ransom from a French Soldier who matches Pistol in cowardice but lacks his bluster. After Pistol leaves with his captive, the Boy, who acted as a translator in the negotiations, comments in a soliloquy on Pistol's bombast: "I did never know so full a voice issue from so empty a heart" (23.68–69). The Boy even anticipates the practice of scholarly commentators of tracing the dramatic lineage of character types: "Bardolph and Nym had ten times more valor than this roaring devil i'th'old play" (ll. 71–72).

The second segment of a two-part scene in *Julius Caesar* also

consists largely of commentary on a character who had been
present during the first part. As scene 11 (IV.i) opens, the three
triumvirs, Antony, Octavius, and Lepidus, are composing a list
of people to be purged, including Lepidus's brother and Mark
Antony's nephew. After sending Lepidus to "fetch" Julius Caesar's will (l. 8), Antony savagely derides him: "This is a slight
unmeritable man, / Meet to be sent on errands" (ll. 12–13).
Antony goes on to compare Lepidus to an ass and to a horse and
calls him a "barren-spirited fellow" and a "property" (ll. 36,
40). But the second segment reflects on the first in another, perhaps more important, respect. The opening of the scene constitutes the first time we have seen the triumvirate together.
They express their seeming solidarity by their willingness to
sacrifice their own relatives. But this solidarity is quickly undercut when, in the second part of the scene, one of the remaining
triumvirs vigorously and protractedly reviles the absent one.

That the triumvirs agreed to the liquidation of their own and
one another's relations in the opening segment seemed to indicate the strength of their bonds to one another. In the second
part those bonds are shown to be fragile indeed, suggesting that
they may become as expendable as the family bonds severed so
expediently in the first part. This scene as a whole, then, gives a
foreshadowing of future historical developments that colors our
response to the conflict in this play between the triumvirs and
the conspirators. After defeating the conspirators, the triumvirs
eventually turn on one another.[6]

In a few two-part scenes the commentary on a character pre-
cedes his appearance. Much of the opening segment of scene 8
(V.i) of *Love's Labor's Lost* is devoted to Holophernes' enumera-

6. Interestingly, one of the reasons that Octavius gives (in *Antony and
Cleopatra*) for his final break with Antony is their disagreement over Lepidus,
but by then the two have completely reversed positions: "Lastly, he frets /
That Lepidus of the triumvirate / Should be deposed" (18 [III.vi].27–29).

tion of Armado's flaws for the edification of Nathaniel and Dull. This denigration ends with the speak-of-the-devil entrance of Armado, accompanied by Moth and Costard. During the course of the second segment, Armado supplies abundant support for Holophernes' accusations. The long speech in which Armado repeatedly and blatantly hints at his intimacy with the King, for example, is indeed "vain, ridiculous, . . . thrasonical, . . . [and] affected" (ll. 12–13).

Yet these adjectives also apply to Holophernes, and each segment exposes Holophernes as much as his rival in foolishness. Early in the first segment Nathaniel praises Holophernes' rhetoric—"witty without affection" (that is, affectation) (l. 4)—but Holophernes' pedantic and mannered speeches attacking Armado both refute Nathaniel's claims and exhibit the very flaws with which Holophernes charges Armado. Nathaniel's misplaced praise of his friend's verbal skill in the opening segment is complemented by Holophernes' misplaced and perhaps hypocritical praise in the second segment of Armado's phrase "posteriors of the day, which the rude multitude call the afternoon" (ll. 86–87). In the second segment Holophernes repeatedly displays his vanity, and Nathaniel's flattery is replaced by Moth's mockery.

Though Moth reserves most of his satiric ammunition for Holophernes, the first salvo he discharges in the second segment is directed at Armado as well. After Holophernes and Armado exchange greetings, Moth comments to Costard that "They have been at a great feast of languages and stol'n the scraps" (ll. 37–38). The first segment had opened, appropriately enough, as Holophernes was literally on his way from dinner, which he used a scrap of mistaken Latin ("Satis quid sufficit") to describe.

Another aspect of the overall structure of this richly comic scene is a droll form of incremental progression. The scene opens with the entrance of three comic characters; these three are joined by three more; and the scene ends with a discussion

of Holophernes' suggestion that they present before the Princess
the pageant of the Nine Worthies.

J. L. Styan maintains that the audience at a Shakespearean
play "frequently hears a statement and then sees an illustration
of it."[7] The organization of an entire scene may be based on this
sequence. In the scene just examined Holophernes' statements
about Armado in the first segment are illustrated by Armado's
speeches in the second segment. A very similar type of two-part
scenic structure is one in which the relationship between the
first and second segments is that of theory and practice. In the
first part of the third scene (I.iii) of *Much Ado about Nothing*,
Don John describes his own personality at some length to Con-
rade. What he reveals is that he is a malcontent and a potential
villain:

> It better fits my blood to be disdained of all than to fashion a
> carriage to rob love from any. In this, though I cannot be said to
> be a flattering honest man, it must not be denied but I am a
> plain-dealing villain. . . . If I had my mouth, I would bite; if I
> had my liberty, I would do my liking. (ll. 26–30, 32–33)

Borachio shortly enters and provides Don John with "food" for
his "displeasure" (l. 62). Don John's first response after Borachio
mentions "intelligence of an intended marriage" is to ask, "Will
it serve for any model to build mischief on?" (ll. 41–42,
43–44). It will. Don Pedro's plan to woo Hero for Claudio provides Don John with an outlet for his malice. The potential villain begins to put his villainy into practice with the help of his
two henchmen.

In the short opening segment of *Antony and Cleopatra*, scene
3 (I.iii), Cleopatra makes explicit her principle of contrariness
in dealing with Antony:

7. *Shakespeare's Stagecraft* (Cambridge: Cambridge Univ. Press, 1967),
p. 208.

. . . If you find him sad,
Say I am dancing; if in mirth, report
That I am sudden sick.

(ll. 3–5)

Charmian challenges the effectiveness of this "method" (l. 7) and advises conciliation instead. But Cleopatra retorts, "Thou teachest like a fool: the way to lose him!" (l. 10). The "infinite variety" by which "she makes hungry / Where most she satisfies" includes infinite contrariety.

Antony shortly enters, and Cleopatra puts her method into practice. She complains, bemoans her situation, and does not permit Antony to respond—five times she ignores his attempts to speak. Eventually he is able to tell her of the military necessity for his departure from Egypt and of his wife's death. Briefly subdued by the latter news, she quickly returns to her earlier tone by actually finding fault with his lack of sorrow for Fulvia. At the very end of the scene she does become self-critical and conciliatory, but it is a conciliation dramatically highlighted for Antony (and for the audience) by her earlier contentiousness. Cleopatra does, however, "lose him" in the sense that she does not dissuade him from going. In the preceding scene Antony repeatedly expressed the necessity of breaking "these strong Egyptian fetters" (2 [I.ii].117), so he may even be insincere when he here tells Cleopatra, "My full heart / Remains in use with you" (3.43–44). Yet she does maintain a hold on him, and he eventually does return to her. Cleopatra's method, which she defends in the first part of this scene and which she puts into practice in the second, has forged fetters Antony is unable to break.

This scene is also the first of four consecutive two-part scenes (I.iii–v and II.i). As I have already argued, the three consecutive two-part scenes in *King John* form a pattern aside from that of mere sequential plot development. Scenes 3 through 6 of

*Antony and Cleopatra* constitute another example of a series of two-part scenes within a particular play that directly reflect on one another.

The leading character in the opening segment of each of these four scenes raises the issue of Antony's whereabouts. The first actually opens with Cleopatra's question, "Where is he?" She is concerned not so much with Antony's physical location as with his state of mind ("If you find him sad, / . . . if in mirth"). Yet his state of mind is inextricably bound up with his conflicting allegiances, which are associated with two locations, Rome and Egypt. In the preceding scene Cleopatra was troubled by an intimation that his mind was reverting to Rome:

> He was disposed to mirth: but on the sudden
> A Roman thought hath struck him.

> (2.83–84)

Thus, the question "Where is he?" is not so easily answered. The question of his physical location is quickly answered by his entrance. But he has come to inform Cleopatra of his decision to depart. Though he is in Egypt, his thoughts have returned to Rome. The scene ends with Antony's attempt to reverse the terms of this paradox:

> Our separation so abides and flies
> That thou residing here goes yet with me,
> And I hence fleeting here remain with thee.
> Away!

> (3 [I.iii].102–05)

Ironically, the next scene (4 [I.iv]) opens with Octavius's complaints to Lepidus that Antony is feasting and carousing in Alexandria rather than assuming his responsibilities as a triumvir. Octavius denounces Antony's degradation at length but, curiously, does not even mention the crisis of Pompey's insurrection, although Antony in the earlier scene cited that crisis as the reason for his departure. In the second part of scene 3 Antony told

Cleopatra, "Sextus Pompeius / Makes his approaches to the port of Rome" and "creeps apace / Into the hearts of such as have not thrived / Upon the present state" (ll. 45–46, 50–52). In the second part of scene 4 a messenger informs Octavius and Lepidus that

> . . . Pompey is strong at sea,
> And it appears he is beloved of those
> That only have feared Caesar.
>
> (4 [I.iv].36–38)

As early as scene 2 Antony had told Enobarbus that the letters he had received from Rome informed him that Pompey

> . . . commands
> The empire of the sea. Our slippery people,
> Whose love is never linked to the deserver
> Till his deserts are past, begin to throw
> Pompey the Great and all his dignities
> Upon his son.
>
> (ll. 185–90)

Shakespeare seems to have constructed scene 4 as a flashback in order to emphasize a parallel with the previous scene. Octavius responds to the news by addressing an appeal to the absent triumvir: "Antony, / Leave thy lascivious wassails" (4.55–56). Having seen the preceding scenes, we are aware, as Octavius is not, that a Roman thought will indeed persuade Antony to leave Egypt. In the second half of the preceding scene Cleopatra confronted Antony in person, and in the second half of scene 4 Octavius, after receiving virtually the same news Cleopatra received in scene 3, addresses Antony in absentia. From our perspective Octavius has already won this particular contest for Antony's commitment.

During the opening segment of scene 5 (I.v), again located in Egypt, Cleopatra asks Charmian, "Where think'st thou he is now?" (l. 19). Her subsequent questions indicate that she is really asking Charmian what she thinks Antony is doing. But the question reminds us that Antony's current physical location is between Egypt and Rome, the poles between which his mind is constantly in transit.

The scene is interrupted this time not by Antony's entrance but by the entrance of a messenger from Antony. Alexas's report that Antony "was nor sad nor merry" (l. 52) leads Cleopatra to commend his "well-divided disposition!" (l. 53). She is right that his disposition is indeed divided, but it is perhaps well divided only in the sense that its division possesses a tragic beauty. Generally light in tone, the scene culminates in a comic image that plays off against the paradox with which Antony ended scene 3. Antony asserted that despite their separation Cleopatra would be with him and he would remain with her. Since his departure Cleopatra has been sending messengers to him "thick" and fast (l. 63). She now asserts, "He shall have every day a several greeting, / Or I'll unpeople Egypt" (ll. 77–78). If Antony cannot be in Egypt, Egypt can go to Antony.[8]

In the fourth of these scenes Pompey, like Caesar in the second, assumes that "Mark Antony / In Egypt sits at dinner" (6 [II.i].11–12). Unlike Caesar, Pompey is pleased at Antony's presumed absence from Rome; he virtually depends on it for the success of his campaign against the triumvirate. He even apostrophizes Cleopatra to "Tie up the libertine in a field of feasts" (l. 23). His words recall the passage in which Octavius apostrophized Antony to leave his lascivious wassails. But Pompey's

8. The focus of the present discussion is on the pattern of connections among this series of scenes. Each scene is, however, internally unified in specific ways unrelated to the overall pattern. In the first segment of scene 5, for example, Cleopatra wonders if Antony is riding his horse: "O happy horse, to bear the weight of Antony! / Do bravely, horse, for wot'st thou whom thou mov'st? (ll. 21–22). Her questions receive answers of sorts in the second segment. Antony was indeed on his horse as the latest messenger to Cleopatra left him, and the horse showed signs of knowing the magnificence of its rider. According to Alexas, it "neighed so high that what I would have spoke / Was beastly dumbed by him" (ll. 49–50).

elaboration of the sensual pleasures that he is confident will detain Antony is ironically interrupted by the entrance of Varrius, who announces, "Mark Antony is every hour in Rome / Expected" (ll. 29–30). Pompey's confidence turns to stoicism.

Although he appears only in the first of these scenes, Antony is the center of attention in all four. One of Shakespeare's techniques to give major characters fullness and roundness—in addition to presenting them directly in varying contexts—is to present them as seen through the eyes of a variety of other characters. In the first of these four scenes, we see Cleopatra's anxiety about Antony's possible intention to depart and then Antony's announcement of his departure and the effect of this announcement on Cleopatra. In the last, we see the effect of his presumed absence from Rome on Pompey and then the effect of the announcement of his impending arrival. In the second, we see the effect of his absence from Rome on Octavius; in the third, the corresponding effect of his absence from Egypt on Cleopatra.

The first and third are set in Cleopatra's Egypt while the second and fourth depict Roman military leaders, who, though opponents, share a Roman contempt for Egyptian sensuality and for Antony's attachment to Cleopatra. Both Octavius and Pompey give elaborate descriptions of the sensual pleasures of Egypt among which they include without distinction Antony's love of Cleopatra and the pleasures of food and drink. In the intervening scene Cleopatra gives some color to these aspersions by referring to herself as a "morsel for a monarch" (5.31). But in the first of these four scenes the dramatized relationship of these lovers is more attractive and more complex than a "lascivious wassail."

Among those plays that contain a series of two-part scenes that reflect on one another, even though the scenes are not consecutive, are *Henry IV, Part One* and *Romeo and Juliet*. Sir Walter Blunt's presence in three two-part scenes in *Henry IV*,

*Part One* gives those scenes a suggestive pattern that can be briefly described. Most of scene 10 (III.ii) is devoted to the reconciliation of Henry IV and his errant son Hal.[9] At the moment this reconciliation is achieved, Blunt enters to announce that the rebels are gathering forces: "A mighty and fearful head they are, / If promises be kept on every hand" (ll. 167–68). His faith restored in his son and heir, Henry gives Hal his instructions, outlines the instructions of other leaders, and ends the scene with a call to immediate action: "Let's away: / Advantage feeds him fat while men delay" (ll. 179–80).

By contrast, scene 14 (IV.iii) opens with a squabble between the rebel leaders near Shrewsbury over whether to attack that night or to delay. Hotspur and Douglas favor attack; Worcester and Vernon, delay. The dispute is still unresolved when Blunt enters to offer terms as a representative of King Henry. Hotspur, the rebel spokesman, refuses to give Blunt an immediate answer and tells him that Worcester will parley with Henry "in the morning early" (l. 110). Thus, not only has this decision been delayed, but the dispute that opened the scene has, by default, been won by the side favoring delay.

The first of these scenes begins with a reconciliation between the two major figures on the King's side. After Blunt enters, the King takes immediate and decisive action. The second opens with the depiction of disunity among the rebel leaders and ends after Blunt's entrance with their decision and action delayed. "Advantage feeds" the King's party "fat while men delay."

Scene 19 (V.iii.1–29) gives a final twist to the implications established by this sequence. The scene occurs during the Battle of Shrewsbury and opens with the separate but simultaneous

9. Actually, other characters enter with the King and the Prince, but Henry immediately dismisses them. That dismissal merely serves to emphasize the privacy of the ensuing conversation and does not really constitute a separate segment.

entrances of Douglas and a character in the panoply of King Henry. The two soldiers trade challenges and fight. After killing his opponent, Douglas is joined by Hotspur and exuberantly declares: "All's done, all's won: here breathless lies the king" (19.16). But the victory proves hollow and Douglas's exuberance turns to frustration when Hotspur identifies the corpse. The "king" is actually Sir Walter Blunt. Once again Blunt has "appeared" in the second segment of a two-part scene; again he is Henry's representative, this time in a more literal sense; and once again his appearance marks a shift in favor of the King's forces. Blunt himself is dead, but he has died in place of the King; Douglas's hollow victory is the closest the rebels come to defeating Henry.[10]

10. Douglas, certainly, is deceived by Blunt's disguise in the first segment of the scene and is surprised and stunned by the "appearance" of Blunt in the second segment. But Shakespeare may have also intended to deceive or misdirect the audience to enhance the dramatic effect of the scene. Blunt's face must be covered by his helmet, or else the disguise would not deceive Douglas who saw Blunt in scene 14 (IV.iii). If the actor playing Blunt can disguise his voice well enough, the audience, at least at first, might presume along with Douglas that he is Henry. A suspicion about his identity might, however, be raised by Douglas's reference to having killed the Lord of Stafford while the latter was disguised as the King. Nevertheless, that Douglas kills an opponent who seems to be the King is startling. Only upon reflection do we deduce that the dead character could not be Henry IV since Henry IV did not die at Shrewsbury. In any case, this scene serves as one link in the ironic connection between Henry IV and Falstaff. Falstaff is a kind of parody father figure in relation to Henry's son and actually does mimic the King earlier in the play. Scene 19 depicts the death of a character who appears to be Henry, at least to the other character onstage, but Douglas's claim that "here breathless lies the king" (l. 16) turns out to be false. Later in the play, the same character who thought he killed the King appears to kill Falstaff. But Falstaff's apparent death, like Henry's, turns out to be a deception, this time almost certainly a deception of the audience as well as of other characters. (See chapter 1 for a discussion of Falstaff's "death.") If, during the earlier scene, we *were* able to penetrate Blunt's disguise, we perhaps felt a certain superiority to the deceived Douglas, who believed he had killed the King, but Shakespeare here punctures our self-satisfaction by deceiving us into believing a monarch of wit

In two similarly constructed scenes in *Romeo and Juliet* the
Nurse acts as a messenger or bearer of tidings to Juliet. The first
of these (10 [II.v]) opens with a long soliloquy by Juliet in which
she complains of the Nurse's slowness in returning from Romeo:

> O, she is lame! Love's heralds should be thoughts,
> Which ten times faster glides than the sun's beams
> Driving back shadows over low'ring hills.
>
> (ll. 4–6)

She deplores the advance of the day from morning to noon without news of Romeo:

> Now is the sun upon the highmost hill
> Of this day's journey, and from nine till twelve
> Is three long hours; yet she is not come.
>
> (ll. 9–11)

Scene 13 (III.ii) opens with an even longer soliloquy by
Juliet. This time she complains of the slowness of time itself,
represented by the sun's motion through the sky, since she will
not be reunited with Romeo until night:

> Gallop apace, you fiery-footed steeds,
> Towards Phoebus' lodging! Such a wagoner
> As Phaëthon would whip you to the west
> And bring in cloudy night immediately.
>
> (ll. 1–4)

---

has been killed—and wins our admiration for having done so after we grate-
fully witness Falstaff's resurrection.

Scene 19 is part of the traditional division V.iii, which actually comprises
three scenes according to the criteria discussed in chapter 1. The first of these
(scene 18) is a unitary group scene without dialogue: "*The* King *enters with his
power. Alarum to the battle*" (opening s.d.). After the King and his troops
presumably exit, "*Then enter* Douglas *and* Sir Walter Blunt." Douglas eventually kills Blunt and is joined by Hotspur. At line 29 these two characters
presumably exit and Falstaff enters. Though Blunt's body remains onstage, the
exit of Douglas and Hotspur clears the stage of living characters and thus ends
scene 19. Scene 20 begins with Falstaff's entrance.

But her second expression of impatience is, unlike the first, imbued with ominousness. In the just-quoted opening passage she is so discontented with the slow progress of the sun that she gives tacit approval to Phaëthon's speedier but disastrous race across the sky. Much of the speech is directed to "civil night," the "sober-suited matron all in black" (ll. 10, 11) who wears a "black-mantle" (l. 15) and is "black-browed" (l. 20). Such imagery seems more appropriate to a funeral than to the consummation of a marriage. The only birds mentioned in the earlier soliloquy were doves, white and associated with love; the only bird mentioned in the later soliloquy is the raven, black and associated with death.

In both scenes Juliet's plaintive meditations are broken off by the approach of her Nurse:

> O God, she comes! O honey nurse, what news?
>
> (10.18)
>
> . . . O, here comes my nurse,
> And she brings news. . . .
> Now, nurse, what news?
>
> (13.31–32, 34)

And the remainder of each scene consists of Juliet's dialogue with the Nurse.[11] In both cases the Nurse's demeanor causes anxiety for Juliet: "O Lord, why lookest thou sad?" (10.21); "Ay me! What news? Why dost thou wring thy hands?" (13.36). And in neither case does Juliet receive a full and clear report from

---

11. The Nurse enters scene 10 with her subordinate servant Peter, but Juliet immediately orders him sent away. The entrance and immediate dismissal of Peter, who does not speak, emphasize the juncture between the two segments of the scene rather than constituting a separate segment. His brief time onstage merely sets up the following dialogue, as the dismissal of the other characters at the beginning of *Henry IV, Part One*, scene 10 (III.ii), sets up the ensuing dialogue between Henry and Hal. Peter's presence is merely the first of the Nurse's maddening dilatory tactics employed to tease Juliet, and his dismissal emphasizes Juliet's impatience and desire for privacy.

the Nurse for some time. The motive for the Nurse's delay in
scene 10 is a desire to tease her charge; her delay in scene 13 is
presumably unintentional and due to genuine confusion brought
on by her distress. At one point in the earlier scene the impa-
tient Juliet asks for a one-word summary of the Nurse's news:

> Is thy news good or bad? Answer to that.
> Say either, and I'll stay the circumstance.
> Let me be satisfied, is't good or bad?
>
> (10.35–37)

Driven to desperation by the Nurse's unintelligible hints of disaster in the later scene, Juliet again asks for a one-word answer:

> If he be slain, say "Ay"; or if not, "No."
> Brief sounds determine of my weal or woe.
>
> (13.50–51)

In neither case does the Nurse respond to Juliet's pleading for a
simple answer.

One of the Nurse's speeches in scene 10 is devoted to a paradoxical catalogue of Romeo's qualities (for example, "He is not
the flower of courtesy, but, I'll warrant him, as gentle as a lamb"
[10.43–44]). This speech is ironically complemented in scene
13 by the catalogue of paradoxical epithets that Juliet applies to
Romeo in her first reaction to the news that he has slain Tybalt.
Some of these epithets even contain echoes of the Nurse's catalogue: "O serpent heart, hid with a flow'ring face!"; "Wolvish-
ravening lamb!" (13.73, 76). One epithet even crossbreeds the
two species of birds mentioned in the two opening soliloquies:
"Dove-feathered raven!" (l. 76).

Nearly the last dilatory tactic employed by the Nurse in the
earlier scene was to ask Juliet, "Where is your mother?" (10.58).
Particular attention is drawn to the question because Juliet twice
repeats it in her annoyed reply. Near the end of the later scene
and at the end of a long speech in which Juliet reaffirms her love

for Romeo and expresses her intense grief at Romeo's banishment, she asks, "Where is my father and my mother, nurse?" (13.127). In addition to being a delaying tactic, the Nurse's question had perhaps been a playful reminder that Juliet has been pursuing her romance with Romeo without the consent or knowledge of her parents. Juliet's question and the Nurse's response in the later scene make explicit the opposing and irreconcilable positions of Juliet and her parents. According to the Nurse, Capulet and Lady Capulet are "Weeping and wailing over Tybalt's corse" (13.128), whereas Juliet is grieving over the banishment of the slayer of Tybalt.

After finally divulging the wedding plans to Juliet in scene 10, the Nurse parted from her to fetch a rope ladder. The Nurse enters scene 13 with these "cords," and at the end of the scene Juliet addresses them in acknowledging the reversal of her earlier expectations of "high fortune" (10.79):

> . . . Poor ropes, you are beguiled,
> Both you and I, for Romeo is exiled.
>
> (13.132–33)

Both scenes end, not incongruously, with the word "farewell" delivered by Juliet; but only the first is an actual parting salutation. The second is a pathetic reference to her imminent separation from Romeo: "And bid him come to take his last farewell" (13.143). Earlier in the scene Juliet quickly revoked the paradoxical epithets she had flung at Romeo. But she cannot revoke the paradox of her "maiden-widowèd" state (l. 135) or the paradox suggested by the phrases "bid him come" and "last farewell."

The ordering of elements in scene 13 is clearly an ironic reflection of the ordering of elements in scene 10. Shakespeare daringly patterned a scene of pathos, the scene in which Juliet learns that her wedding day will be the day of her husband's exile, on a prior scene of comic bantering and joy, the scene in which Juliet learns of the plans for her immediate wedding to Romeo.

As we have seen, most two-part scenes, even if clearly unified by linear narrative or character development, are also unified in a variety of other ways. The second segment of a scene may contain verbal echoes of the first or a situation that somehow parallels the first. The second segment may directly comment or ironically reflect upon the first or upon characters who appear in the first. The two segments may deal with the same theme in complementary ways. Some two-part scenes within a given play, furthermore, reflect on one another as units.

In developing my argument in this chapter, I may have given the misleading impression that Shakespeare's overriding purpose was to unify his scenes. It was not. But the structural unity and independence of individual scenes provided Shakespeare with a framework within which he could pursue larger artistic goals. The development of dramatic elements such as character, theme, plot, and imagery is facilitated and enhanced in his plays by the very scenic unity these elements help to create. It is, finally, impossible to tell the dancer from the dance.

# Six ✗ Multipartite Scenes

Like two-part scenes, scenes that contain a series of three or more distinct character groupings are more than mere collections of incidents that do not happen to be interrupted by a cleared stage. Despite their greater complexity, such scenes exhibit internal artistic unity similar to that exhibited by the two-part scenes examined in the preceding chapter.

Many multipartite scenes achieve artistic coherence by developing a single, almost self-contained, dramatic issue. The sole issue of scene 29 (V.i) of *Henry V*, for example, is Fluellen's humiliation of Pistol, and this scene has the structure of a miniature play. The opening dialogue between Fluellen and Gower provides the exposition. Gower asks his companion, "Why wear you your leek today?" (ll. 1–2). Fluellen explains that he has been insulted by "the rascally, scauld, beggarly, lousy, pragging knave, Pistol" (ll. 5–6):

> He is come to me, and prings me pread and salt yesterday, look you, and bid me eat my leek. It was in a place where I could not breed no contention with him; but I will be so bold as to wear it in my cap till I see him once again, and then I will tell him a little piece of my desires. (ll. 8–13)

The subject of these remarks promptly enters—Shakespeare had no compunction about such timely entrances—and conflict immediately ensues. Fluellen insults Pistol and sarcastically requests him to eat the leek. Pistol attempts to outface his antagonist, but the conflict escalates as Fluellen resorts to striking

Pistol. The climax comes when Pistol submits and eats the leek. And Fluellen adds monetary insult to gustatory injury by forcing Pistol to accept a groat.

Fluellen leaves, and the next segment of the scene brings the conflict to a resolution of sorts. As soon as Fluellen is out of hearing, Pistol declares, "All hell shall stir for this!" (l. 70). Gower calmly points out the foolishness of such displays of empty bombast. Then, in a tone of exhortation rather than malice, he reproves Pistol for his past coxcombry and takes pains to make Pistol understand the justice and inevitability of Fluellen's retaliation: "I have seen you gleeking and galling at this gentleman twice or thrice. You thought, because he could not speak English in the native garb, he could not therefore handle an English cudgel" (ll. 75–78). Gower finally urges Pistol to amend his behavior—"henceforth let a Welsh correction teach you a good English condition" (ll. 79–80). His advice is a kind of peace treaty offered to Pistol by a representative of genuine soldiery.

But Gower's sober counsel of upright conduct is not the last word in this play within a play. Left alone to soliloquize, Pistol at first almost becomes a figure of pathos. Not only has he been humiliated and beaten, but his wife has died, he is homeless, and he feels old and weary. But the scene ends with a comic upturn as Pistol displays the resilience of his knavery: "To England will I steal, and there I'll steal" (l. 88). Ironically, he will even make his punishment for former vainglory the basis of new displays of vainglory: "And patches will I get unto these cudgeled scars, / And swear I got them in the Gallia wars" (ll. 89–90).

The center of attention has shifted from Fluellen's indignation in the opening segment before Pistol's arrival to Pistol's irrepressibility in the final segment after the other characters have left. The middle two segments of the scene also balance one another: the second segment in which the choleric Fluellen forcibly teaches Pistol a lesson is balanced by Gower's phlegmatic and almost conciliatory instruction in the third segment. Although it may not be one of the high points of Shakespearean drama, this particular multipartite scene involving four distinct character groupings has a very tight internal coherence.

Some multipartite scenes include episodes from different narrative strands in a single unified structure. The fifth scene (III.ii) of *The Taming of the Shrew* occurs on the wedding day of Petruchio and Kate. Most of the scene concerns the unconventional behavior of the bridegroom. The scene as a whole displays a nearly symmetrical structure; the segments after the offstage wedding balance the segments before the wedding. In the opening segment characters express dismay at Petruchio's failure to arrive and his possible absence from the wedding ceremony; in the final segment characters comment on Petruchio's departure with Kate and their consequent absence from their own wedding feast. The early segment in which Biondello describes the zany wardrobe of the still offstage Petruchio is balanced by the later segment in which Gremio describes Petruchio's zany behavior at the offstage wedding. Each of these descriptions of Petruchio's offstage zaniness is followed by Petruchio's entrance. In his first appearance onstage in the scene, he peremptorily refuses to change his clothes; in his second, he peremptorily refuses to stay for the wedding feast.

But at the center of the scene occurs a segment that focuses on the subplot, a brief moment of stasis that serves to set off the two major and complementary subdivisions of the scene from one another. That central segment is a dialogue between Tranio and Lucentio in which they discuss the plan for Lucentio to obtain the hand of Bianca. The comparison between the main plot and subplot that has been implicit throughout the play and that will receive an explicit and ironic twist in the final scene is strengthened by the juxtaposition of the two plot lines within this scene. Lucentio has already won the love of "sweet Bianca"

(l. 136), and his efforts are now mainly directed at securing her
father's consent through secret machinations engineered by
Tranio. Petruchio, on the other hand, has had no trouble securing Baptista's consent; his efforts are directed at taming the
woman whom he marries offstage while Tranio and Lucentio
confer. Yet at times during the scene Petruchio acts as if he were
in Lucentio's position. He describes the shrewish Kate as "pa-
tient, sweet, and virtuous" (l. 194). Lucentio wishes he could
elope with Bianca:

> 'Twere good, methinks, to steal our marriage,
> Which once performed, let all the world say no,
> I'll keep mine own despite of all the world.

> > (ll. 139–41)

Later in the scene Petruchio declares, "I will be master of what
is mine own. . . . Touch her whoever dare" (ll. 228, 232), as if
he were eloping with a woman whom he married against her
father's consent and in "despite of all the world." Similar ironies
occur elsewhere in the scene. After Petruchio's first appearance
in his bizarre costume, Tranio implores him, "Go to my cham-
ber; put on clothes of mine" (l. 112). Tranio's clothes, however
conventional, are actually Lucentio's and are worn by Tranio in
disguise as his master; however bizarre, Petruchio's clothes are
his own and are not a disguise. At the end of the scene, Baptista
asks Tranio, who has taken the place of Lucentio, to take the
place of Petruchio at the wedding feast. This is somehow appropriate because Petruchio is the main agent in the main plot,
the taming of Kate, whereas Tranio, rather than Lucentio, is the
main agent in the subplot, the main deviser and executor of the
machinations to secure Bianca for Lucentio. And Baptista's suggestion that Bianca take Kate's role at the wedding feast foreshadows the ironic substitution in the final scene, after the wedding of Lucentio and Bianca, when Bianca at least briefly takes
the role of shrew from her sister. The mainplot and subplot are

counterpoised throughout the play and interwoven to form a single unified play. One way in which this unity is created is that the two plots are counterpoised and interwoven within individual unified scenes.

Most of scene 12 (IV.ii) of *Othello*, sometimes referred to as the "brothel scene," consists of a single dramatic movement. The climax of the scene is the dialogue in which Othello brutally accuses Desdemona of being a whore. The earlier segments dramatically prepare for this climax. As the scene opens, Othello questions Emilia about Desdemona's behavior toward Cassio. Though he regards Emilia's testimony with skepticism, Othello's language is controlled, and at one point his belief in Desdemona's guilt even seems to waver—in response to one of Emilia's avowals, he says, "That's strange," (l. 11). But after he sends Emilia to bring Desdemona, he dismisses Emilia's reliability as a witness ("yet she's a simple bawd," l. 20) in a brief soliloquy. The extinguishment of a faint glimmer of hope just before the entrance of Desdemona increases the dramatic tension, and the tension increases further when Othello openly characterizes Emilia as a bawd ("Your mystery, your mystery!" l. 30) as he orders her away. After the climactic dialogue with Desdemona, Othello summons Emilia and resumes the pretense that he is in a brothel ("We have done our course; there's money for your pains," l. 92). The segments that follow Othello's departure show the aftermath of his accusation; we see the effect on Desdemona. She is at first disoriented but eventually sends Emilia for Iago, whom she asks to intercede with her husband. The deceived Othello's cruel accusation of the innocent Desdemona and her declaration of her innocence are now balanced by the cruel irony that Desdemona kneels before Iago as she had before Othello, swears her innocence to the villain who has maliciously convinced Othello of her guilt, and asks this villain to help her. A lesser irony is that in the same scene in which Othello makes a prolonged and intense denunciation of his wife,

Emilia repeatedly and vigorously but unwittingly denounces her husband: "If any wretch have put this in your head, / Let heaven requite it with the serpent's curse" (ll. 15–16; see also ll. 129–32, 135, 138–46).

But the scene does not end with Desdemona's appeal to Iago. After she and Emilia exit, Roderigo joins Iago onstage. The ensuing dialogue is superficially unrelated to the earlier action of the scene. The portion of this dialogue that substantively advances the plot is Iago's explanation of his plan for "the removing of Cassio" (l. 227). Yet only one-third of the long final segment (75 lines of prose in the Signet edition) is devoted to a discussion of that plan. Most of the dialogue concerns Roderigo's accusation that Iago has acted falsely. To the earlier ironies in the scene is added an ironic parody of Othello's climactic accusation of Desdemona. Othello falsely accused Desdemona of being a whore, and now Roderigo rightly accuses Iago of not turning Desdemona into a whore. Desdemona denied Othello's accusation ("By heaven you do me wrong!"—l. 80), and Iago denies Roderigo's ("You charge me most unjustly," l. 183). But the innocent Desdemona was unable to convince Othello of her faithfulness, whereas the duplicitous Iago is able to convince Roderigo that he is acting in good faith.

Roderigo's denunciation of Iago's "scurvy" dealings also recalls Emilia's denunciations of the "scurvy fellow" who has poisoned Othello's mind against Desdemona (ll. 193, 139). Iago dismissed Emilia's maledictions with a series of brief replies: "Fie, there is no such man! It is impossible"; "Speak within door"; "You are a fool. Go to" (ll. 133, 143, 147). During most of the final segment, Iago reacts to Roderigo's charges with a series of similarly brief and dismissive responses, including the following: "Well, go to; very well"; "Very well"; "You have said now?" (ll. 191, 195, 201). And finally, Roderigo's accurate charge that Iago has failed to procure Desdemona, has failed as a bawd, recalls Othello's mistaken aspersion that Iago's wife has been a procurer, a bawd, for Desdemona. Roderigo's temporary defiance is a very inconsequential element in the plot and, were it not for such ironic connections with the rest of the scene, would hardly justify the extended treatment it receives, especially at this point in the play. Roderigo has been complaining since the very opening lines of the play, but his most sustained and vehement reproach of Iago so far in the play occurs in this scene, the scene in which Othello makes his first sustained and explicit accusation of Desdemona.

The scene as a whole is thus unified by the series of accusations that ironically reflect on one another. The scene is also unified by an almost symmetrical balance between features in the early portion of the scene, before Othello's exit, and features in the later portion of the scene, after Iago's entrance. In the opening dialogue Emilia tries to convince Othello that Desdemona will be faithful and offers her own soul as surety:

> I durst, my lord, to wager she is honest,
> Lay down my soul at stake. . . .
> . . . . . . . . . . . . . . . . . . . . . . . . . . . . . .
> For if she be not honest, chaste, and true,
> There's no man happy.
>
> (ll. 12–13, 17–18)

In the closing dialogue Iago tries to convince Roderigo that Desdemona will be unfaithful and offers his own life as surety: "If thou the next night following enjoy not Desdemona, take me from this world with treachery and devise engines for my life" (ll. 214–17). As already noted, Desdemona's declaration of her innocence before Othello ironically balances her declaration of her innocence before Iago.

Othello dominates the first half of the scene. He wrongly accuses Desdemona of being a whore and Emilia of being a bawd. Iago, though outwardly passive and reticent for most of his time onstage, is the dominant figure in the second half of the scene.

Set in contrast to the vehement but false accusations delivered
by Othello are the soothing but false assurances Iago gives first
to Desdemona ("I pray you be content. . . . All things shall be
well," ll. 164, 169) and then to Roderigo ("And you shall be
satisfied," l. 244). On the other hand, Iago is the object of two
valid accusations. But the first accuser is unaware of the identity
of the villain she denounces, and the second accuser is eventually mollified. Iago is in control of circumstances even though
his control is subtle and insidious rather than open; he is, as the
audience is aware, even in control of the character who dominated the first half of the scene.

Scene 12 presents a series of segments that depict the rising
action, climax, and aftermath of one narrative action and then a
seemingly unrelated final segment. Yet the scene as a whole is
unified by a larger structure that encompasses the final segment.
This scene has a more complex unity than it would have had if
the final segment were not included, but it is unified nonethe-
less. It displays on a small scale the kind of unity through multiplicity that Madeleine Doran found characteristic of Elizabethan
drama.

Even scenes composed of a series of incidents that form a
closely linked narrative sequence, a single narrative development, often reveal a pattern of parallelism or symmetry among
the segments of the scene. This double structure is especially
evident in scenes in which the linear narrative development is
coupled with successive increments in the number of characters
onstage.

In scene 24 (III.x, except opening s.d.) of *Antony and Cleopatra*, for example, the number of participants progressively increases, and the three segments of the scene parallel one another.[1] The scene opens with a soliloquy by Enobarbus in which

1. The opening stage direction of the traditional division III.x describes two
military progressions, after each of which the stage is presumably cleared
(scenes 22 and 23). Then Enobarbus enters to begin scene 24.

he despairingly describes the flight of Cleopatra's ships from the
battle off the coast of Actium. Then Scarus enters, adds his own
condemnation of Cleopatra, and informs Enobarbus of the subsequent ignominious retreat of Antony's ships. These two lieutenants of Antony are joined by a third, Canidius, who echoes
Scarus's condemnation of Antony and reports the consequences
of Antony's flight. Antony's action at sea has undermined the
loyalty of his land forces. Canidius announces:

> To Caesar will I render
> My legions and my horse; six kings already
> Show me the way of yielding.
>
> (24.32–34)

Thus, as the number of participants in the scene progressively
increases, we are informed of the progressive decline in Antony's fortunes. The final character to enter not only augments
the dire information presented by the first two characters but
actually contributes to Antony's decline by deciding to render
unto Caesar what had been Antony's.

A longer and more intricate scene, which also progresses
from a soliloquy to a trio, is the fourth scene (II.ii) of *The Tempest*. Caliban enters the stage alone, bearing wood, cursing
Prospero, and complaining of the spirits sent by Prospero in the
forms of apes, hedgehogs, and adders to punish him. Mistaking
the approaching Trinculo for one of these spirits, Caliban lies
down in the ridiculous hope of escaping observation. He is,
however, observed by Trinculo who at first regards him as a
preternatural creature—a "strange fish!" (l. 28), a "monster"
(l. 31), a "strange beast" (l. 31)—which could earn a man a
fortune by being exhibited in England. Trinculo's speech opens
and closes with references to the threatening weather, and he
employs similar figurative language in both references: "Yond
same black cloud, yond huge one, looks like a foul bombard that
would shed his liquor" (ll. 20–22) and "I will here shroud till

the dregs of the storm be past" (ll. 40–41). The second segment
of the scene ends as Trinculo crawls under Caliban's cloak to
escape the coming storm.

But Trinculo's figurative description proves accurate in an unexpectedly literal way, for liquor does arrive—in the bottle carried by Stephano. The song Stephano sings elicits a plea for
mercy from Caliban, which in turn draws Stephano's attention to
the curious animate object prostrate before him. Stephano's first
tentative explanation for this phenomenon—"Have we devils
here? Do you put tricks upon's with savages and men of Inde,
ha?" (ll. 57–59)—recalls Caliban's opening complaint about
the "spirits" who assume various shapes to bedevil him. But
Stephano then concludes, as Trinculo had after noticing the solitary Caliban, that this four-legged creature is a "monster of the
isle" (l. 65) and considers, more seriously than Trinculo had,
the possibility of making his fortune by bringing this freak back
to civilization. He pledges his friendship to the monster by giving Caliban a drink.

Recognizing Stephano's voice, Trinculo is now the one to suspect supernatural agents, and he cowers as Caliban had: "I
should know that voice. It should be—but he is drowned; and
these are devils. O, defend me!" (ll. 89–90). When Trinculo
finally calls out, Stephano reverts to the devil theory too: "Doth
thy other mouth call me? Mercy, mercy! This is a devil, and no
monster. I will leave him; I have no long spoon" (ll. 98–100).
Stephano finally drags Trinculo out from under Caliban's cloak,
and the two reassure one another of their identities—Stephano
facetiously asks his comrade to swear to his escape from drown-
ing by kissing "the book" (l. 130), that is, by drinking from the
bottle. And Caliban swears his obedience to Stephano in the
same way.

The third segment of the scene began with Stephano's tavern
song and nearly ends with Caliban's drunken song:

No more dams I'll make for fish,
  Nor fetch in firing
  At requiring.

(ll. 182–84)

Yet he has just told Stephano, "I'll fish for thee, and get thee wood enough" (l. 163). Exultant over the imagined change in his condition, Caliban ignores the contradictions of his own words. He vigorously declares his "freedom" (l. 188), but he has only exchanged Prospero for what he himself calls "a new master" (l. 187). Stephano and Trinculo finally solve the cases of mistaken identity that arise during the course of the scene, but Caliban remains very much mistaken about the identity of Stephano. Caliban's mistake is the inverse of the devil theory earlier propounded by the other two characters; he regards Stephano as a "god" (l. 150).

The scene is very tightly structured. The opening segment consists solely of Caliban's speech at the end of which he lies prostrate; the second segment consists solely of Trinculo's speech at the end of which he imitates Caliban's action by joining him under the cloak. The connection between these characters is carried to the utmost when the next character to enter mistakes the pair for one creature. Stephano himself continues the pattern of repetition by echoing comments made by each of the characters in the opening segments of the scene and even supplying a literal counterpart to Trinculo's figurative language. The final segment, furthermore, is an inverted reflection of the opening segment. The scene began with Caliban grudgingly performing a service for Prospero, cursing his master, and complaining of his condition. It ends ironically with Caliban praising and willingly serving a new, far less worthy master and rejoicing in his anticipated condition.

The fourth scene (II. ii) of *The Comedy of Errors* also involves a progressive increase in the number of characters onstage and contains a series of more conventional cases of mistaken identities. Antipholus of Syracuse opens the scene with a short soliloquy that reveals his still inadequate understanding of the confusion he is encountering in Ephesus. He is then joined by Dromio, whom he mistakenly chastises for the behavior of Dromio's Ephesian twin in a previous scene. The servant denies his master's account and is consequently beaten. At approximately the same point in this conversation that the language shifts from blank verse to prose, the basis of the humor shifts from the cross-purposes arising from the "error" to a mutual indulgence in burlesque dialectics upon propositions such as "There's a time for all things" (l. 64).[2]

The last segment of the scene parallels the preceding segment. Adriana, married to Antipholus's Ephesian twin, enters with her sister Luciana and proceeds to berate the confused Syracusan Antipholus whose seeming equivocation adds insult ("contempt," l. 173) to injury ("wrong," l. 172). The object of this assault had just berated the confused Dromio and become enraged at that character's denials. The parallel is strengthened by the rhetorical similarity of the two harangues. Antipholus asked a series of sarcastic questions: "You know no Centaur? You received no gold?" (l. 9), and so on. Adriana employs a series of sarcastic negatives: "I am not Adriana, nor thy wife" (l. 113), and so on. In each case these sarcasms burst without warning upon the unsuspecting victim. The parallel is also a reversal, for the scourger has become the scourged. Again, as in the previous segment, the antipathy dissolves and the dissolution is again marked by a change in the language—this time from blank verse to couplets. Though still unenlightened and confused, the four characters fall to bantering.

2. See Ludwig Borinski, "Shakespeare's Comic Prose," *Shakespeare Survey* 8 (1955): 64, for a discussion of burlesque dialectics in Shakespearean drama.

In this scene, as in the ones just discussed, Shakespeare combines two structural devices, a progressive increment in the number of characters involved and a parallelism of incident between individual segments. This combination produces effects similar to those produced by a theme and variation in a musical composition. The theme is first played by Antipholus and Dromio. It is then repeated with variations in the instrumentation: two treble voices are added, and Antipholus is demoted to the part played by his servant in the original presentation of the theme. Dromio, on the other hand, faces the same music in both segments. He is undeservedly excoriated first by Antipholus and then by the sisters (both times as a result of Antipholus's encounter with the other Dromio). A confrontation between two characters is followed by a confrontation between two pairs of characters.

Not all scenes possessing an incremental structure open with soliloquies. *Richard II*, for example, contains a set of scenes in each of which the initial entrance of a group of characters is followed by a series of entrances of other characters later in the scene. And, once again, these scenes directly reflect on one another. Scene 7 (II.iii) is the first scene depicting Bolingbroke after his provocative return to England from exile. Only two very brief scenes (occupying a total of sixty-eight lines) intervene between the scene of Bolingbroke's return and that of Richard's return from Ireland (10 [III.ii]). The similarity of scenic structure aids the contrast established between the characters and situations of Bolingbroke and Richard. In both scenes the leading character is on the move with his retinue, and each opens with that character's one-line question concerning location:

> *Bolingbroke.* How far is it, my lord, to Berkeley now?
>
> (7.1)

> *Richard.* Barkloughly Castle call they this at hand?
>
> (10.1)

Bolingbroke is accompanied by his soldiers and by Northumberland, who in the course of a rather sycophantic speech gives details about the imminent assembly of Bolingbroke's forces. The two leaders are then joined by Northumberland's son, Harry Percy, who brings news of Worcester's defection from Richard and who tenders his own service to Bolingbroke. The next characters to enter, Ross and Willoughby, also pledge their allegiance to the invader.

The final pair of entering characters, however, put Bolingbroke on the defensive. Lord Berkeley, as an emissary of the Duke of York, regent during Richard's absence, asks him to explain his defiant and armed incursion. Before Bolingbroke can reply, the Duke himself appears and proceeds to upbraid him. York then alludes to his military exploits of the distant past and declares,

> Were I but now the lord of such hot youth
> . . . . . . . . . . . . . . . . . . . . . . . . . . . . . . . . .
> O, then, how quickly should this arm of mine,
> Now prisoner to the palsy, chastise thee,
> And minister correction to thy fault!
>
> (7.98, 102–04)

Because he is the prisoner of age rather than the lord of youth, his declaration, which sounds like stern resistance, is in fact an implicit capitulation. Bolingbroke is tactful, respectful, and politic in allowing York thus to save face. Though York attempts to maintain a moral superiority and asserts his political neutrality to the end, his acquiescence places him in Bolingbroke's camp.

If York had simply added his support to that already voiced by Northumberland, Percy, Ross, and Willoughby, our sense of the irresistibility of Bolingbroke's ascendancy would not have been so strong. York defends his reluctant acquiescence as simply the acceptance of the inevitable: "Things past redress are now with me past care" (l. 170, the last line of the scene). Ironically,

York's grudging submission at the end of the scene does more to establish the impression of Bolingbroke's strength than Northumberland's obsequious sycophancy at the beginning.

The first segment of scene 10 provides an ironic contrast with the opening of the earlier scene. Like Bolingbroke, Richard is accompanied by supporters, but Richard himself rather than one of his followers is the main speaker and his speeches do not concern the assembly of his forces, at least not his human forces. Instead, he first sets forth an elaborate and majestic but improbable claim of support from the terrain of England itself: "This earth shall have a feeling, and these stones / Prove armèd soldiers" (ll. 24–25). The Bishop of Carlisle suggests that "heaven" (l. 30) is also on their side but rather obscurely implies that heaven helps them that help themselves. Aumerle is blunter:

> He means, my lord, that we are too remiss,
> Whilst Bolingbroke through our security
> Grows strong and great in substance and in power.
>
> (ll. 33–35)

Scene 7, partly by means of its incremental structure, actually depicted what Aumerle is now describing—Bolingbroke's growth in substance and in power. Yet Richard chastises Aumerle and develops at great length the first of the Bishop's two propositions. In the closing lines of this speech, Richard himself ironically calls attention to the contrast between the nature of the support on which he is depending and that which Bolingbroke has secured:

> For every man that Bolingbroke hath pressed
> To lift shrewd steel against our golden crown,
> God for his Richard hath in heavenly pay
> A glorious angel; then, if angels fight,
> Weak men must fall, for heaven still guards the right.
>
> (10.58–62)

The second segment of scene 7 began with the entrance of
Percy, who brought news that Worcester had defected and had
"dispersed / The household of the king" (ll. 27–28). The second segment of scene 10 begins with the entrance of Salisbury,
who brings news that "all the Welshmen . . . / Are gone to
Bolingbroke, dispersed and fled" (ll. 73–74). Richard's own
skepticism about the likelihood of aid from stones and angels is
revealed by his sudden shift from unrealistic optimism to un-
qualified pessimism:

> Have I not reason to look pale and dead?
> All souls that will be safe fly from my side,
> For Time hath set a blot upon my pride.
>
>                                      (10.79–81)

Yet he just as abruptly reverts to the opposite extreme and cites
another improbable source of support: "Is not the king's name
twenty thousand names?" (l. 85).

But then Scroop enters. The joint entry of Ross and Willoughby in scene 7 was emblematic of the swelling ranks of Bolingbroke's supporters; Scroop now brings Richard news of the swell
of support for Bolingbroke among the general populace: "both
young and old rebel" (10.119). Scroop's entrance initiates another downturn in Richard's outlook. After Scroop reveals the
further news of the executions of Bushy, Bagot, and Green,
Richard delivers a long discourse on the vulnerability of kings
("let us sit upon the ground / And tell sad stories of the death of
kings: / How some have been deposed," ll. 155–57 ff.), which
matches in eloquence his earlier long discourses on the invul-
nerability of kings. As he had done in the preceding segment,
however, Richard abruptly reverts from unmitigated defeatism
to baseless optimism: "An *easy* task it is to win our own" (l. 191;
my emphasis). But when Scroop eventually delivers the further
news that York has defected, Richard not only returns to despair
but orders the disbandment of his remaining forces: "Go to Flint

Castle: there I'll pine away . . . / That power I have, discharge, and let them go" (ll. 209, 211). York's reluctant acquiescence was the climax of Bolingbroke's rising fortunes in the earlier scene, and the report of that event provides the climax of the disintegration of Richard's world in this scene.

Upon his return to England in scene 7, Bolingbroke's fortunes rose and the breadth of his support widened in successive stages. Each of the characters who entered after the start of the scene except Berkeley (whose brief opposition only heightened the effect of York's subsequent capitulation) contributed to our impression of Bolingbroke's growth in power. During scene 10, only two characters join those already onstage, but the first brings Richard news of a major setback, and the second brings news of three separate calamities. (By delivering his information piecemeal, Scroop functions almost as the equivalent of three separate messengers.) Upon his return to England, Richard is forced to confront in successive stages the disintegration of his power.

The similarities in structure between scenes 7 and 10 provide the ground for indirect contrast not only between Bolingbroke's situation and that of Richard but between the personalities of the two characters. In scene 7 Bolingbroke shows determination, political astuteness, and an ability to form bonds with his supporters—qualities that have led to his ascendency. In scene 10 Richard reveals inconstancy, political naiveté, and self-absorption—qualities that have led to the decline in his fortunes.

The indirect contrast established by scenes 7 and 10 is replaced by direct confrontation in the very next scene, which is, appropriately, the third and last incremental scene in the play. Scene 11 (III.iii) opens, as scene 7 had, with a dialogue between Bolingbroke and Northumberland, who are again accompanied by soldiers but this time by York as well. As in scene 7, the first subsequent character to enter is Harry Percy, and thus Bolingbroke is in company with the three most prominent adherents who had appeared in the earlier scene. Bolingbroke delivers a long speech in which he couches his demands and threats in dignified and respectful language.

As this speech reaches its culmination, Richard appears on the walls accompanied by the same group of adherents who had appeared in scene 10.[3] Bolingbroke retires to a distant part of the stage at the entrance of Richard, who admonishes Northumberland. Richard alludes, as he had in scene 10, to God's concern for anointed kings, but instead of claiming divine protection, he now only prophesies divine retribution:

> . . . God omnipotent,
> Is mustering in his clouds on our behalf
> Armies of pestilence, and they shall strike
> Your children yet unborn and unbegot
> That lift your vassal hands against my head.
>
> (11.84–88)

Acceding to Bolingbroke's demands as presented by Northumberland, Richard gives vent, at first privately in asides to Aumerle and then publicly, to his bitterness at having to make such concessions and to his sense of utter defeat.

Richard then comes down to the main stage with his attendants and confronts Bolingbroke directly for the first time since the latter's banishment. Bolingbroke's dialogue with York that concluded scene 7 provided a foretaste of this confrontation. There Bolingbroke was respectful, but York pointed out that this

3. The relevant stage direction in the first Quarto (1597) does not list the characters accompanying Richard on the walls, but that in the First Folio does. Earlier in the scene, furthermore, Percy enumerates those of Richard's adherents who are in the castle: "with him are the Lord Aumerle, Lord Salisbury, / Sir Stephen Scroop, besides a clergyman / Of holy reverence—who, I cannot learn" (11. 26–28). Northumberland identifies the "clergyman" as the Bishop of Carlisle. If these four characters, who are the very same ones who appeared with Richard in the previous scene, are in the castle, they almost certainly would join him on the walls.

respectfulness was belied by his actions. York told the kneeling
invader, "Show me thy humble heart, and not thy knee" (7.83).
When Bolingbroke kneels at the approach of Richard in scene
11, Richard also calls attention to the incongruity of Bolingbroke's genuflection:

> Me rather had my heart might feel your love,
> Than my unpleased eye see your courtesy.
>
> (ll. 190–91)

Though Bolingbroke presumably rises, he continues to speak as
a dutiful subject presenting a just grievance. York's acknowledgment at the end of scene 7 of the futility of opposing Bolingbroke
is now echoed by Richard's similar acknowledgment:

> What you will have, I'll give, and willing too,
> For do we must what force will have us do.
>
> (ll. 204–05)

Of the many specific echoes in scene 11 of the two earlier
incremental scenes, I will discuss only one further example.
Upon his entrance in scene 7 Berkeley addresses Bolingbroke
as "My Lord of Hereford" (l. 69). Bolingbroke objects to Berkeley's disregard for his claim to the title of Lancaster, and Berkeley
replies,

> Mistake me not, my lord; 'tis not my meaning
> To race one title of your honor out.
>
> (7.74–75)

Near the beginning of scene 11 York objects to Northumberland's omission of the word "King" in a reference to "Richard."
Bolingbroke's intervention in the dispute sparks a punning jibe
by York:

> *Bolingbroke.* Mistake not, uncle, further than you should.
> *York.* Take not, good cousin, further than you should,
>   Lest you mis-take: the heavens are over our heads.
>
> (11.15–17)

Bolingbroke had bristled at Berkeley's omission of his rightful title; now the issue is no longer whether Bolingbroke will be granted the title of Lancaster but whether he will deny Richard the rightful title of "King" by taking that title and the kingship for himself.

Earlier chapters of this study demonstrated that one feature of the dramatic structure of some Shakespearean plays consists of the pattern established within an individual play among similarly structured unitary or two-part scenes. As the preceding discussion of the three incremental scenes in *Richard II* indicates, Shakespeare also constructed patterns involving similarly structured multipartite scenes, despite the greater complexity of such scenes.

As I pointed out in chapter 5, more than twice as many two-part scenes involve the entrances of new characters than involve the exit of characters who entered at the beginning of the scene. Similarly, the canon contains far fewer multipartite scenes that involve a progressive depletion of characters onstage than ones that involve a progressive increase.

Among the handful of such strict depletion scenes is scene 12 (IV.i) of *Much Ado about Nothing*, which comprises Claudio's renunciation of Hero and the aftermath of that renunciation. Except for the attendants, the characters who enter as the scene opens fall into two groups—not precisely, as at a typical wedding, the friends of the bride and the friends of the groom but those (Hero, Leonato, Beatrice, Benedick, and the Friar) who expect to participate in or witness a wedding and those who, as the audience is aware, have come to make a fiasco of the ceremony. The latter group includes the villainous deceiver Don John and his dupes, Don Pedro and Claudio.

Claudio heightens the shock of his accusation first by allowing the ceremony to proceed for a while before making his renunciation clear and then by unnecessarily cruel exaggeration of Hero's supposed crime:

But you are more intemperate in your blood
Than Venus, or those pamp'red animals
That rage in savage sensuality.

(ll. 58–60)

Claudio's accusation is seconded by Don Pedro and Don John.
Hero and Leonato are both thunderstruck; she utters a series of
very brief speeches in her defense, and he issues only very brief
speeches in trying to comprehend and in reacting to the situation. Leonato finally asks, "Hath no man's dagger here a point
for me?" (l. 108), and at virtually the same moment Hero
swoons. Fittingly, the actual malicious creator of the episode,
Don John, is the one to end it by calling on Don Pedro and
Claudio to leave with him.

Left onstage for the second segment of the scene are the slandered Hero, her relatives, and her friends who now include Benedick. Granting complete credence to the charges against his
own daughter, Leonato reviles her, as viciously as Claudio had,
while she is still recovering her senses. Less emotionally involved, Benedick and the Friar do not accept the charges at face
value and react more responsibly. Benedick shows concern for
Hero ("How doth the lady?" l. 112), tries to get at the truth
("Lady, were you her bedfellow last night?" l. 146), and eventually deduces the actual state of affairs:

Two of them have the very bent of honor;
And if their wisdoms be misled in this,
The practice of it lives in John the bastard,
Whose spirits toil in frame of villainies.

(ll. 185–88)

Near the end of the segment he even vows allegiance to Hero's
cause despite his former friendship with the Prince and the
Count.

The Friar expresses faith in Hero's chastity and devises a plan
of action. Without hesitation and without any apology to his

daughter, Leonato shifts from vilifying Hero to swearing revenge against her slanderers even though—since he has not personally witnessed the contrived encounter between Borachio and Margaret—he himself has proven guilty of an even less understandable gullibility than that shown by Claudio and Don Pedro and has proven guilty of an even less understandable lack of trust in Hero, who is his own child.

In any case, Leonato and the Friar finally escort Hero offstage, and Benedick is left alone with Beatrice for the final segment of the scene. He tries to woo her, but Beatrice insists on linking his courtship with the issue of the outrage committed against her cousin. She delays revealing the shocking nature of this link, just as Claudio in the opening segment had delayed making his shocking accusation. And her command to "Kill Claudio" (l. 288) in the midst of a wooing episode is perhaps even more shocking to us than Claudio's accusation in the midst of a wedding ceremony had been because we are less prepared for it. We are as unprepared as Benedick, whom Beatrice has skillfully manipulated into declaring "Come, bid me do anything for thee" (l. 287).[4] Her startling two-word response is one of the great moments of the theater.[5] Benedick at first chooses not to take her seriously, but she is in earnest, and she strives to enforce his compliance by threatening to forsake him and by challenging his manhood. Despite his friendship with Claudio, Benedick had, near the end of the preceding segment, vowed to join those whom Claudio had slandered, and at the end of this, the

4. Throughout the scene our responses are probably closest to those of Benedick. In the opening segment Benedick is detached enough to comment, "This looks not like a nuptial" (l. 67). We commend his reactions in the second segment, and we know his deduction about the probable culprit to be accurate. Finally, we are as stunned as he by Beatrice's command in the last segment.

5. The effect of Beatrice's command is enhanced by the contrast, noted by D. A. Traversi and others, between its abruptness and her earlier polished and free-flowing language; see *An Approach to Shakespeare*, 3rd ed. (Garden City, N.Y.: Anchor Books, 1969), pp. 275–76.

final segment of the scene, he vows to his beloved to kill his former friend: "Enough, I am engaged. I will challenge him. I will kiss your hand, and so I leave you. By this hand, Claudio shall render me a dear account. . . . And so farewell" (ll. 330– 32, 334). The scene that began with Claudio's refusal to take an expected vow of devotion to Hero ends with Benedick's vow to kill Claudio as a demonstration of his devotion to Beatrice.

Thus, this scene progressively narrows in scope from an opening segment depicting a disrupted public ceremony to a segment depicting the private adoption of a secret plan by a small group of characters, and finally, to an intimate tête-à-tête between two lovers. In the opening segment a ceremony of unification was broken by discord and renunciation. In the second segment discord, perpetuated by a father's attack on his own daughter, is replaced, after Leonato's abrupt volte-face, by a uniting of all the remaining characters in a conspiracy to follow the Friar's plan.

But in the final segment one of the lovers suggests and the other agrees to pursue a course of action entirely independent of and at odds with that plan—the Friar's goal of ultimately reconciling Claudio and Hero will be thwarted if Benedick kills Claudio. Beatrice and Benedick are thus isolated to a certain extent from the other adherents of Hero's cause, and the bond between them is intensified by this isolation and by the gravity of the command that Beatrice has laid on Benedick and he has accepted. The sundering of one pair of lovers in the opening segment has, as critics have often noted, ironically resulted in this strengthening of the bond between the other pair in the closing segment.[6] The

6. Richard Levin elaborates on this point in a discussion of the Church scene in *The Multiple Plot in English Renaissance Drama* (Chicago: Univ. of Chicago Press, 1971). Beatrice and Benedick "had been maneuvered into this romance as the passive dupes of a joke contrived by the characters in the main plot; now, even though they are again responding to an event in that plot, their actions arise out of the attachment between them—out of her readiness to rely completely on him in this crisis, and his to risk everything for her—which thereby generates a dynamic of its own independent of its derivative, comic

scene is a brilliant theatrical and dramatic creation, and part
of its brilliance, as I hope this analysis suggests, lies in its
structure.

The most spectacularly artificial example of a scene constructed on the basis of a progressive depletion of the number of
characters onstage is the opening scene of *Henry VI, Part Two.*
It begins with the simultaneous entrance of two large groups of
characters: Henry VI, Gloucester, Somerset, Buckingham, Cardinal Beaufort, and attendants from one door; and from the
other, York, Suffolk, Queen Margaret, Salisbury, and Warwick.
As Henry's proxy in France, Suffolk had espoused Margaret of
Anjou and now presents her to the King, who exchanges formal
compliments with his new Queen. Gloucester begins to read the
articles of peace with France but falters in ill-disguised distaste
at the item granting Anjou and Maine to Margaret's father. The
Cardinal finishes reading the document.

After the newlyweds, the matchmaker, and their attendants
have left, Gloucester bitterly complains about the concessions
that have been made to bring about this marriage. Other nobles
concur in the misgivings expressed by Gloucester, who departs
after noting the personal animosity between himself and the Cardinal. As if in demonstration of Gloucester's final assertion, the
Cardinal opens the next segment by denouncing Gloucester at
length. Buckingham responds by suggesting a joint effort to re-
move Gloucester from the protectorship. After the Cardinal
leaves, he, in turn, becomes the topic of unfavorable comments
by Somerset and Buckingham.

---

origin." Their love "has, in this crucial scene, achieved and demonstrated its
autonomous validity" (p. 92). Even A. P. Rossiter, who regards *Much Ado*,
and the romantic comedies in general, as trivial or superficial in comparison
with Shakespeare's plays in the tragicomic mode, grudgingly finds special
merit in this scene: "The place where we can hardly not notice little *points* of
contact with the tragi-comedy outlook is the Church-scene"; *Angel with
Horns*, ed. Graham Storey (London: Longmans, 1961), p. 80.

When those two exit, they are immediately personified as "Pride" and "Ambition" by Salisbury, who suggests to Warwick and York, "Join we together for the public good" (1 [I.i].178, 197) against Somerset, Buckingham, Suffolk, and the Cardinal. York and Warwick assent without hesitation, but in an aside York indicates his motive is self-aggrandizement rather than a concern for the public good. The scene that began with a public, highly formal, almost ceremonial segment finally ends with a soliloquy. Left alone, York rails against the other peers in general and makes explicit his intention of seizing the crown.

Thus, the scene contains six segments created by five successive exits of individual characters or of groups, and after each exit—to quote Don M. Ricks—"the characters remaining upon the stage conspire against those who have just left." The complicated antagonisms and motives of characters are thus presented in the easiest fashion for the audience to absorb and remember. As the number of conspiracies and counter-conspiracies mounts, the number of characters onstage decreases. The scene is "almost a dramatic 'table of contents' to the rest of the play."[7]

One of the few other depletion scenes in the canon happens to be the very last scene (43 [V.v]) in *Henry VI, Part One*, and the similarity in structure of that scene to the first of *Part Two* is one clear link between the two plays.[8] As the final scene of *Part One* begins, Henry VI is in conference with three leading nobles, Suffolk, Gloucester, and Exeter. Suffolk's eloquence has brought Henry to the point of agreeing to an espousal to Margaret of Anjou despite Gloucester's objections, objections Gloucester will reiterate in the first scene of *Part Two* after the marriage has become a fait accompli. Suffolk's smooth rhetoric and sophistry

7. Ricks, *Shakespeare's Emergent Form*, p. 67.
8. This link does not establish the priority of composition of the two plays. If Shakespeare wrote *Part Two* before *Part One*, he could have constructed the last scene of *Part One* along the same structural lines as the already-written opening scene of *Part Two*.

win Henry's approval for the match. Henry, who is among the
first group to depart in scene 1 of *Part Two*, is the first to leave
this scene. After a brief expression of trepidation, Gloucester
(whose exit also marks the end of the second segment of *Part
Two*, scene 1) leaves with Exeter.

Suffolk is left alone at the end of this scene, as York is at the
end of the other, and, like York, Suffolk reveals his ambition to
obtain supreme power:

> Margaret shall now be queen, and rule the king;
> But I will rule both her, the king, and realm.
>
> (43.107–08)

York's soliloquy is longer, more impressive, and shows more
awareness of the complex series of factions that must be played
off against one another to secure control; and York's bid for
power eventually comes closer to fulfillment than Suffolk's,
though York himself dies in *Part Three* without having obtained
the crown.

Even more striking than the link between the first scene of
*Part Two* and the last of *Part One* is the connection between the
first scene of *Part Two* and a later scene in the same play. The
structure of scene 24 (V.i) is an inverted imitation of the structure of the opening scene. Whereas the earlier scene is a strict
depletion scene in which the number of characters onstage gradually diminishes by means of a long series of exits, the later one
is a strict incremental scene in which the number of characters
onstage gradually increases by means of a long series of entrances. Scene 1 ends with York's soliloquy in which he vows:

> A day will come when York shall claim his own.
> . . . . . . . . . . . . . . . . . . . . . . . . . . . . . . . . .
> And, when I spy advantage, claim the crown.
> . . . . . . . . . . . . . . . . . . . . . . . . . . . . . . . . .

Nor shall proud Lancaster usurp my right,
Nor hold the scepter in his childish fist.

(ll. 237, 240, 242–43)

York is accompanied onstage at the beginning of scene 24 by his
Irish army but by no other notable characters. He is the only
character to speak in the segment, and he announces the imminent fulfillment of the vow he made in his earlier soliloquy:

From Ireland thus comes York to claim his right,
And pluck the crown from feeble Henry's head.

(24.1–2)

Among the verbal and thematic echoes in this speech of the
soliloquy are his reference to himself in the third person, his
assertion of his right to the crown, not only of England but of
France, and his contempt for Henry's weakness. As Buckingham
approaches, York confides to the audience, "I must dissemble"
(l. 13), just as he confided in scene 1 his ulterior motives, particularly his intention to deceive the contending nobles. Despite
the bravado of his opening declaration, York is forced to play the
same dissembling role he played in the earlier segments of scene
1 rather than openly seizing the crown. After Buckingham asks
the reason for his armed return to England, York reveals in an
aside, "Scarce can I speak, my choler is so great. / . . . But I
must make fair weather yet awhile" (24.23, 30). He is still doing
what he complained in scene 1 of having had to do at that time:
"So York must sit, and fret, and bite his tongue" (1.228). Even
Buckingham's news of the arrest of York's enemy Somerset is
unwelcome because York is now deprived of his excuse for having landed an army in England and he has no choice but to
disband it.

The King then enters, and York is forced into a submissive
role. York is further relegated to the role of observer during the
next segment of the scene. He temporarily ceases to be the cen-

ter of attention after Alexander Iden enters with the head of
Cade.

But the subsequent entrance of Somerset at liberty and accompanied by the Queen enrages York, who openly denounces
Henry and asserts his own claim to the crown. Somerset arrests
York, who offers his sons as bail. Two of those sons, Edward and
Richard, then enter, shortly followed by Lord Clifford and his
son. York and Clifford trade abuse and threats, and York's sons
support their father. The last two characters to swell the progress
of this scene are the earls of Warwick and Salisbury who now
openly side with York, with whom they had aligned themselves
near the end of scene 1. The conflict has reached the point at
which it can be settled only by battle, and that battle occupies
the remaining scenes of the play.

Scene 1 began with Suffolk's ceremonial presentation of
Queen Margaret to King Henry, a ceremony that marked the
culmination of peace between England and France. Near the
end of the segment Suffolk knelt to receive a new rank as a
reward from Henry. But the harmony and order suggested by this
ceremonial beginning were shattered as each successive exit in
the scene exposed more and more festering animosities, although no direct conflict occurred.

Open conflict is avoided in scene 24 until after Iden's presentation of Cade's head to Henry, a presentation that marks the end
of an internal disorder and that Henry rewards by conferring
knighthood on the kneeling Iden. But each entrance after that
ceremony heightens the pitch of open conflict among the nobility
of England.

Scene 24 thus turns scene 1 inside out—segments of progressive exposure of latent hostility involving fewer and fewer characters in the one are complemented by segments of progressively more intense open conflict involving more and more
characters in the other. The public reading of the peace terms
between England and France in the first segment of scene 1 is

complemented by the challenges to war that are exchanged in the last and most public segment of scene 24. In each of these scenes a series of distinct narrative episodes actually constitutes a unified dramatic movement, the dramatic depiction of social disharmony or disintegration.

Though ingeniously constructed, these scenes in two of the three parts of *Henry VI* are highly artificial and rather mechanical. Yet, as we have seen, Shakespeare used similar, but less obtrusive, incremental and depletion structures for scenes in later, more mature plays, such as *Richard II*, *Much Ado about Nothing*, *Antony and Cleopatra*, and *The Tempest*.

Progressive enlarging and progressive narrowing of the scope of a scene are only two types of formal patterns that Shakespeare employed. Other multipartite scenes are constructed on a clearly symmetrical pattern. In a number of three-part scenes, for example, the identical set of characters appears in both the opening and the closing segments. The middle segment begins either with the exit of one of the characters who opened the scene and who later returns to the stage or with the entrance of another character whose eventual departure restores the original grouping of characters.

The simplest and most common variation of this type of symmetrically constructed scene is one in which the same character is alone onstage at the beginning and at the end of the scene but shares the stage with another character or with a group of characters during the middle segment of the scene. The final scene (9 [V.i.370–end]) of *A Midsummer Night's Dream* follows this pattern.

This scene is a curious kind of bonus scene since the preceding scene (8 [V.i.1–369]) ends as emphatically, and as conventionally, as the final scene of almost any other Elizabethan comedy. After the conclusion of the play within a play ("Pyramus and Thisbe") near the end of scene 8, Theseus refuses Bottom's offer of an epilogue: "No epilogue, I pray you; for your play needs no excuse. . . . Let your epilogue alone" (8.354–55, 360–61). Despite Theseus's facetiousness, we might reasonably infer that the play we are watching, which certainly needs no excuse, will not have an epilogue (especially since few Elizabethan plays do have epilogues). Theseus does, however, call for a "Bergomask" (l. 360). One conventional way to conclude a comedy in the Elizabethan theater was with a dance; *Much Ado about Nothing*, for example, ends in this manner. But here the bergomask is followed by a speech of Theseus that concludes,

> A fortnight hold we this solemnity,
> In nightly revels and new jollity.

> (ll. 368–69)

This speech fits the conventional pattern of a speech concluding a comedy without an epilogue or final dance. Valentine ends *The Two Gentlemen of Verona*, for example, by telling Proteus,

> . . . our day of marriage shall be yours;
> One feast, one house, one mutual happiness.

> (20 [V.iv].173–74)

All the characters onstage leave after Theseus's speech, as all the characters onstage leave after Valentine's, but only a scene has ended, not the play. Puck enters alone. Denied Bottom's epilogue to the play within a play, an audience might well presume that Puck will deliver the epilogue to the play itself despite the contradiction of Theseus's dictum. But no—after twenty lines of Puck's rhymed soliloquy, which describes the night and which does not acknowledge the audience, Oberon, Titania, and the train of fairies enter. In the second segment of the scene, the king and queen of the fairies express their intention to bless the palace and then lead another dance. Rather than ending the play, this dance, like the earlier one, is followed by what seems to be a formal peroration, again delivered by the ranking male figure onstage. But *A Midsummer Night's Dream* is still not over.

After delivering his speech, Oberon leaves with Titania and their trains, but Puck remains onstage.

Although the play "needs no excuse," Puck now does deliver an epilogue. (As I noted in chapter 2, an epilogue can constitute a separate scene, but like a soliloquy it may also be merely an element in a longer, continuous scene.) The actor who has played Puck addresses the audience and makes a plea for applause. But, like the speaker of the Epilogue to *The Tempest*, he retains his fictional role:

> And, as I am an honest Puck,
> If we have unearnèd luck
> Now to scape the serpent's tongue,
> We will make amends ere long;
> Else the Puck a liar call:
> So, good night unto you all.
> Give me your hands, if we be friends,
> And Robin shall restore amends.
>
> (9.61–68 [V.i.430–37])

The repeated promises to make "amends" thus have a witty double meaning. Spoken by the actor in his role as a performer, they simply mean that the Chamberlain's Men will present pleasing plays in the future. Spoken by the actor in the role of Puck, which he has not relinquished, they mean that he and his fellow fairies will perform services for members of the audience who applaud. This piquant breakdown of the barrier between the world of enchantment and the everyday world is aided by the series of false endings to the play. We are repeatedly led to believe that we are leaving the world of the play only to find that world repeatedly reasserting itself. Even after a final dance and a final speech by Theseus, we are given not an immediate epilogue but a multipartite scene, a quaint and lyrical scene involving all the fairies. The epilogue that at last does end the play is part of that scene, and its speaker retains his fairy role. The final segment balances the opening segment in which the actor playing Puck, perhaps unexpectedly, fully retained his fictional role. The symmetrical structure of the scene thus contributes to the interpenetration of fiction and reality, to the delightful prolongation of our dream.

Another scene with a simple, symmetrical pattern occurs in the Battle of Shrewsbury sequence in *Henry IV, Part One*. At a point after the stage has been cleared of living characters, Falstaff enters "*solus*" to begin scene 20 (V.iii.30–end [see chap. 5, n. 10]). He discovers and comments contemptuously upon the body of Sir Walter Blunt: "There's honor for you! Here's no vanity!" (20.3–4 [V.iii.32–33]). Despite the danger of the battle, the presence of the corpse, and his reference to the slaughter of the men under his command, Falstaff's speech is full of humor and of puns in particular. Hal then enters, scolds Falstaff for standing idly, and asks to borrow his sword, which Falstaff, after blatantly lying about his exploits, refuses to give up, offering instead his pistol "that will sack a city" (20.26–27 [V.iii.55–56]). Falstaff is again punning, for his "pistol" turns out to be a bottle of sherris sack. Hal asks, "What, is it a time to jest and dally now?" (20.28 [V.iii.57]). But, as Hal well knows, to Falstaff nearly any time is "a time to jest and dally." In an earlier rhetorical question, posed at the start of his very first dialogue with Falstaff, Hal drew attention to Falstaff's disregard for "time":"What a devil hast thou to do with the time of the day?" (2 [I.ii].6).

After throwing the bottle at Falstaff, Hal leaves to rejoin the fray. Alone again, Falstaff repeats the sentiments he expressed in his opening soliloquy: "I like not such grinning honor as Sir Walter hath. Give me life" (20.31–33 [V.iii.60–62]). And his short speech contains still more puns. Falstaff has the last word as well as the first word in the scene. He adopts the dead Blunt as his foil in the opening and closing segments and treats Hal as straight man and butt in the middle segment.

The segregation of this episode from the surrounding epi-

sodes—it qualifies as an independent scene because it is immediately preceded and followed by moments in which the stage is
clear of living characters—is significant. This very unusual
"battle scene" is dominated by an antichivalric character; it is
the chivalric character who is made to seem the intruder. The
Falstaffian point of view is thus given greater prominence and
greater independent stature as an opposing principle than it
would have if segments dominated by Falstaff's humor were
merely included in longer scenes in which other episodes focused
on combat or on the formation of military strategy.

Macbeth begins a scene during the Battle of Dunsinane with a
short soliloquy. Despite the extremity of his circumstances,
Macbeth clings to a delusive hope: "What's he / That was not
born of woman? Such a one / Am I to fear, or none" (*Macbeth*,
27 [V.vii].2–4). Young Siward then enters and, in spite of his
declaration of moral superiority, is slain by Macbeth. This victory only confirms Macbeth's deluded hope, which he reasserts
in a brief soliloquy that ends the scene:

> Thou wast born of woman.
> But swords I smile at, weapons laugh to scorn,
> Brandished by man that's of a woman born.
>
> $(27.11–13)^9$

Despite their differences, the two scenes just discussed have
a structural similarity which, in turn, contributes to a broad
similarity in function—to make dramatic what otherwise might
not have been dramatic, a character's adherence to an attitude.

---

9. Scene 27 is not coextensive with V.vii. The stage becomes cleared of
living characters at Macbeth's exit after line 13. Macduff then enters, delivers
a soliloquy, and exits (scene 28)—for a discussion of this solo scene, see
chapter 2. Malcolm and Siward then enter, have a brief dialogue, and exeunt
(scene 29). It is not clear how or when Young Siward's body makes its departure; no stage direction mentions its removal, but neither Macduff nor the pair
of characters who subsequently occupy the stage acknowledge the presence of
the corpse.

Each scene opens with a declaration of opinion in a soliloquy by a character who, in some sense, occupies a position of moral isolation. After a confrontation with another character that points up the moral isolation of the first character, each scene ends with the original character's reaffirmation of his opinion in another soliloquy.

The third scene (II.i) of *The Comedy of Errors* is a symmetrically constructed three-part scene in which a character's attitude, revealed in the opening segment, is not only reaffirmed but intensified in the final segment. In this case the initial and final segments are not soliloquies but dialogues between Adriana and her sister Luciana. In the opening conversation Adriana expresses her impatience with the tardiness of her husband Antipholus (of Ephesus) and her opinion that wives should not put up with mistreatment from their husbands. Luciana exercises the theory of the Great Chain of Being to justify unquestioning obedience to a husband by a wife, but Adriana rebuts her sister's advocacy of patience by an *ad feminem* diversion: if Luciana were married she would change her tune.

The women are then joined by Dromio (of Ephesus), who in the previous scene mistook Antipholus of Syracuse for his master. Dromio's oblique complaints about the beating he has received lead to what Ludwig Borinski has termed a "vexing dialogue."[10] Dromio responds to Adriana's questions truthfully, but his answers annoyingly play on her words and are frustratingly uninformative. Eventually, he does give an explicit, though hilariously capsulated, report of his encounter with "Antipholus." Adriana sends the understandably reluctant Dromio a second time to fetch his master, and the two sisters are again alone. The attitude toward her husband that Adriana revealed in the opening dialogue leads her, in the closing dialogue, to interpret the strange behavior of her "husband" as effrontery and his refusal to come

10. "Shakespeare's Comic Prose," p. 64.

home as due to a liaison with another woman. Adriana's impatience has turned to jealousy, her discontent to bitterness and outrage. Luciana's attempts to mollify her are rejected even more stridently than in the opening segment.

The symmetry of scene 3 exposes an interesting feature of this comedy of errors: the confusion and conflict created by the errors themselves are exacerbated and prolonged by the misinterpretations of those errors, misinterpretations that result from the preexisting attitudes or temperaments of the characters.

In the first segment of scene 7 (II.iv) of *Julius Caesar*, which takes place on the morning of Caesar's assassination, Portia reveals her anxiety in her distracted and confused instructions to the young servant Lucius. The Soothsayer then enters, and Portia questions him. She learns that he has had premonitions of dire events and that he intends to warn Caesar. After the departure of the Soothsayer, Portia reveals her increased apprehensiveness in her asides and reveals her distracted state by allowing the boy, or thinking she has allowed the boy, to hear her ruminations:

> . . . Ay me, how weak a thing
> The heart of woman is! O Brutus,
> The heavens speed thee in thine enterprise!
> Sure the boy heard me—Brutus hath a suit
> That Caesar will not grant—O, I grow faint.
>
> (ll. 39–43)

This three-part scene is another one in which the same characters appear in the opening and closing segments. And it provides yet another example of Shakespeare's use of this particular scenic structure in widely differing contexts in order to dramatize the continuance in or intensification of a character's preexisting state of mind.

Symmetrical three-part scenes in which one or more of the original characters leave during the course of the scene and then

return before the end and thereby restore the initial grouping
are, not unexpectedly, rare. One example is the long scene that,
except for the Epilogue, concludes *Henry V*. King Henry and his
English lords enter the stage from one door, and from the other
door enter the King of France, Queen Isabel, Princess Katherine,
and the Duke of Burgundy, with other French lords and attendants. The leaders of the recently belligerent parties exchange
formal, conciliatory greetings. Henry is the only speaker on the
English side; the King and Queen speak for the French; and the
Duke of Burgundy, who casts himself in the role of mediator,
delivers by far the longest speech, in which he elaborately describes the havoc wreaked on the garden of France by the late
war. Though the cordiality of tone makes clear that the ratifica-
tion of a peace treaty is only a formality, the French King asks
for a bilateral negotiation of the final terms. The purely formal
nature of this consultation is confirmed when Henry, rather than
participating in person, sends his lieutenant lords to negotiate,
offstage, with the French King.

Henry stays onstage with Princess Katherine, whose betrothal
to him is the "capital demand" among his peace terms (30
[V.ii].96). Katherine's waiting woman, Alice, also remains.
While the public, ceremonial negotiations are being conducted
offstage, Henry negotiates onstage for Katherine's love in the
plain terms of a soldier. His vigorous suit is eloquent in its own
fashion, and he wins her affection and a kiss. Henry pays for the
kiss with a personal compliment that nevertheless alludes to the
political context of this courtship: "You have witchcraft in your
lips, Kate: there is more eloquence in a sugar touch of them than
in the tongues of the French council; and they should sooner
persuade Harry of England than a general petition of monarchs"
(ll. 279–83).

And at this very point the French council and French monarch
return to the stage with the rest of the characters who exited
earlier in the scene. That Burgundy immediately begins to ban-

ter with Henry indicates that the offstage negotiation was as amicably concluded as the onstage wooing. The French King has already submitted to all terms except a trivial one to which he now submits at Henry's request.

The opening segment focused on political reconciliation, the middle segment on private courtship. These two strands and the interrelationship between them are given equal prominence in the final segment. King Charles tells Henry,

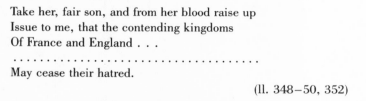

> Take her, fair son, and from her blood raise up
> Issue to me, that the contending kingdoms
> Of France and England . . .
> . . . . . . . . . . . . . . . . . . . . . . . . . . . . . . . . .
> May cease their hatred.
>
> (ll. 348–50, 352)

Henry then kisses Katherine in a public, ceremonial manner— "bear me witness all, / That here I kiss her as my sovereign queen" (ll. 357–58)—after having, in the preceding segment, virtually stolen a kiss from her in private. The double significance of this union is the subject of the Queen's prayer:

> God, the best maker of all marriages,
> Combine your hearts in one, your realms in one!
>
> (ll. 359–60)

In the final line of the scene (and of the play except for the Epilogue) Henry makes an appeal—"may our oaths well kept and prosp'rous be!" (l. 374)—that applies both to the marriage vow to be taken by Katherine and himself and to the oaths of surety taken by the political leaders of England and France. The structure of the scene directly reflects the balancing and unifying of the two issues with which the scene deals.

A symmetrical three-part scene in *King Lear* involves the exit and subsequent return of one character. In scene 30 of *Henry V*, a group of characters leaves the stage to take part in a matter of state offstage and then returns to report the result; in scene 24

(V.ii, except opening s.d.) of *Lear*, Edgar exits, leaving Gloucester onstage, to take part in the battle near Dover and then returns to report the outcome. Still keeping his identity secret,
Edgar asks his father in the opening segment of this scene to
"pray that the right may thrive" (l. 2) and tells him, "If ever I
return to you again, / I'll bring you comfort" (ll. 3–4). One of
Shakespeare's minor audacities in this audacious play is that the
entire battle takes place offstage. Instead of witnessing the battle itself, we watch the lone, silent figure of Gloucester and wait
with him to learn of the outcome.

In this case the symmetrical structure contributes to the irony
of the scene. When Edgar returns, he brings not "comfort" but
news that Lear and Cordelia have lost and have been captured.
The first segment began with Edgar's instruction, "Here, father,
take the shadow of this tree / For your good host" (ll. 1–2). The
final segment also begins with Edgar's instructions, but these
contrast with the earlier one not only in content but in tone and
in poetic rhythm: "Away, old man; give me thy hand; away!"
(l. 5). Even the tenderly ambiguous "father" has changed to the
less personal "old man."

Gloucester at first refuses to move: "a man may rot even here"
(l. 8). Edgar's response includes one of the most familiar passages in drama:

> What, in ill thoughts again? Men must endure
> Their going hence, even as their coming hither:
> Ripeness is all. Come on.
>
> (ll. 9–11)

Taken out of context Edgar's words could be reduced to the plati-
tude that men must endure their dying as well as their being
born. But the dramatic brilliance of the lines lies in the way this
generalized moral plays against the literal situation. The opening segment of the scene began with Gloucester having had to
endure "coming hither" ("Here, father") and he is now being

asked to endure "going hence" ("Away, old man"). In the opening segment Edgar had personified the shadow of the tree ("your good host") under which he places Gloucester. In the final segment Gloucester reverses the metaphor—it is he who has become like the fruit of a tree ("a man may rot even here"). In context, Edgar's declaration, "Ripeness is all," which is so evocative out of context, takes up Gloucester's metaphor, but the word "ripeness" restores the healthy implications of his own earlier metaphor of the tree's shadow as a "good host." Concentrating our attention too much on the generalized implications of Edgar's words obscures their actual dramatic function. What rouses Gloucester from despair is not so much the philosophical content of the statement as his companion's courageous demonstration of a kind of wit in the face of disaster. In a way, Edgar is as good as his word; he does bring Gloucester "comfort," but of a different sort than he had hoped to bring.

The main function of the symmetrical structure of the scene may be to provide a ground for ironic contrast between the opening and closing segments, but by being ironic himself, by bravely confronting the disaster and bringing Gloucester to overcome his despair in the final segment, Edgar becomes the source of a similarity between the opening and closing segments that underlies the contrasts—both reveal his capacity for noble action.[11]

11. I presume that I am not the first reader to notice a possible allusion to Psalm 23:4 in Edgar's opening speech in this scene: "Here, father, take the shadow of this tree / For your good host; pray that the right may thrive. / If ever I return to you again, / I'll bring you comfort" (24 [V.ii].1–4); "Yea, thogh I shulde walke through the valley of the shadow of death, I wil feare no euil: for thou art with me: thy rod and thy staffe, they comfort me" (Geneva Bible, Ps. 23:4). Although Edgar is a human rather than a divine comforter, the allusion is not inappropriate. Edgar has certainly been a shepherd to the blind Gloucester, and in the final segment of the scene he continues his efforts to restore Gloucester's soul. Edgar has been attempting to do for Gloucester what the psalm seems at least in part designed to do for one who recites it—to instill faith and courage, to instill these in the face of conditions of hardship and hostility.

Some of Shakespeare's scenes involving longer series of character groupings also have symmetrical structures. Scene 1 (I.i)
of *Richard III* begins with Richard's famous soliloquy. Richard
manipulates other characters, stage-manages the action to such
an extent, at least in the early part of the play, that it is only
fitting that he provide the prologue as well. In the first thirteen
lines he explains the current situation—"Now" is the first word
in the play and is repeated in lines 5 and 10. Yet he is not an
objective expositor. Even more resonant than his repetitions of
the word "now"—each occurrence of which is as the first or
second word in a line—are his repetitions of the pronoun "our."
The word occurs six times and begins three consecutive lines
(6–8). Richard would seem to be a spokesman for the House of
York were it not for the rising sarcasm in his descriptions of the
change from war to the frivolous pastimes of peace.

Sarcasm is eventually replaced by the explicit assertion of his
isolation from his fellow Yorkists. A decided shift occurs in line
14: "But I, that am not shaped to sportive tricks . . ." The
speech turns to a direct revelation of Richard's character, his
motives, and his "plots" (l. 32). After having avoided the pronoun "I" in the first thirteen lines, he uses it nine times in the
remainder of the soliloquy—six times as the first or second word
of a line. In four of those instances the word is further set off
because it is followed by a marked pause or break in the syntax.

The one plot Richard explains in detail is the elimination of
his elder brother, the Duke of Clarence. This explanation is
followed by the entrance of Clarence himself, who is being es-
corted to the tower by Brakenbury and guards. Richard feigns
ignorance of the circumstances of Clarence's arrest and then
blames it on the connivance of the Queen and her relatives. He
joins in Clarence's expression of disgust at the manipulation of
King Edward by the Queen, by her kindred, and by the King's
mistress, Jane Shore, and indicates his fellow feeling and alliance with Clarence:

We are not safe, Clarence, we are not safe.

(l. 70)

Brother, farewell. I will unto the king;
And whatsoe'er you will employ me in,
Were it to call King Edward's widow sister,
I will perform it to enfranchise you.
Meantime, this deep disgrace in brotherhood
Touches me deeper than you can imagine.

(ll. 107–12)

Richard's antipathy to the Queen's relatives is genuine enough, but his expressions of support for Clarence are feigned—his involvement in Clarence's disgrace is indeed deeper and of a different sort than Clarence can imagine. In a short soliloquy after Clarence's departure with his guards, Richard again refers, this time sardonically, to his intentions concerning his brother:

Simple plain Clarence, I do love thee so
That I will shortly send thy soul to heaven.

(ll. 118–19)

Richard's next interlocutor is Lord Hastings, who has been newly delivered from prison and who vows, "I shall live, my lord, to give them thanks / That were the cause of my imprisonment" (ll. 127–28). Richard not only associates Clarence's grievance with that of Hastings but implicitly establishes himself as an ally and fellow adversary of the Queen's kindred:

No doubt, no doubt; and so shall Clarence too,
For they that were your enemies are his
And have prevailed as much on him as you.

(ll. 129–31)

But these lines have a second, insidious meaning. Clarence's most dangerous enemy is not any of the Queen's relatives but an unrecognized enemy, Richard himself. Richard's remark, which outwardly establishes an alliance, thus carries the implication that Hastings as well as Clarence may have a potential enemy in Richard. And he does, of course, as we discover later.

A series of parallels, reinforced by the structure of the scene, is thus established between Clarence and Hastings. One meets Richard on the way to the Tower, the other meets him having just been released from the Tower. Both are declared enemies of the same court faction, and both trust Richard and regard him as an ally. Thus, although Richard does not announce a plot against Hastings during this scene, we might anticipate the eventual completion of the parallel between Clarence and Hastings. Both will indeed be sent to their deaths by Richard. [12]

Alone once again after Hastings exits, Richard contradicts his protestations to Clarence and Hastings. He had told Clarence, "I will deliver you, or else lie for you" (l. 115), that is, or else go to prison in Clarence's stead. He does intend to lie, to go to Edward "With lies well steeled with weighty arguments" against Clarence (l. 148). After expressing his concern to Hastings about the ailing King, he now declares, "God take King Edward to his mercy / And leave the world for me to bustle in!" (ll. 151–52). His plot against Clarence already developing to his satisfaction, Richard turns his thoughts to another facet of his program for seizing power—his marriage to Lady Anne.

12. The first words spoken by Richard after Hastings departs are momentarily ambiguous: "He cannot live" (l. 145). The pronoun could refer to Clarence, or it could refer to Hastings, the character who has just left; as later becomes clear, Richard is actually referring to King Edward. Other details occurring during the course of the play contribute to the parallel established in the opening scene. Clarence, for example, fails to see the significance of a premonitory dream in which Richard "stumbled, and in falling / Struck" Clarence "overboard" (4 [I.iv].18–19). Hastings later dismisses Stanley's premonitory dream about Richard (10 [III.ii].25–27). And after Hastings has been condemned, he regrets his foolish condemnation of Stanley's premonition and couples it with another omen, one that recalls Clarence's dream of a fatal stumble: "Stanley did dream the boar did raise our helms, / And I did scorn it and disdain to fly. / Three times today my footcloth horse did stumble, / And

The scene thus has a symmetrical five-part structure. The first, middle, and final segments are soliloquies in which Richard reveals his ruthlessness and ambition. The second and fourth segments depict Richard's encounters with figures who are paralleled in several ways but most notably in both being deceived about Richard's character and intentions. Not only do the alternations between soliloquy and deception economically establish Richard's duplicity and moral isolation, but the success of the deceptions gives credibility to the expressions of confidence in the soliloquies delivered before, between, and after the two deceptions.

Shakespeare evidently felt that this scenic structure was an effective one for introducing a duplicitous, Machiavellian villain; in a later play he used the same structure for a similar purpose. The focus of *King Lear* is not so exclusively on Edmund's villainy as that of *Richard III* is on Richard's: the scene that exposes Edmund's character and that corresponds to the opening scene of *Richard III* is understandably not the first in the play—but it is the second.

The first, third, and final segments of this scene are soliloquies in which Edmund reveals many of the same qualities that Richard revealed in his three soliloquies. In the second and fourth segments Edmund, like Richard, deceives two separate characters, one of whom is his brother, against whom he is plotting.

In his opening soliloquy Edmund, like Richard in his opening soliloquy, complains of his birth, though Edmund's complaint is virtually the opposite of Richard's. Richard acknowledges that he is "not shaped for sportive tricks" (1 [I.i].14) and is "rudely stamped" (l. 16), and he blames Nature:

---

started when he looked upon the Tower, / As loath to bear me to the slaughter-house" (12 [III.iv].81–85).

I, that am curtailed of this fair proportion,
Cheated of feature by dissembling Nature,
Deformed, unfinished, sent before my time
Into this breathing world scarce half made up.

(ll. 18–21)

Edmund, on the other hand, complains,

. . . Why bastard? Wherefore base?
When my dimensions are as well compact,
My mind as generous, and my shape as true,
As honest madam's issue?

(2 [I.ii].6–9)

Rather than being "unfinished" by "dissembling Nature," Edmund boasts of being born with "more composition" (l. 12), that is, completeness, as a result of being conceived "in the lusty stealth of nature" (l. 11); and he has made Nature his goddess. In the last section of his soliloquy, Edmund, like Richard, reveals his intention to compensate ruthlessly for the disadvantage of his birth and alludes to his plot against his elder brother.

In this case the next character to enter is not the soliloquizer's brother but his father. By means of a forged letter, Edmund plants a seed of suspicion in Gloucester's mind against Edgar and cleverly nurtures that seed with a lame defense of his brother. Edmund has chosen the perfect moment to initiate his deception. Gloucester enters in a state of disillusionment and dismay:

Kent banished thus? and France in cholor parted?
And the king gone tonight? prescribed his pow'r?
Confined to exhibition? All this done
Upon the gad? Edmund, how now? What news?

(ll. 23–26)

That the news Edmund reveals with disingenuous reluctance so perfectly conforms to the pattern of events on Gloucester's mind

clearly contributes to Gloucester's readiness to indict his innocent son. Gloucester himself calls attention to this pattern of
events in his last speech before exiting:

> These late eclipses in the sun and moon portend no good to
> us. . . . Love cools, friendship falls off, brothers divide. In cit-
> ies, mutinies; in countries, discord; in palaces, treason; and the
> bond cracked 'twixt son and father. This villain of mine comes
> under the prediction, there's son against father; the king falls
> from bias of nature, there's father against child. (ll. 106–07,
> 109–15)

Gloucester is perhaps right about this pattern but wrong in his
specific interpretation of its application to his own family.

In the central soliloquy of the first scene of *Richard III*,
Richard expressed contempt for the mental powers of the character he had just deceived ("Simple plain Clarence"). In the
central soliloquy of the scene now under discussion, Edmund
expresses contempt for the "foppery" (l. 121) of Gloucester's
ascription of human villainy to "planetary influence" (l. 128).

But as Edgar, the intended victim of Edmund's plot, enters,
Edmund feigns belief in such portents. He then informs Edgar
of Gloucester's displeasure with him, a displeasure Edgar ascribes to an unknown villain. In the earlier play Richard promised his brother to mollify Edward, whose anger he has actually
inflamed and intends to further inflame. Edmund, who has inflamed and intends to further inflame Gloucester's suspicions of
Edgar, makes a similar false claim to his brother: "I do serve
you in this business" (l. 182).

Edmund, like Richard, cannot resist the temptation to make
statements that, for his own entertainment, have ironic implications unsuspected by the character he is in the act of deceiving.
Richard told Clarence, "I will deliver you, or else lie for you."
Edmund tells Edgar, "I am no honest man if there be any good
meaning toward you" (ll. 177–78). Such passages indicate Ed-

mund's and Richard's enjoyment of the actual process of deception and their confidence in their powers of manipulation.

These particular aspects of the characters of the two villains
are also evident in their soliloquies, especially in their final ones
in the two scenes. In his closing soliloquy Richard looks forward
with exuberant confidence to the challenge of wooing Anne—
"What though I killed her husband and her father" (l. 154).
Buoyed by the success of his deceptions, Edmund in his final
soliloquy again expresses disdain for his dupes and looks forward with relish to future success:

> A credulous father, and a brother . . .
> . . . on whose foolish honesty
> My practices ride easy. I see the business.
> Let me, if not by birth, have lands by wit.
> All with me's meet that I can fashion fit.
>
> (ll. 183, 185–88)

Edmund's reference to overcoming his birth recalls his opening
soliloquy. Richard's confident anticipation of wooing Anne recalls
and contradicts his disqualification of himself as a lover in his
opening soliloquy. That disqualification, it now becomes clear if it
was not clear then, was merely ironic self-detraction and a face-
tious excuse for his villainy. Actually, Richard, like Edmund,
believes nothing is beyond his powers of manipulation.

An example of a symmetrically constructed scene that Shakespeare wrote late in his career is the eighth scene (III.iii) of *The
Winter's Tale*, the much-discussed bear scene. One of the "Six
Points of Stagecraft in *The Winter's Tale*" analyzed in an article
by Nevill Coghill is the way in which this scene effects an appropriate transition from the tragic first half of the play to the comic
second half. The two genres merge in the tragic-comic death of
Antigonus and the grotesque-tender description of offstage disaster provided by the Clown.[13] William H. Matchett extends

13. *Shakespeare Survey* 11 (1958): 31–41.

Coghill's analysis by calling attention to the undisguised the-
atricality of the scene and the experimental nature of its strange
mixture of tones. In addition, Matchett describes the effect of
these features of the scene on an audience: "The insistent way in
which Shakespeare forces us out of mere passive participation in
an ongoing story into an active disorientation . . . leaves us no
choice but to question our own responses."[14]

Both the transitional function of the scene and its self-con-
scious artifice are further revealed by a close examination of its
structure. For a brief moment at the center of this central, pivot-
al scene, the stage is occupied only by the infant Perdita, who
was falsely assumed by Leontes in the tragic first half of the play
to be the product of his wife's adultery and who as an adult is
restored and reconciled to her father in the comic second half.
The segments following this moment strangely mirror the segments that precede it.

The scene opens with the entrance of three characters: old
Antigonus, the "Babe" he is carrying, and a Mariner. After the
Mariner expresses his concern about the threatening weather
and warns Antigonus about the predatory animals of Bohemia,
Antigonus sends him back to the ship and then delivers a long
soliloquy during which he sets down the infant he has been instructed to abandon. The Mariner's warning about predators was
not idle, for Antigonus eventually makes his exit "*pursued by a
bear*" (s.d. after l. 57). No scene break occurs because the stage
has not been cleared of living characters. That the sole occupant
of the stage is presumably a doll, a mere prop, is another example, like the intrusion of the "bear," of the conspicuous the-
atricality of the scene noted by Matchett. Nevertheless, that doll
does represent a living character.[15]

14. "Some Dramatic Techniques in *The Winter's Tale*," *Shakespeare Survey*
22 (1969): 102.

15. As if to confirm the status of the doll as a full-fledged character, the
stage direction at the beginning of the scene does not take the form "*Enter*

Old Antigonus is shortly replaced onstage by the Old Shepherd.[16] As unlikely as it may seem, the scene, in a way, begins
to reverse itself. Antigonus exited after "losing" a child; the
Shepherd enters in search of his lost sheep and finds the lost
child. The quaintly comic prose of the Old Shepherd could
hardly be further from the grave, formal blank verse of Antigonus, but both men are deeply moved by the child's predica-
ment, Antigonus in abandoning the "poor wretch" (l. 48) and the
Shepherd in taking up the "poor thing" (l. 74). Despite the differences in their diction, their speeches contain other parallels.
At the moment he lays the baby down, Antigonus hopes she will
be found and saved "if Fortune please" and calls her "pretty"
(l. 47). At the moment he discovers the baby, the Old Shepherd
also defers to a higher power and repeatedly uses the term of
admiration and endearment used by Antigonus: "Good luck,
an't be thy will, what have we here? Mercy on's, a barne! A very
pretty barne; a boy or a child, I wonder? A pretty one, a very
pretty one" (ll. 67–70). Antigonus suffers from the mistaken
impression that Perdita is illegitimate, and he is grieved at the
tragic consequences of her "mother's fault" (l. 49). Arriving at
the same conclusion about the child's parentage, the Shepherd
expresses his assumption in comic terms: "This has been some
stair-work, some trunk-work, some behind-door work; they were
warmer that got this than the poor thing is here" (ll. 72–74).

---

Antigonus, *carrying a baby, and a* Mariner," but rather, lists "Babe" separately and not even immediately after the character who is carrying the prop
that represents the infant: "*Enter* Antigonus, *a* Mariner, Babe." Compare the
stage direction after line 19 of *Titus Andronicus*, scene 12 (V.i), a scene the
continuity of which is not affected by the status of the baby as a living character: "*Enter a* Goth, *leading of* Aaron *with his child in his arms.*"

16. The latter character is identified as the "Old Shepherd" in "The Names
of the Actors" in the 1623 Folio, and the Clown calls him "old man" in line
116 of this scene. Antigonus's advanced age is indicated by 3 [II.i].174 and 5
[II.iii].161, 165.

And, though superficially contrasted in tone, the remarks of both old men are tinged with tenderness.

Antigonus had sent the Mariner away to be alone while leaving the baby. Alone in discovering the baby, the Shepherd now calls for his son, the Clown. In the opening segment the Mariner had warned his aged companion of the threat to the ship at sea posed by the storm and of the threat of wild creatures on land. In the final segment, the Clown tells the Old Shepherd that the ship has been destroyed in the storm and that Antigonus has been attacked by a bear. Both disasters are still virtually in progress offstage: "the men are not yet cold under water, nor the bear half dined on the gentleman; he's at it now" (ll. 102–03).

The affinity between the Old Shepherd and Antigonus is strengthened by the Shepherd's response: "Would I had been by, to have helped the old man!" (ll. 104–05). Shakespeare put these words of fellow feeling for one old man in the mouth of the other even at the risk of having future expositors point out that the Clown has not indicated the age of the bear's victim. And only a few lines after the Shepherd applies the words "old man" to the person dismembered, literally unmade, by the bear, the Clown finds the gold left by Antigonus with Perdita and calls the Shepherd "a made old man" (l. 116). Leaving the child and the gold led to the undoing of one old man, but finding that child and that gold will be the making of another old man.

Both of the adult characters who appear in the opening segments of the scene are disturbed by and ashamed of the "business" they are about (ll. 14, 33). While alone, Antigonus laments, "my heart bleeds; and most accursed am I / To be by oath enjoined to this" (ll. 51–52). Earlier, the Mariner even saw a connection between the threatening weather and their dubious mission: "In my conscience, / The heavens with that we have in hand are angry / And frown upon's" (ll. 4–6). It is, according to the Mariner, an "ill time" (l. 3).

By contrast, the scene ends with the Shepherd's comment, "'Tis a lucky day, boy, and we'll do good deeds on't" (ll. 134–35). Considering the proximity of disaster, one might regard his sentiment as tactless. But both he and his son have already shown their comically expressed but genuine sorrow for the victims of the disasters and have already shown their spontaneous charity and good intentions. The Shepherd decided to take care of the forsaken child before he discovered the gold, and the Clown intends to bury the remains of Antigonus despite the storm. These simple men give instinctive voice to their true feelings without a sense of impropriety and act on those feelings. The actions of Antigonus and the Mariner, on the other hand, go against their own instinctive feelings.

Antigonus and the Mariner have done their "ungentle business" in an "ill time" and have been punished. The prophecy made by Hermione in Antigonus's dream, that he would never again see his wife Paulina, has come true. The Shepherd and the Clown have done their "good deeds" on a "lucky day" and have been rewarded. The prophecy made to the Old Shepherd that he "should be rich by the fairies" (l. 114) is fulfilled, although the agency of his enrichment is not the fairies but perhaps the same heavens that frowned upon the pair of men who appeared in the opening segment of the scene. On the one hand, the scene effects a transition from the tragic first half of the play to the comic second, yet on the other hand, the scene possesses a tightly knit internal structure.

The almost mirrorlike reversal in the second half of this scene of what occurred in the first half is incomplete. The ill fortune of Antigonus and the Mariner is balanced by the good fortune of the Shepherd and the Clown and the forsaken baby is taken up; but the lives of Antigonus and the Mariner are over. Similarly, although the reconciliations in the second half of the play balance the cruel severances of the first half and, for example, Florizel becomes a new son to Leontes, some of what has been lost, such as the life of Leonte's own son Mamillius, cannot be recovered.

This scene has certain structural similarities with scene 24 (V.ii, except opening s.d.) of *King Lear*, which was discussed earlier. In the middle of each scene the stage is occupied by a silent, essentially helpless figure—a baby in one case and the blind, feeble Gloucester in the other—while we await news of portentous offstage action. What follows this central stasis in each scene ironically echoes what preceded it. Furthermore, although our worst fears are confirmed in the final segment of each scene, our response is complicated by an element creating an unexpected incongruity in tone—Edgar's intrepid demonstration of a kind of wit despite the disaster that has occurred offstage in *Lear* and the disorienting burst of clownishness in the very description of offstage disasters in *The Winter's Tale*.

Many of the complex scenes examined in this chapter exhibit a pattern based on parallelism or some more complicated form of symmetry among the individual segments. The opening, middle, and closing segments of the second scene of *Lear* are soliloquies delivered by Edmund, while the second and fourth depict his dialogues, first with his gullible father and then with his gullible brother. The pattern of the scene contributes to the efficient and forceful revelation of Edmund's character. The closing segments of scene 8 of *The Winter's Tale* mirror the opening segments: the first half of the scene consists of a dialogue between two characters followed by a soliloquy delivered by one of them, and the second half consists of a soliloquy followed by a dialogue between the soliloquizer and another character. This pattern is appropriate because the action depicted in the closing segments is a mirrorlike reversal of the action depicted in the opening segments. Just as some plays contain patterns of similarly constructed scenes, some multipartite scenes contain patterns of similar types of segments.

The foregoing discussion of representative multipartite scenes,

although necessarily selective, confirms and extends conclusions reached earlier in this study. The examples presented in
this chapter suggest that Shakespeare repeatedly used a particular multipartite scenic structure to serve a particular set of dramatic functions, just as he repeatedly used a specific unitary or
two-part scenic structure to serve a specific set of dramatic functions. And just as some individual plays contain patterns of similarly constructed unitary or two-part scenes, some individual
plays contain patterns of multipartite scenes with similar or
complementary structures.

More fundamentally, the examples presented in this chapter
suggest that, despite their generally greater length and complexity, multipartite scenes, like unitary and two-part scenes, possess an internally coherent artistic unity. Many multipartite
scenes are inherently unified because they present a single, almost self-contained narrative episode. Some scenes, though not
encompassing a self-contained narrative episode, do focus on a
limited or intermediate dramatic issue. The single *narrative* episode of Hamlet's initial confrontation with the Ghost, for example, is divided into two multipartite scenes which, as I argued in
chapter 1, comprise two distinct *dramatic* movements, each
with its own exposition, rising action, climax, and denouement.
The structure of such scenes thus resembles the structure normally associated with an entire play.

Some scenes, on the other hand, incorporate more than one
narrative episode. Many of the scenes discussed in this chapter
and in the preceding chapter incorporate disparate narrative elements yet possess an internal artistic unity. In chapter 1 I discussed the complex unity of scene 7 (II.ii–iv) of *King Lear*,
which begins with the morning quarrel of Kent and Oswald and
ends as the night and the storm approach and which includes
Edgar's "Poor Tom" soliloquy. Such scenes are unified in one—
or more than one—of a variety of ways. Some focus on the revelation of a single character's personality; some develop a single

theme; some establish suggestive parallels between different lines of action. In some, the series of distinct narrative episodes actually constitutes a unified dramatic movement.

In some cases, the relationship of an individual segment to the multipartite scene of which it is a part resembles the relationship of an individual scene to the play of which it is a part. William Empson's comment about scenes in Elizabethan drama—that they "stand out as objects in themselves, to be compared even when they are not connected"—applies to the segments within some multipartite scenes. Edgar's "Poor Tom" soliloquy, for example, stands out as an object in itself yet is closely tied to the rest of the scene of which it is a part by common themes, by verbal echoes, and by the implicit comparison between Kent and Edgar. The Elizabethan drama, as Madeleine Doran has argued, achieved its unity, paradoxically, "by making the parts independent as free members"—achieved its unity through multiplicity.[17] It is not surprising that in Shakespeare's plays, some "free members," some scenes that stand out as objects in themselves, should display structural similarities to the whole of which they are parts; it is not surprising that some individual scenes achieve unity through multiplicity.

17. Empson, "Double Plots," p. 55; and Doran, *Endeavors of Art*, p. 6. These passages were discussed in chapter 1.

# Afterword

Many of the specific kinds of scenic structures that have been examined in this study, though used by Shakespeare throughout his career, are highlighted in a particular play. One or two choral scenes occur in a number of plays, but *Henry V* has five. One or two solo scenes by nonchoral figures occur in plays throughout the canon, but four occur in *Cymbeline*. Duets appear frequently, but only *King Lear*, with five, has more than three. Two-part scenes are not uncommon, but *King John* includes three in a row and *Antony and Cleopatra* four in a row. A number of plays from *The Comedy of Errors* to *The Tempest* contain a single multipartite scene involving a progressive increment of characters onstage, but *Richard II* contains three, two of which are consecutive.

Scenes that depict physical action without dialogue—most of which are "excursions" during battle—are naturally concentrated in the history plays. Yet the three parts of *Henry VI* contain about half (13 of 27) of the total of such scenes in the entire canon. Though battles are important in the narrative action of a number of plays written later than *Henry V*, none of those plays contains an excursion that constitutes a separate scene. Episodes of physical combat are either incorporated into scenes involving dialogue or are eliminated entirely. In an audacious theatrical move, for example, Shakespeare does not show us any of the decisive battle in *King Lear*; rather, he shows us a pre-battle procession of the forces led by Lear and Cordelia and then, while the battle is being decided, shows us an old, blind man sitting silently by a tree.

Although I have concentrated in this study on the internal structure of individual scenes, I hope I have given some insights into Shakespeare's "system of 'construction by scenes.'" I have given some attention to particular sequences of scenes and, furthermore, have tried to demonstrate that two or more scenes with similar structures in the same play almost invariably reflect upon one another in a variety of ways and create patterns that serve to bind together the play as a whole. The five unitary duets in the seemingly loosely structured *King Lear*, for example, form a surprisingly symmetrical pattern. The patterns of some sets of similarly constructed scenes serve the function of establishing indirect conflict. Although conflict is generally presumed to be the very essence of drama, including comedy, Duke Senior and Duke Frederick are never presented in direct conflict in *As You Like It*; they never even appear onstage together. By presenting their differences in juxtaposed scenes and by presenting the differences between their courts in contrasting sets of similarly constructed unitary group scenes, Shakespeare makes those differences dramatic. Suggestive sequential patterns of scenes and patterns involving scenes located in different parts of a play are important elements of Shakespeare's overall dramatic structure and deserve further investigation. [1]

As I argued in chapter 1, the flexibility of the scene made it an ideal structural unit for a drama that achieved its unity through multiplicity. The lifeblood flowing through Shakespeare's plays is his incomparable language, but the element that gives

1. A few critics, however, have begun to investigate this feature of Shakespeare's craftsmanship. See, e.g., the chapter, "Design in Groups of Scenes," in Rose, *Shakespearean Design*, and the chapter, "The Juxtaposition of Scenes," in Nevill Coghill, *Shakespeare's Professional Skills* (Cambridge: Cambridge Univ. Press, 1964).

each of those plays organic structure is the pattern of relationships among individual scenes. Appropriately enough, perhaps
the earliest surviving literary allusion to Shakespeare makes the
basic structural unit of his plays a part of his name. In *A
Groatsworth of Wit* (1592) Robert Greene accused an "upstart"
playwright of believing himself to be "the only Shake-scene in a
country." No true conception of Shakespeare's overall dramatic
structure can ignore the essential role of the most important
common structural denominator found in all his plays, the individual scene.

# Appendix ✠ A Catalogue of the Scene Divisions in Shakespeare's Plays

The following charts correlate the traditional divisions of Shakespeare's plays into acts and scenes, with the divisions into scenes on the basis of the criteria set forth in chapter 1. Those criteria may be summarized as follows:

1. The continuity of a play is not broken, and hence a scene division does not occur, unless the stage is cleared of all living characters. Living characters include a baby even though probably represented by a doll and exclude corpses even though represented by actors.

2. The continuity of a play is not broken, and hence a scene division does not occur, even if the stage is technically cleared for a moment, if either the exiting or the entering characters express awareness of the presence of the other group.

3. If continuity is not maintained either by the continuous presence onstage of a character or set of characters or by the awareness of departing or of entering characters of the other group, then a break between scenes occurs even if the location of the second of two consecutive episodes is the same as the first and no discernible fictive time has elapsed between the episodes.

4. If two sets of characters occupy the stage at the same time they belong to the same *dramatic scene* even if they are unaware of one another's presence and, furthermore, even if they are in separate fictive locations.

The traditional divisions and the lineations cited in this catalogue are those provided in *The Complete Signet Classic Shakespeare*, Sylvan Barnet, gen. ed. (New York: Harcourt, 1972). The plays are arranged in alphabetical order. Three plays generally considered to be collaborations—*The Two Noble Kinsmen, Pericles*, and *Henry VIII*—are included in the appendix but have been excluded from consideration in the analyses and tabulations presented in the text. (The figure of 780 scenes in the canon, for example, does not include the 75 scenes in these plays.) Several cases of problematic scene divisions in addition to those discussed in the notes to this appendix are examined in earlier sections of this study.

## All's Well That Ends Well

| | | |
|---|---|---|
| 1–I.i | 9–III.i | 17–IV.ii |
| 2–I.ii | 10–III.ii | 18–IV.iii |
| 3–I.iii | 11–III.iii | 19–IV.iv |
| 4–II.i | 12–III.iv | 20–IV.v |
| 5–II.ii | 13–III.v | 21–V.i |
| 6–II.iii | 14–III.vi | 22–V.ii |
| 7–II.iv | 15–III.vii | 23–V.iii (333 lines) |
| 8–II.v | 16–IV.i | and Epilogue |

## Antony and Cleopatra

| | | |
|---|---|---|
| 1–I.i | 10–II.v | 19–III.vii |
| 2–I.ii | 11–II.vi | 20–III.viii |
| 3–I.iii | 12–II.vii | 21–III.ix |
| 4–I.iv | 13–III.i | 22–⎱ III.x, opening |
| 5–I.v | 14–III.ii | 23–⎰ s.d. ("Canid- |
| 6–II.i | 15–III.iii | ius . . . *Alar-* |
| 7–II.ii | 16–III.iv | *um*")[1] |
| 8–II.iii | 17–III.v | 24–III.x, except |
| 9–II.iv | 18–III.vi | opening s.d. |

1. "Canidius *marcheth with his land army one way over the stage, and* Taurus, *the lieutenant of* Caesar, [with his army] *the other way. After their going in is heard the noise of a sea-fight. Alarum.*" As it is likely that these processions of armies are successive rather than simultaneous, the stage direction constitutes two separate scenes (22 and 23). After the departure of the

| | | |
|---|---|---|
| 25–III.xi | 32–IV.v | 39–IV.xi |
| 26–III.xii | 33–IV.vi | 40–IV.xii |
| 27–III.xiii | 34–IV.vii.1-3 | 41–IV.xiii |
| 28–IV.i | 35–IV.vii.4-end | 42–IV.xiv |
| 29–IV.ii | 36–IV.viii | 43–IV.xv |
| 30–IV.iii | 37–IV.ix | 44–V.i |
| 31–IV.iv | 38–IV.x | 45–V.ii |

**As You Like It**

| | | |
|---|---|---|
| 1–I.i | 9–II.vi | 17–IV.i |
| 2–I.ii | 10–II.vii | 18–IV.ii |
| 3–I.iii | 11–III.i | 19–IV.iii |
| 4–II.i | 12–III.ii.1-10 | 20–V.i |
| 5–II.ii | 13–III.ii.11-end | 21–V.ii |
| 6–II.iii | 14–III.iii | 22–V.iii |
| 7–II.iv | 15–III.iv | 23–V.iv (198 lines) |
| 8–II.v | 16–III.v | and Epilogue |

**The Comedy of Errors**

| | | |
|---|---|---|
| 1–I.i | 5–III.i | 9–IV.iii |
| 2–I.ii | 6–III.ii | 10–IV.iv |
| 3–II.i | 7–IV.i | 11–V.i |
| 4–II.ii | 8–IV.ii | |

**Coriolanus**

| | | |
|---|---|---|
| 1–I.i | 7–I.vii | 13–II.iii |
| 2–I.ii | 8–I.viii | 14–III.i |
| 3–I.iii | 9–I.ix | 15–III.ii |
| 4–I.iv | 10–I.x | 16–III.iii |
| 5–I.v | 11–II.i | 17–IV.i |
| 6–I.vi | 12–II.ii | 18–IV.ii |

---

second of these processions and after the offstage sound effects, Enobarbus
enters to begin scene 24.

| | | |
|---|---|---|
| 19 – IV. iii | 24 – IV. vi | 28 – V. iii |
| 20 – IV. iv | 25 – IV. vii | 29 – V. iv |
| 21 – IV. v. 1-2 | 26 – V. i | 30 – V. v |
| 22 – IV. v. 3-4 | 27 – V. ii | 31 – V. vi |
| 23 – IV. v. 5-end | | |

### Cymbeline

| | | |
|---|---|---|
| 1 – I. i | 19 – III. vii | 29 – V. ii from s. d. |
| 2 – I. ii | 20 – IV. i | after l. 10 ("*The* |
| 3 – I. iii | 21 – IV. ii. 1-100 | *battle con-* |
| 4 – I. iv | 22 – IV. ii. 101-end | *tinues. . . .*") |
| 5 – I. v | 23 – IV. iii | to middle of |
| 6 – I. vi | 24 – IV. iv | s. d. after l. 13 |
| 7 – II. i | 25 – V. i | ("*They rescue* |
| 8 – II. ii | 26 –⎫ V. ii, first two | Cymbeline *and* |
| 9 – II. iii | 27 –⎭ sentences of | *exeunt*") |
| 10 – II. iv | opening s. d. | 30 – V. ii from middle |
| 11 – II. v | ("*Enter* | of s. d. after l. |
| 12 – III. i | *. . . go out*")² | 13 ("*Then en-* |
| 13 – III. ii | 28 – V. ii from third | *ter . . .*") to end |
| 14 – III. iii | sentence of | of V. ii |
| 15 – III. iv | opening s. d. | 31 – V. iii |
| 16 – III. v | ("*Then enter* | 32 – V. iv |
| 17 – III. vi. 1-27 | *again . . .*") to | 33 – V. v |
| 18 – III. vi. 28-end | l. 10 | |

### Hamlet

| | | |
|---|---|---|
| 1 – I. i | 3 – I. iii | 5 – I. v |
| 2 – I. ii | 4 – I. iv | 6 – II. i |

2. "*Enter* Lucius, Iachimo, *and the* Roman Army *at one door, and the* Briton Army *at another*, Leonatus Posthumus *following like a poor soldier. They march over and go out*." As it is likely that these processions of armies, like those in *Antony and Cleopatra* (see above, n. 1), are successive rather than simultaneous, the stage direction constitutes two separate scenes. During the course of the traditional division V. ii, the stage is cleared four times (see chap. 5, n. 5).

7 – II.ii
8 – III.i
9 – III.ii
10 – III.iii
11 – III.iv

12 – IV.i
13 – IV.ii
14 – IV.iii
15 – IV.iv
16 – IV.v

17 – IV.vi
18 – IV.vii
19 – V.i
20 – V.ii

## Henry IV, Part One

1 – I.i
2 – I.ii
3 – I.iii
4 – II.i
5 – II.ii.1-94
6 – II.ii.95-end
7 – II.iii
8 – II.iv
9 – III.i
10 – III.ii

11 – III.iii
12 – IV.i
13 – IV.ii
14 – IV.iii
15 – IV.iv
16 – V.i
17 – V.ii
18 – V.iii, opening
  s.d. (*"The* King
  . . . *battle"*)

19 – V.iii.1-29, not
  including open-
  ing s.d.
20 – V.iii.30-end
21 – V.iv, opening
  s.d. (*"Alarum.*
  *Excursions"*)
22 – V.iv, except
  opening s.d.
23 – V.v

## Henry IV, Part Two

1 – Induction:
  Rumor
2 – I.i
3 – I.ii
4 – I.iii
5 – II.i
6 – II.ii
7 – II.iii
8 – II.iv

9 – III.i
10 – III.ii
11 – IV.i (226 lines)
  and IV.ii
12 – IV.iii
13 – IV.iv (132 lines)
  and IV.v
14 – V.i
15 – V.ii

16 – V.iii
17 – V.iv
18 – V.v.1-5
19 – V.v, s.d. after
  l. 5 (*"Trum-*
  *pets . . . stage"*)
20 – V.v.6-end
21 – Epilogue

## Henry V

1 – Prologue
2 – I.i
3 – I.ii
4 – II. Chorus
5 – II.i

6 – II.ii
7 – II.iii
8 – II.iv
9 – III.Chorus
10 – III.i

11 – III.ii.1-54
12 – III.ii.55-end
13 – III.iii
14 – III.iv
15 – III.v

16 – III. vi                  s.d. (*"Alarum.*          27 – IV. viii
17 – III. vii                     *Excursions"*)       28 – V. Chorus
18 – IV. Chorus           23 – IV. iv, except          29 – V. i
19 – IV. i                        opening s.d.          30 – V. ii
20 – IV. ii                   24 – IV. v                31 – Epilogue:
21 – IV. iii                  25 – IV. vi                   Chorus
22 – IV. iv, opening      26 – IV. vii

## Henry VI, Part One

1 – I. i                      15 – II. iii              s.d. (*"Alarum:*
2 – I. ii. 1-21               16 – II. iv                   *excursions"*)
3 – I. ii, s.d. after l.      17 – II. v                33 – IV. vii. 1-32, not
   21 (*"Here . . .*       18 – III. i                   including open-
   *loss"*)               19 – III. ii. 1-17            ing s.d.
4 – I. ii. 22-end             20 – III. ii. 18-35       34 – IV. vii. 33-end
5 – I. iii                    21 – III. ii. 36-40       35 – V. i
6 – I. iv. 1-22               22 – III. ii, s.d. after  36 – V. ii
7 – I. iv. 23-end                l. 40 (*"An alar-*   37 – V. iii, opening
8 – I. v, opening                *um: excursions"*)       s.d. (*"Alarum.*
   s.d. (*"Here . . .*   23 – III. ii. 41-114          *Excursions"*)
   *him"*)              24 – III. ii. 115-end     38 – V. iii. 1-29, not
9 – I. v, except              25 – III. iii                 including open-
   opening s.d.          26 – III. iv                  ing s.d.
10 – I. vi                    27 – IV. i                39 – V. iii, s.d. after
11 – II. i. 1-38              28 – IV. ii                   line 29 (*"Excur-*
12 – II. i, s.d. after l.     29 – IV. iii (53 lines)       *sions . . . fly"*)
   38 (*"The* French        and IV. iv            40 – V. iii. 30-44
   *. . . shirts"*)      30 – IV. v                41 – V. iii. 45-end
13 – II. i. 39-end            31 – IV. vi               42 – V. iv
14 – II. ii                   32 – IV. vii, opening     43 – V. v

## Henry VI, Part Two

1 – I. i                      4 – I. iv                 7 – II. iii
2 – I. ii                     5 – II. i                 8 – II. iv
3 – I. iii                    6 – II. ii                9 – III. i

| | | |
|---|---|---|
| 10 – III.ii | 17 – IV.v | 24 – V.i |
| 11 – III.iii | 18 – IV.vi | 25 – V.ii.1-30 |
| 12 – IV.i[3] | 19 – IV.vii, opening | 26 – V.ii.31-65 |
| 13 – IV.ii | s.d. (*"Alar-* | 27 – V.ii.66-71 |
| 14 – IV.iii, opening | *ums . . . rest"*) | 28 – V.ii, s.d. after |
| s.d. (*"Alar-* | 20 – IV.vii, except | l. 71 (*"Fight.* |
| *ums . . . slain"*) | opening s.d. | *Excursions"*) |
| 15 – IV.iii, except | 21 – IV.viii | 29 – V.ii.72-end |
| opening s.d. | 22 – IV.ix | 30 – V.iii |
| 16 – IV.iv | 23 – IV.x | |

**Henry VI, Part Three**

| | | |
|---|---|---|
| 1 – I.i | 8 – II.iii, except | 13 – III.i |
| 2 – I.ii | opening s.d. | 14 – III.ii |
| 3 – I.iii | 9 – II.iv, opening | 15 – III.iii |
| 4 – I.iv | s.d. (*"Excur-* | 16 – IV.i |
| 5 – II.i | *sions"*) | 17 – IV.ii |
| 6 – II.ii | 10 – II.iv, except | 18 – IV.iii.1-27 |
| 7 – II.iii, opening | opening s.d. | 19 – IV.iii.28-end |
| s.d. (*"Alarum.* | 11 – II.v | 20 – IV.iv |
| *Excursions"*) | 12 – II.vi | 21 – IV.v |

3. The stage direction that opens IV.i—*"Alarum. Fight at Sea. Ordnance goes off"*—may constitute a separate scene without dialogue. But since this "fight" is not of particular dramatic relevance, it is more likely that *"Fight at Sea"* refers merely to sound effects associated with a naval battle. Compare the unambiguous direction that follows the two military processions in *Antony and Cleopatra* (see above, n. 1): *"After their going in is heard the noise of a sea-fight."* Although *The First Part of the Contention Betwixt the Two Famous Houses of York and Lancaster* is a bad quarto of *Henry VI, Part Two,* the stage direction at the corresponding point in that play is probably accurate: *"Al-armes within, and the chambers be discharged, like as it were a fight at sea"*; See *The First Part of the Contention . . . ,* ed. James Orchard Halliwell, in *Dodsley's Old Plays,* Supplement (London: Shakespeare Society, 1853), 4: 47. Though bound together, the individual plays in this volume have independent pagination.

| 22 – IV. vi | s.d. (*"Alarum* | 29 – V. iv |
| 23 – IV. vii | *and excursions"*) | 30 – V. v |
| 24 – IV. viii | 27 – V. ii, except | 31 – V. vi |
| 25 – V. i | opening s.d. | 32 – V. vii |
| 26 – V. ii, opening | 28 – V. iii | |

## Henry VIII

| 1 – Prologue | 8 – II. iii | 15 – V. ii (35 lines) |
| 2 – I. i | 9 – II. iv | and V. iii |
| 3 – I. ii | 10 – III. i | 16 – V. iv |
| 4 – I. iii | 11 – III. ii | 17 – V. v |
| 5 – I. iv | 12 – IV. i | 18 – Epilogue |
| 6 – II. i | 13 – IV. ii | |
| 7 – II. ii | 14 – V. i | |

## Julius Caesar

| 1 – I. i | 8 – III. i | 14 – V. ii |
| 2 – I. ii | 9 – III. ii | 15 – V. iii. 1-50 |
| 3 – I. iii | 10 – III. iii | 16 – V. iii. 51-90 |
| 4 – II. i | 11 – IV. i | 17 – V. iii. 91-end |
| 5 – II. ii | 12 – IV. ii (52 lines) | 18 – V. iv |
| 6 – II. iii | and IV. iii | 19 – V. v |
| 7 – II. iv | 13 – V. i | |

## King John

| 1 – I. i | 5 – III. ii. 1-10, not | 7 – III. ii. 11-end |
| 2 – II. i | including open- | 8 – III. iii |
| 3 – II. ii (74 lines) | ing s.d. | 9 – IV. i |
| and III. i | 6 – III. ii, s.d. after | 10 – IV. ii |
| 4 – III. ii, opening | line 10 (*"Alar-* | 11 – IV. iii. 1-10 |
| s.d. (*"Alarums,* | *ums, excursions,* | 12 – IV. iii. 11-end |
| *excursions"*) | *retreat"*) | 13 – V. i |

14–V.ii                16–V.iv                18–V.vi
15–V.iii               17–V.v                 19–V.vii

## King Lear

1–I.i                  10–III.iii             21–IV.vii
2–I.ii                 11–III.iv              22–V.i
3–I.iii                12–III.v               23–V.ii, opening
4–I.iv                 13–III.vi                  s.d. ("*Alar-*
5–I.v                  14–III.vii                 *um* . . .
6–II.i                 15–IV.i                    *exeunt*")
7–II.ii (176 lines),   16–IV.ii               24–V.ii, except
   II.iii (21 lines),  17–IV.iii                  opening s.d.
   and II.iv           18–IV.iv               25–V.iii
8–III.i                19–IV.v
9–III.ii               20–IV.vi

## Love's Labor's Lost

1–I.i                  5–IV.i                 8–V.i
2–I.ii                 6–IV.ii                9–V.ii, including
3–II.i                 7–IV.iii                  "The Song"
4–III.i

## Macbeth

1–I.i                  8–I.vii, except        16–III.iv
2–I.ii                    opening s.d.        16a–III.v is gener-
3–I.iii                9–II.i                    ally believed
4–I.iv                 10–II.ii                  to be non-
5–I.v                  11–II.iii                 Shakespearean
6–I.vi                 12–II.iv               17–III.vi
7–I.vii, opening       13–III.i               18–IV.i
   s.d. ("*Hautboys*   14–III.ii              19–IV.ii
   . . . *stage*")     15–III.iii             20–IV.iii

21 – V. i                    25 – V. v                    29 – V. vii. 24-end
22 – V. ii                   26 – V. vi                   30 – V. viii. 1-34[4]
23 – V. iii                  27 – V. vii. 1-13            31 – V. viii. 35-end
24 – V. iv                   28 – V. vii. 14-23

4. If genuine, a stage direction after line 34—"*Enter* [Macbeth and Mac-duff] *fighting, and* Macbeth *slain*"—would constitute a separate scene. The preceding direction—"*Exeunt* [Macbeth and Macduff], *fighting. Alarums*"—created a cleared stage. After having slain Macbeth, Macduff presumably exits carrying Macbeth's body—even though no stage direction so indicates—since neither Macduff nor Macbeth's body is onstage when Malcolm, Siward, Ross, Thanes, and Soldiers subsequently enter. After Malcolm, Ross, and Siward discourse, mainly about the death of Siward's son, for twenty lines, occurs the stage direction "*Enter* Macduff, *with* Macbeth's *head*." The earlier stage direction "*Enter fighting, and* Macbeth *slain*" diminishes the dramatic effectiveness of the sequence and creates seemingly unnecessary difficulties. In the first place, that Macbeth and Macduff should "*exeunt fighting*" only to turn around and immediately "*enter fighting*" creates what seems to be a rather pointless break in the continuity of the action. More importantly, Macduff's entrance with Macbeth's head, though visually striking, is anticlimactic if we already know of Macbeth's death. Sylvan Barnet, among others, has argued that "the inconsistent stage directions concerning Macbeth's death (one calls for him to be slain on stage, another suggests he is both slain and decapitated offstage) indicate some sort of revision" (*The Complete Signet Classic Shakespeare*, p. 1231). These difficulties would be eliminated by the omission of the single stage direction "*Enter fighting, and* Macbeth *slain*." If this stage direction were omitted, there would be no pointless break in the continuity and no needless violation of the convention against an immediate reentry, a convention to which Shakespeare almost always adheres. Furthermore, we would be kept in the dark about the outcome of the combat between Macbeth and Macduff for twenty lines and would learn of Macbeth's death only when we see his severed head. The anticlimax noted earlier would be replaced by suspense culminating in a genuine *coup de théâtre*. The effect would be similar to that of a sequence in *Cymbeline*. At the end of scene 21 (IV. ii. 1 – 100) Guiderius and Cloten "*Fight and Exeunt*." Belarius and Arviragus then enter and speculate about Cloten and about the outcome of his combat with Guiderius. The two characters onstage and the audience first learn that outcome when Guiderius enters carrying, as is clear from the ensuing dialogue, Cloten's head. A plausible explanation for the insertion of the dubious stage direction in *Macbeth* is that, after Shakespeare's retirement from the King's Men, the leaders of the company or the editors of the 1623 Folio felt that the play would be improved, despite the introduction of several difficulties, if the villain received his deserts onstage rather than offstage.

## Measure for Measure

| | | |
|---|---|---|
| 1 – I.i | 7 – II.iii | 12 – IV.iii |
| 2 – I.ii | 8 – II.iv | 13 – IV.iv |
| 3 – I.iii | 9 – III.i (269 lines) | 14 – IV.v |
| 4 – I.iv | and III.ii | 15 – IV.vi |
| 5 – II.i | 10 – IV.i | 16 – V.i |
| 6 – II.ii | 11 – IV.ii | |

## The Merchant of Venice

| | | |
|---|---|---|
| 1 – I.i | 8 – II.v | 15 – III.iii |
| 2 – I.ii | 9 – II.vi | 16 – III.iv |
| 3 – I.iii | 10 – II.vii | 17 – III.v |
| 4 – II.i | 11 – II.viii | 18 – IV.i |
| 5 – II.ii | 12 – II.ix | 19 – IV.ii |
| 6 – II.iii | 13 – III.i | 20 – V.i |
| 7 – II.iv | 14 – III.ii | |

## The Merry Wives of Windsor

| | | |
|---|---|---|
| 1 – I.i | 9 – III.ii | 17 – IV.iv |
| 2 – I.ii | 10 – III.iii | 18 – IV.v |
| 3 – I.iii | 11 – III.iv | 19 – IV.vi |
| 4 – I.iv | 12 – III.v | 20 – V.i |
| 5 – II.i | 13 – IV.i | 21 – V.ii |
| 6 – II.ii | 14 – IV.ii.1-102 | 22 – V.iii |
| 7 – II.iii | 15 – IV.ii.103-end | 23 – V.iv |
| 8 – III.i | 16 – IV.iii | 24 – V.v |

## A Midsummer Night's Dream

| | | |
|---|---|---|
| 1 – I.i | 5 – III.ii.1-412 | 7 – IV.ii |
| 2 – I.ii | 6 – III.ii.413-end | 8 – V.i.1-369 |
| 3 – II.i | (51 lines) and | 9 – V.i.370-end |
| 4 – II.ii (156 lines) | IV.i | |
| and III.i | | |

## Much Ado about Nothing

| | | |
|---|---|---|
| 1–I.i | 7–III.i | 13–IV.ii |
| 2–I.ii | 8–III.ii | 14–V.i |
| 3–I.iii | 9–III.iii | 15–V.ii |
| 4–II.i | 10–III.iv | 16–V.iii |
| 5–II.ii | 11–III.v | 17–V.iv |
| 6–II.iii | 12–IV.i | |

## Othello

| | | |
|---|---|---|
| 1–I.i | 6–II.iii | 11–IV.i |
| 2–I.ii | 7–III.i | 12–IV.ii |
| 3–I.iii | 8–III.ii | 13–IV.iii |
| 4–II.i | 9–III.iii | 14–V.i |
| 5–II.ii | 10–III.iv | 15–V.ii |

## Pericles

| | | |
|---|---|---|
| 1–I.Chorus | 11–II.iv | 21–IV.ii |
| 2–I.i.1-143 | 12–II.v | 22–IV.iii |
| 3–I.i.144-end | 13–III.Chorus | 23–IV.iv |
| 4–I.ii | 14–III.i | 24–IV.v |
| 5–I.iii | 15–III.ii | 25–IV.vi |
| 6–I.iv | 16–III.iii | 26–V.Chorus |
| 7–II.Chorus | 17–III.iv | 27–V.i |
| 8–II.i | 18–IV.Chorus | 28–V.ii[5] |
| 9–II.ii | 19–IV.i.1-92 | 29–V.iii.1-83[6] |
| 10–II.iii | 20–IV.i.93-end | 30–V.iii.84-end |

5. The 1609 Quarto of *Pericles* contains no stage directions at the beginning of the passage that was later designated V.ii or at the beginning of the passage later designated V.iii. The dialogue of the traditional division V.ii consists solely of Gower's choral speech. But most modern editors follow Malone in inserting a stage direction calling for the entrance of Thaisa, Maidens, Cerimon, and Ephesians before Gower's entrance. According to these editions these characters remain onstage after Gower's departure at which point (the beginning of V.iii) they are joined by Pericles, Lysimachus, Helicanus, and Marina. If these interpolated stage directions were correct, then the passage

# Richard II

| | | |
|---|---|---|
| 1 – I. i | 8 – II. iv | 15 – V. ii |
| 2 – I. ii | 9 – III. i | 16 – V. iii |
| 3 – I. iii | 10 – III. ii | 17 – V. iv |
| 4 – I. iv | 11 – III. iii | 18 – V. v |
| 5 – II. i | 12 – III. iv | 19 – V. vi |
| 6 – II. ii | 13 – IV. i | |
| 7 – II. iii | 14 – V. i | |

# Richard III

| | | |
|---|---|---|
| 1 – I. i | 9 – III. i | 17 – IV. ii |
| 2 – I. ii | 10 – III. ii | 18 – IV. iii |
| 3 – I. iii | 11 – III. iii | 19 – IV. iv |
| 4 – I. iv | 12 – III. iv | 20 – IV. v |
| 5 – II. i | 13 – III. v | 21 – V. i |
| 6 – II. ii | 14 – III. vi | 22 – V. ii |
| 7 – II. iii | 15 – III. vii | 23 – V. iii. 1-18 |
| 8 – II. iv | 16 – IV. i | 24 – V. iii. 19-271 |

---

from the beginning of V. ii through V. iii. 83 (at which point the stage almost certainly becomes empty) would compose a single scene uninterrupted by a cleared stage. Yet the other characters supposedly onstage during Gower's monologue neither say nor do anything during his speech, and Gower never refers to their presence. In my opinion a different staging is more likely. Gower enters, delivers his monologue, and exits with no other characters onstage. After his exit Thaisa, Maidens, Cerimon, and Ephesians enter from one door, and then Pericles, Lysimachus, Helicanus, and Marina enter at another. Presumably, the reason some editors feel compelled to place the entry of the first of these groups at an earlier point is that the location of V. iii. 1–83 is the temple of Diana, and the entrance of the priestesses and the native Ephesians only a moment before the entry of the visitors might seem odd. But such entrances—in which a resident or host group enters at virtually the same moment as a visiting group—occur elsewhere in Shakespeare's plays. (See, e.g., the stage direction at the beginning of *Henry V*, scene 30 [V. ii], and that at the beginning of *Cymbeline*, scene 12 [III. i].) If the above analysis is correct, then a cleared stage does in fact occur at Gower's exit, and a new scene begins at the beginning of the traditional V. iii.

6. See n. 5 above.

25 – V.iii.272-end          27 – V.iv, except            *um* . . .
26 – V.iv, opening             opening s.d.              *slain*")
   s.d. (*"Alarum;*       28 – V.v, opening          29 – V.v, except
   *excursions*")            s.d. (*"Alar-*              opening s.d.

## Romeo and Juliet

1 – Prologue:              7 – II.i (42 lines)         16 – III.v
   Chorus                     and II.ii                17 – IV.i
2 – I.i                    8 – II.iii                  18 – IV.ii
3 – I.ii                   9 – II.iv                   19 – IV.iii
4 – I.iii                  10 – II.v                   20 – IV.iv (28 lines)
5 – I.iv (114 lines)       11 – II.vi                     and IV.v
   and I.v                 12 – III.i                  21 – V.i
6 – II.Prologue:           13 – III.ii                 22 – V.ii
   Chorus                  14 – III.iii                23 – V.iii
                           15 – III.iv

## The Taming of the Shrew

1 – Induction. i           4 – III.i                   10 – IV.iv.1-72
2 – Induction. ii          5 – III.ii                  11 – IV.iv.73-end
   (142 lines), I.i        6 – IV.i.1-167              12 – IV.v
   (253 lines), and        7 – IV.i.168-end            13 – V.i
   I.ii                    8 – IV.ii                   14 – V.ii
3 – II.i                   9 – IV.iii

## The Tempest

1 – I.i                    5 – III.i                   8 – IV.i
2 – I.ii                   6 – III.ii                  9 – V.i
3 – II.i                   7 – III.iii                 10 – Epilogue
4 – II.ii

## Timon of Athens

1 – I.i                    3 – II.i                    5 – III.i
2 – I.ii                   4 – II.ii                   6 – III.ii

| | | |
|---|---|---|
| 7–III.iii | 12–III.vi.107-end | 17–V.i.116-end |
| 8–III.iv.1-102 | 13–IV.i | 18–V.ii |
| 9–III.iv.103-end | 14–IV.ii | 19–V.iii |
| 10–III.v | 15–IV.iii | 20–V.iv |
| 11–III.vi.1-106 | 16–V.i.1-115 | |

## Titus Andronicus

| | | |
|---|---|---|
| 1–I.i (496 lines) | 5–II.iv | 10–IV.iii |
| and II.i | 6–III.i | 11–IV.iv |
| 2–II.ii | 7–III.ii | 12–V.i |
| 3–II.iii.1-191 | 8–IV.i | 13–V.ii |
| 4–II.iii.192-end | 9–IV.ii | 14–V.iii |

## Troilus and Cressida

| | | |
|---|---|---|
| 1–Prologue | 10–III.iii | 19–V.iv |
| 2–I.i | 11–IV.i | 20–V.v.1-44 |
| 3–I.ii | 12–IV.ii | 21–V.v.44-end |
| 4–I.iii | 13–IV.iii | 22–V.vi |
| 5–II.i | 14–IV.iv | 23–V.vii.1-8 |
| 6–II.ii | 15–IV.v | 24–V.vii.9-end |
| 7–II.iii | 16–V.i | 25–V.viii |
| 8–III.i | 17–V.ii | 26–V.ix |
| 9–III.ii | 18–V.iii | 27–V.x |

## Twelfth Night

| | | |
|---|---|---|
| 1–I.i | 8–II.iii | 15–III.iv.278-end |
| 2–I.ii | 9–II.iv | 16–IV.i |
| 3–I.iii | 10–II.v | 17–IV.ii |
| 4–I.iv | 11–III.i | 18–IV.iii |
| 5–I.v | 12–III.ii | 19–V.i, including |
| 6–II.i | 13–III.iii | Feste's final song |
| 7–II.ii | 14–III.iv.1-277 | |

## The Two Gentlemen of Verona

| | | |
|---|---|---|
| 1–I.i | 8–II.v | 15–IV.iii |
| 2–I.ii | 9–II.vi | 16–IV.iv |
| 3–I.iii | 10–II.vii | 17–V.i |
| 4–II.i | 11–III.i | 18–V.ii |
| 5–II.ii | 12–III.ii | 19–V.iii |
| 6–II.iii | 13–IV.i | 20–V.iv |
| 7–II.iv | 14–IV.ii | |

## The Two Noble Kinsmen

| | | |
|---|---|---|
| 1–Prologue | 10–II.iv | 19–IV.ii |
| 2–I.i | 11–II.v | 20–IV.iii |
| 3–I.ii | 12–III.i | 21–V.i.1-68 |
| 4–I.iii | 13–III.ii | 22–V.i.69-136 |
| 5–I.iv | 14–III.iii | 23–V.i.137-end |
| 6–I.v | 15–III.iv | 24–V.ii |
| 7–II.i | 16–III.v | 25–V.iii |
| 8–II.ii | 17–III.vi | 26–V.iv |
| 9–II.iii | 18–IV.i | 27–Epilogue |

## The Winter's Tale

| | | |
|---|---|---|
| 1–I.i | 6–III.i | 11–IV.iii |
| 2–I.ii | 7–III.ii | 12–IV.iv |
| 3–II.i | 8–III.iii | 13–V.i |
| 4–II.ii | 9–IV.i | 14–V.ii |
| 5–II.iii | 10–IV.ii | 15–V.iii |

# Index of Scenes Discussed